Copyright © 2023 Steven M. Stroum
Published by THE VENMARK CORPORATION

All rights reserved.
No part of this book may be reproduced in any form or by any electronic or mechanical means, including information storage and retrieval systems, without written permission from the author, except for the use of brief quotations in a book review.

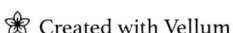 Created with Vellum

DISCLAIMER

Disclaimer: The names of former employees and clients of The Venmark Corporation in this book have been changed to protect the privacy of those individuals; except for family members and a few others. Any resemblance to actual people, living or dead, is purely coincidental.

CONTENTS

1. Send Me Back to the War
2. Learning How to Become a Winner
3. If You Want Something, Ask For It
4. Planting the Seeds of Change in San Francisco
5. A Sales Manager who Didn't Want Steak
6. A Taste of Entrepreneurship Gone Sour
7. Where Do I Go From Here With My Life
8. Embarking on an Entrepreneurial Journey
9. Learn on the Fly and Fake it Till You Make It
10. Growing Pains, Tumult, and Critical Decisions
11. Blurred Lines: Business and Personal
12. Honor in Korea and Betrayal Back Home
13. Twin Light Manor and the Changing Tides
14. Letting Go and Becoming My Own Person
15. We've Been Trying to Get Rid of You
16. Low Pricing Can Kill Your Business
17. Business Success and Life-Altering Revelations
18. The Internet Changed Everything... and Nothing
19. Are You an S.O.B?

20. The Final Year That Never Happened
21. My Business is My Art and My Art is My Business
22. Entrepreneurs are the Real American Heroes

Dedicated to Peggy and Ellen, the girls from Framingham.

INTRODUCTION

People have a lot of opinions when it comes to the characteristics that make a successful entrepreneur. Assumptions about the entrepreneur title are thrown around on social media outlets like LinkedIn, and every time I come across yet another one, this line comes to mind: "an entrepreneur is not an entrepreneur, is not an entrepreneur." I borrowed that idea from S.I. Hayakawa, the semanticist and former Senator, who wrote many years ago, "A cow is not a cow, is not a cow." In other words, even though they are all cows; not all cows are the same. The same logic applies to entrepreneurs. Not all entrepreneurs are the same, even though they are all entrepreneurs. There is the blue-collar entrepreneur and the white-collar entrepreneur.

The white-collar entrepreneur is the lucky one who was bright enough and fortunate enough to attend a top university like MIT or Stanford and found it fairly easy to attract funding and a team to build their startup company. You know, venture capitalists, IPOs, etc. In other words, using other people's money to fund the company and mitigate your risk. Then there's the guy or gal who gets laid-off or terminated and has to strike out on his or her own to make a living. One of my clients started that way. He lost his job as a machinist and found a customer who helped him purchase a machine which he placed in his garage. Today he has a large plant with nearly one hundred machines and dozens of employees and customers. He is a blue-collar entrepreneur.

A blue-collar entrepreneur is typically someone who grew up in a working-class family and always wanted to be his or her own boss, but has no idea how to start a business. When presented with an opportunity, the blue-collar entrepreneur dives head-on into the water, with limited resources. I am a blue-collar entrepreneur, and I earned the title when I lost my job. Unlike the aforementioned white-collar entrepreneur, however, who typically has a Plan B and other survival options in the event the business fails, the blue-collar entrepreneur is like a prize fighter. He or she enters the ring expecting to win. There is no Plan B because not succeeding is not an option. There are no backup resources. For me, starting and building my business was brutally tough at times and I wanted to quit more than once, but I am glad I stuck with it, fought those feelings, and got up each time that I got knocked down. Now I've been in business for over forty-six years.

This is a book about empowerment. About my personal growth while in business. I share my experiences, warts and all. I describe how I learned how to succeed in college, how to win sales contests at work, and how I started my own business with only $300 at twenty-eight years old and turned it into a million-dollar company. In this book I include the good and bad decisions that I made and what my reasoning was in order to help you learn from them, and

I provide actual detailed how-to sales and marketing tips and tricks. Most importantly, I candidly share my personal journey from the effect of growing up as the youngest child in a flawed family to quitting college during the Vietnam War, enlisting in the U.S. Air Force, and returning to school as a disabled veteran. Then a year after graduation, my wife and I moved to San Francisco and I describe in very specific terms how and what I learned about myself while there that prompted me to move back home to Boston and become an entrepreneur.

The entrepreneurial highway is riddled with potholes, twists, turns, and bumps. Once you start your business you will be amazed at how many of them will come your way. There will be issues and experiences that are impossible to predict and even more difficult to comprehend. For me, my early business success spawned depression and revealed family issues that had previously been repressed by my drive to succeed. An opportunity to travel overseas and represent Massachusetts for the International Rotary Foundation was an incredible experience and created unfathomable personal and business issues that changed me forever.

Despite the challenges and disappointments, being your own boss and controlling your own life is worth every twist, turn, bump, and detour along the road. As Theodore Roosevelt wrote, *"Far better it is to dare mighty things, to win glorious triumphs even though checkered with failure than to take the ranks with those poor spirits who neither enjoy much nor suffer much because they live in the grey twilight that knows not victory nor defeat."*

I hope my story inspires you to become an entrepreneur. I've tried to tell it in an entertaining and meaningful way, designed to help you grow awareness and avoid the pitfalls and painful circumstances that I've personally experienced as a blue-collar entrepreneur. On the flip side, I hope it will help you achieve your business and personal goals. Like a prize fighter, you may not win the fight, but you never want to enter the ring thinking that you're going to lose. Even if you get knocked down, get up and change your stance; then do battle in the next round and the rounds after. Ultimately, you'll hear the winning bell ring! Blue collar entrepreneurs are the independent-thinking, hard-working champs for the American Dream!

1

SEND ME BACK TO THE WAR

It was November 1966 and I was a freshman at Northeastern University with a student draft deferment. There were about 375,000 US troops in Vietnam at that time and the war was raging. But, so was the anti-war movement in the United States. In 1964 the movement began by left wing groups and college students. By mid-1966, because of the rise of American casualties and increased draft calls, middle-class families for whom military service was not on the agenda, started to take notice. More and more people were questioning authority. Also, Martin Luther King, Jr. was marching for civil rights while Atlanta and other cities experienced race riots for the first time. President Lyndon Johnson was in the White House and the seeds were being sown for the fury of 1968.

I was majoring in education and while I had some wonderful teachers and a group of nice classmates, I wasn't particularly motivated. My mother was a teacher and was a heavy influence on me at that time. Perhaps that's why I majored in education. Attending college was something that was expected but I didn't feel like I belonged there at the time. I quit college and enlisted in the U.S. Air Force. My oldest brother was an Air Force veteran and my other brother was an Airman stationed in Thailand. At that time, the Dean of Freshman, Dean Call, assured me that I could return to Northeastern after my four years of military service. So, I left college while in good academic standing.

It was a youthful decision. I had set the gears into motion: my classmates were throwing a goodbye party for me and deep down in my gut, at the very pit of my stomach, I knew that I had made a huge mistake. I was conflicted. The impulsive decision was made and I had to act like it was the right thing for me. Pride is powerful, especially for a teenager and, again, I had already enlisted. I was committed and moving ahead. I am grateful that I enlisted in the Air Force, where it was unlikely that I would see action on the ground in Vietnam like I would have had I been drafted into the Army. Ironically, I received a draft notice the following week. News travels fast when you lose your 2-S student draft deferment!

I was scheduled to leave the following February for basic training at Lackland Air Force Base in San Antonio, TX. Quitting college was a mistake and I knew it. The evening I told my father that I quit college and enlisted in the Air Force he couldn't control his anger. We were standing in the kitchen when he looked at me and said, "You're stupid, just like your brothers and you're a quitter!" Three sons and none chose to attend and graduate from college. The disappointment in his eyes was palpable and it felt like the lowest moment of my life.

When February, 1967 came and I left for basic training I promised myself that nobody would ever call me stupid or a quitter, ever again. A father's words play a critical role in the motivation of a son and rather than being angry at him I wanted to make him proud of me. Perhaps it was because I knew that "I was stupid." In basic training I became a squad leader, and it took me about two weeks to learn how to become a team player and not an autocratic fool like my father.

One night I was summoned to the drill sergeant's office. I stood at the door and announced myself, "Airman Stroum, Sir." His reply was, "Enter." And then the lights went out and a musty green military blanket was thrown over my head. I could feel the roughness of the fabric scratching against my face when all of a sudden, boots that were tied together by their laces were swung indiscriminately and landing all over my body, arms, and head. Punches were thrown at me from all angles. All hell broke loose and the beating didn't stop until I bit someone's arm, tasted his blood and heard him scream.

The incident lasted less than five minutes, but I learned something that night about 'going along to get along' and the next four weeks of basic training were an easier adjustment for me. I never found out who was responsible for the ordeal, but the result was a sense of belonging which spurred me to be highly motivated to succeed. I was proud to be in the United States Air Force and even remember looking up at the American flag one day while marching in basic training and saying to myself, "I would be proud to die for my country."

My next assignment was technical school at Lowry Air Force Base in Denver, CO where I would study to become a munitions specialist. To my surprise, the coursework was every bit as stringent as the college courses that I had taken, and it actually meant more because our promotions and income were based on success. This was real life! What's more, a mistake with munitions can literally cost you an arm and a leg, if not your life and the lives of others.

Denver, CO in June is a marvelous place to be. The mountains are breathtaking and the weather can vary considerably. For example, I remember on June 17, 1967 it snowed almost a foot and a half and the next day it was nearly 80 degrees outside. We had to shovel the snow off of the drill pad (large marching area) afterwards, while it was in the eighties outside. Typical Air Force training: you had to get used to performing unpleasant tasks for the team. In retrospect, I really understand the importance and value of that training on the development of self-discipline.

Marching was actually fun. We'd take pride in the symmetry of nearly one hundred Airmen acting as one and getting it right. When everyone was in-step, marching was neat. You could hear it and see it. They lined us up in rows of four, by height. The formation was referred to as a Flight. At just shy of six feet tall I always ended up in the middle of the flight toward the back.

A couple of weeks before the aforementioned snowy day, I experienced a very dark day. I was the only Jewish person in our flight and only one or two guys knew it. George Aubee from Cranston, RI knew and he was a friend of mine. It wasn't something you advertised in those days for fear of potential problems with bigotry. And there was no shortage of bigots in the military.

It was early June of 1967 and I was marching along in formation when I heard the airman directly behind me chant, "Hut, Two, Three, Four, Kill One Jew, Kill Some More; Hut, Two, Three, Four, Kill One Jew Kill Some More." I felt the blood rush to my cheeks and the hair stand up on the back of my neck, blocking off any positive thought process or logic and triggering furious anger. In response, I turned around and grabbed the guy by his shirt with my left hand and while twisting his shirt, ripped off a button as I clenched my fist and cocked my right arm to throw a punch directly at his jaw. He was much bigger than me, but I didn't care. I wanted to smash every pimple on the ugly sonofabitch's face! My friend George grabbed my arm and stopped the punch.

He saved me from getting into a lot of trouble and then whisked me aside to cool off before we resumed marching. I remembered in basic training when our flight was marched to an area by the drill sergeant to watch two airmen with pick axes breaking up a poured concrete foundation in the hot Texas sun. They had hidden in our barracks attic and skipped a general meeting. Their grueling punishment made an impression on all of us to stay in line and follow instructions or face severe consequences.

Fortunately, nobody in authority caught on to what was happening on the drill pad that day. That big ugly sonofabitch who said "Kill Jews" during the Israeli Six Day War was a bigoted fool who I nearly went to the brig over. I didn't want to get into trouble and that was the end of the incident. Pride can be a powerful motivator and take you over in the face of blatant bigotry.

That experience in Denver was the first of two hurtful antisemitic experiences that would influence my life. I have never felt like a victim, but I have certainly made choices that guided me towards entrepreneurship and independence. Later experiences would confirm that building my own business would be the best way to get a fair shake in our prejudiced society. Jews didn't choose to work outside of large, mostly Protestant, corporations by accident. There was nothing new about antisemitism in the United States during the sixties. In fact, during the Civil War, General

Ulysses S. Grant issued an order of expulsion against Jews from the portions of Tennessee, Kentucky, and Mississippi which were under his control. The order, however, was quickly rescinded by President Abraham Lincoln.

While at Lowry AFB in Denver, I befriended the sergeant who was responsible for the new base assignments after graduation from tech school. Most of us were going to jungle training school in Pensacola, FL in preparation for duty in Vietnam. I mentioned to the sergeant that my brother was stationed in Thailand and that I'd really like to be considered for any assignments in that location. As it turned out, there was one at Nakhon Phanom Royal Thai Air Force Base (NKP), Thailand. The base was located at the Northeast tip of Thailand on the Mekong River adjacent to Laos, about 30 miles from Vietnam. I lobbied and got the assignment. I was the only airman in my flight not headed to Vietnam. Obviously, I was thrilled to have pulled that off.

The flight to Bangkok, Thailand from Travis AFB in San Francisco took about twenty-six hours. We wore the same clothes and ate breakfast for every meal. We were packed onto a C141 Aircraft, seated backwards with no windows. The flight was beyond boring and at one point I walked up to the back of the aircraft to have a cup of coffee and a smoke. While chatting with another airman there I discovered that he was stationed at my brother's base in South Thailand and he knew him. What were the odds of that happening?

When we got to Bangkok we were transferred to a smaller C130 transport plane and headed northeast up to NKP. That aircraft was noisy, vibrated constantly, and the ride was rather bumpy. It was about 11:00 p.m August 9, 1967 when we arrived at the base and what I remember most about walking out of the plane was how clear and pitch black the night skies were. There was no ambient light. It was darker than I had ever seen before and the stars were bright and vivid. It was almost as though you could reach out and grab a constellation for yourself. The air was fresh and clean too.

When I got off the tarmac and was signing in at the desk inside the small terminal, the welcoming airman, Jack McManus, assigned me to his hooch which would be my home for the next year. He felt chemistry with me and he was right. There were four roommates in the hooch and we all came from different backgrounds, but got along really well.

A hooch is a wooden structure with screened sides that are elevated about four feet off the ground with a plank walkway around it. The elevation helped keep the scorpions, snakes, and other varmints and insects from paying us a visit; especially during the torrential rains of monsoon season which was between July and October. The rains during the summer only lasted for a few hours a day. But, by mid-September and October they were much more persistent.

My metal locker was right next to the screen door to the hooch and I always kept a light bulb on inside of the locker so that the heat it generated would dry my clothes and prevent them from getting musty. Being on the bottom bunk I had to make sure to bang my boots upside down every morning to check for scorpions and other bugs.

When I first arrived at the munitions area which we called the bomb dump, I was assigned to a storage crew. There we received munitions from incoming cargo planes, logged them into our system and stored them in a small metal hut or an open field. The work schedule in the "bomb dump" was 12 hours per day for six days on and one day off.

Over the next several weeks I would then move to the buildup crew where we assembled munitions and got them ready for the transport crew who took them to the flight line where the load crew put them onto the aircraft. Our crews had local Thai civilians who helped us and the cultural differences made for some funny memories.

Knowing that munitions were harmless without a detonator attached, we would throw small missiles around and the Thais would scatter! It was mean, but we were young G.I.s. In return, the Thais would take a plastic baggie of live locust bugs from their back pocket and eat them; still alive and buzzing as they swallowed. They knew that it freaked us out and we had fun goofing on each other. Sometimes they would put a bug on a heavy wire and roast it with a torch before eating it.

We flew about 40 bombing missions a day on small planes from NKP. The pilots bombed the Ho Chi Minh trail which was the main supply route from North Vietnam to the South and only 35 air miles away from us. When they returned from a mission, pilots would take out a template with the cutout of a truck and then use red spray paint to record their "kill" on the side of the plane. Quite impersonal!

Finally, I got the opportunity to move to an inside job in the munitions control area where there were several large plexiglass sections where we used grease pencils to make notations about each function; following a particular munitions load from storage, through buildup, to transport, and finally loaded onto the planes. All of the dates, times, and who authorized the activities were noted. That is what we did before computerized Microsoft Excel® spreadsheets were invented!

There were four of us working in munitions control and

we had to make certain that the area was manned around the clock. Again, we worked 12 hours per day for six days a week to make that happen. Then one day I proposed a new work schedule to the NCOIC (non-commissioned officer in charge). I said, "Sarge, I know you want the munitions control area covered 24/7, but do you care how we divide up the hours?" He said, no, why do you ask?" I told him that the four of us would each like to work 12 hours on and 24 hours off and he agreed to the idea. During that conversation the Sarge said to me, "Stroum, you're a Jew aren't you? I replied, "Yes" and he continued, "Then why aren't you an officer? "I said, "Because I screwed up and enlisted in the Air Force just like you, Sarge," and we both laughed. We had a good rapport.

Being in the Air Force was like having a civilian job. We'd get up in the morning and clean up at the bath area which was down the covered walkway from our hooch. No marching in formations anymore. The walk did get tough, however, during monsoon season with the intense wind-blown rain storms. The rain came at you vertically and horizontally, swallowing you up. You couldn't avoid getting soaked. Then you'd walk to breakfast in the dining hall where there were pretty Thai waitresses and round lazy Susan turn-tables on each table with condiments and sugar. It wasn't bad at all. You'd walk through the line for breakfast yourself, fill your tray, and the girls would then bring your coffee refills, toast or whatever else you wanted afterwards.

Many of our after-work hours were spent drinking. We'd go over to the Airman's club where a beer was a dime and mixed drinks were 15 cents. On the weekends there was live music. The Thai band members couldn't speak a word of English, but sang Beatles and Rolling Stones songs flawlessly in front of the big crowds. Sometimes local prostitutes were there and danced on the tabletops, advertising their wares. They were all inspected by an Air Force nurse as a way to control venereal diseases and had a VD control number which they proudly wore on a badge. "Me clean, me clean," was heard frequently. Their numbers were also displayed on a chalk board at the club entrance.

As it turned out, I was at NKP for my nineteenth birthday on November 20, 1967 and I went to the base post office and collected my mail after work. Fortunately, there were several birthday cards which I stuffed into my fatigue shirt pocket before heading to the Airman's club. Receiving mail from friends and family was emotional nourishment when you were halfway around the world dealing with extreme heat, humidity, and monsoons.

I sat at the bar, ordered a beer, lit a cigarette, and began reading my birthday cards. Naturally, I got a little weepy as I chain-smoked and reread each card several times. Then a fellow airman who I'd never met before sat down next to me and noticed the stack of cards in front of me. He said, "Hey, is it your birthday? I said, "Yes," and then he said, "Let me buy you a beer." Well, that scenario repeated itself at the midnight shift change and I got the same question from another guy. By then I was pretty drunk and continued drinking with my new friend until 6:00 a.m. The last drinking partner I had was kind enough to walk me back to my hooch and when I opened the screen door and it banged up against my metal locker as I slipped and fell, it made a loud noise and woke up my roommates who actually started applauding. They were good natured and knew that I needed to eat something after drinking for 12 hours straight and escorted me, or should I say, carried me to breakfast. Quite a memorable nineteenth birthday! A story I've shared frequently since then.

Meanwhile, I had an awful skin rash for about a month or two and it was getting much worse. Bright red raised, scaly dots were all over my body; especially my torso, thighs, and butt where there was no sun exposure. The hot humid days helped make things worse and the itching was awful. So, about a week after my birthday, I was air-evacuated on another C130 transport plane South to Korat AFB in Thailand for medical treatment. It was a little larger base, just Northeast of Bangkok by about 125 miles, with more medical personnel. My skin condition baffled them and instead of simply returning to NKP, I was air-evacuated to Clark AFB in the Philippines. The same thing happened at Clark and then I was off to Tachikawa Air Base hospital in Japan. All these moves without much more than a small gym bag with two uniforms, a change of underwear, and a shaving kit.

Tachikawa, or "Tachi," as it is known, was a conduit where all of the injured from Vietnam passed through. The hospital at Tachi was filled with injured American servicemen from Vietnam and it was my home for two weeks. The base at Tachikawa was established in 1945 and was turned over to the Japanese in 1969. However, during the Vietnam era it was very busy because it had a 6,500 foot long airstrip which could accommodate large C141 aircraft full of injured soldiers, marines, sailors, and airmen.

Believe me, I felt blessed by only having a skin condition and being ambulatory. Most of my comrades there had been pretty shot up and severely injured. It wasn't rare to hear painful moans at night while these poor men tried to fall asleep. While there, I had a rather large skin biopsy and the doctors concluded that I had lichen planus which was a skin rash triggered by the immune system. Not contagious, but very itchy and bothersome; caused by a virus and stress. The sweltering moist heat of Thailand didn't help my rash either.

This intense moisture in the air was evident when water would literally fall off planes during takeoff, and it could be seen in the permanent dampness of the wooden sides of our hooch.

My next stop from Tachikawa, Japan was Chelsea Naval Hospital near Boston, MA. One of the first three hospitals commissioned to treat Naval personnel, it was established in 1836 and ultimately decommissioned in 1974. It was about 30 miles from my folks' home in Newton, just west of Boston. The flight was another huge C141 transport and we landed briefly to refuel at Elmendorf Air Base in Anchorage, Alaska where it was about ten below zero. Since I was never initially scheduled to leave Southeast Asia, I didn't have a dress blue uniform or a coat, so I was freezing.

I arrived at the Chelsea Naval Hospital a day before Christmas 1967 and because of the holiday season they immediately let me make arrangements to go home. So, I called my buddy Larry to pick me up. He asked where and I looked out the window and saw the Prudential Center building, a Boston landmark. "Pick me up at the North side door," I said and I took a taxi there.

The anti-war movement in Boston, with all of the colleges and universities, was boiling over. There I was, standing outside wearing military fatigues with a black baseball cap which had white lettering that read "456th Munitions Maintenance Squadron Nakhon Phanom, Thailand." I felt like a pariah and was actually spat upon. I was very angry, but quickly let it go and actually felt sorry for the people doing it. I hadn't been home for a year and the anti-war movement wasn't part of my reality. I felt hurt and confused. Why were my sacrifices not appreciated? A year later, though, I'd be marching on the Boston Common chanting "Hut, two, three, four, we don't want your fucking war!"

After the holidays, early in January, 1968 I reported to the Chelsea Naval hospital for treatment. I had to soak in a bathtub for one hour every day. My skin was inflamed and broken out, and while the doctors prescribed a medication, they offered no explanation of its side effects or purpose. Military doctors have a tendency to prescribe without providing details. They just gave me a large bottle of medicine called Serax which I didn't realize was a very strong anti-depressant. I took it as instructed until one night when I drank a little too much and fell asleep while driving my new 1968 Volkswagen bug home from a party. I did wake up, though, after hitting the left side of a 1961 Oldsmobile. A week later I flushed the remaining Serax pills down the toilet.

The "therapy" tub at Chelsea Naval Hospital was in the back of an ordinary bathroom, under a broken window, and the mops that were used for cleaning the floors in hospital wards were stored there; filthy, wet and smelly, likely infiltrated with bacteria. So, every day before I could take my therapeutic soak I had to thoroughly wash the tub. The broken window also let the cold January air inside. It was crazy! It made no sense to me at all and I made that point to the dermatologist who was treating me.

Fortunately my family's home was fairly close to the hospital and I was able to arrange to live at home and take my baths there. It wasn't straightforward though. Seemingly nothing in the military was. After soaking in the tub on that the first day, I reported to the ward nurse who coldly said, "Okay airman, grab a mop and swab the decks." She was an old gray haired woman with a stern look. I asked her what she meant by swab the decks and she said, "Mop the floors."

I replied, "Major, I cannot do that because I have a skin condition and will perspire which will make it worse. In fact, the Air Force air-evacuated me for treatment here from the war zone in Southeast Asia." She wanted to hear no part of my explanation. "Then go to the brig immediately!" she said.

As someone who had never been in serious trouble before, thought of going to a military jail was quite frightening. When I reported to the brig, the sailor in charge said to me, "Did Major Crawford, the nurse from the ward send you down here?" "Yes," I replied. He laughed and said, "She's a fucking whacko! Do you have a military driver's license?" I said, "Yes." Then he told me that I'd be assigned to his team and shuttle people back and forth to the Fargo Building in South Boston and other places.

It turned out to be a great assignment which lasted a couple of weeks until I was sent to Andrews AFB Hospital in Washington, DC for another diagnosis and additional treatment. I was assigned to a ward there with a nice group of guys. The guy in the bed across from me was named Blue. He was a funny dude; a black guy with a stomach disease who had to take a white, chalky medicine several times daily and would joke about the white stains on his dark brown skin from spilled doses during the night.

My first order of business was a thorough physical examination and another skin biopsy. A doctor went around every square inch of my body which was covered with bright red scaly lesions and circled one that was right in the middle of my ass with a ballpoint pen. I said, "Doc, I have lesions all over my body, can you please select one that isn't going to interfere with my sitting down?" So, he found one on my shoulder that didn't interfere with my daily activities and healed fairly quickly.

Within a few days the lab results concluded that I had psoriasis. Specifically, guttate psoriasis which is different from the more common plaque-type patches. Guttate psoriasis involved red, scaly drop-like lesions that appeared virtually everywhere on my body. I was literally covered from head-to-toe. In fact, it was so severe that they photographed sections of my body to use for teaching purposes.

Treatment began soon afterwards. My regimen consisted of UV light treatment and coal tar baths. Yes, the same black tar that you find on freshly paved roads. Finally, I had to cover myself with black coal-tar cream from head to toe. Very smelly, unpleasant, and difficult to wash off. In the meantime, since there was a war going on and I was hospitalized as a result, Red Cross volunteers would visit regularly. When I didn't feel like talking, I'd make sure the black and yellow coal-tar soaked and stained sheets were exposed, and the dismayed volunteers would be gone in minutes. They were totally grossed out and it worked every time!

After several weeks of treatments, it was early March 1968 and I became aware that the Air Force allowed you to be honorably discharged if you couldn't serve in the war zone. Because my psoriasis was so severe, the primary dermatologist treating me wanted to have me assigned to Andrews Air Force Base so that he could continue my treatment for a year. I really didn't want to be in limbo for a year because of a medical condition, and I was certain that I wanted to go back to college.

This was my grandstand play to try and make up for quitting college in the middle of the Vietnam War. I said, "Doc, I'm a munitions specialist and there is not a job for me here at Andrews, *please send me back to the war*. If I can't go back to NKP in Thailand then I want to be discharged from the Air Force." It worked! In fact, I wrote up the official medical discharge paperwork with the doctor and hand carried it to the hospital administrators and other doctors involved with the decision to get their signatures. I would be receiving an honorable medical discharge with a service connected disability.

While awaiting my final discharge date, I wrote a letter to the Dean of Freshman at Northeastern University to reapply for admission to classes the following September. To my dismay, I received a letter a week later from Dean Kennedy stating that their academic standards had changed since I had left Northeastern and that I no longer qualified for admission to the university even though I was in good academic standing when I left. Needless to say, I was furious. Frankly, I don't recall whether I wrote back to Dean Kennedy or called his office, but I requested and was granted an appointment with him when I returned to Boston.

I received a Medical Discharge with a 10% service connected disability on March 25, 1968 and flew home to Boston where my dad picked me up at Logan Airport. I had hoped for a 20% disability because then I'd qualify for free tuition, books, and expenses for five years of college. Someone who I was casually talking with about the situation suggested that I contact the Jewish War Veterans and have them appeal the 10% judgment and try for the life-changing 20%. I figured what the hell: there's nothing to lose. Fortunately, they ended up getting me a 30% disability rating. Just as I had learned back at tech school by asking for an assignment in Thailand, being assertive in life was important.

Now all I had to do was deal with Dean Kennedy again. When I went to meet with him, I was in a grey business suit, white shirt, and striped tie, exuding the confidence of a professional, nineteen-year-old veteran. When I entered his office, I noticed that there were many pictures of children on a credenza behind him. After thanking him for taking the time to meet with me I said, "Are those your children?" He said, "Yes, I have nine children." I complimented him on his beautiful family and then said, "You know, I just spent four months in five different hospitals as a result of my service in the Vietnam War to protect your beautiful nine children and all I'm simply asking of you is that Northeastern University keep its word to me since I had left in good academic standing less than two years ago. I was assured at that time by Dean Call that I could return to Northeastern after my military service was over." His facial expression showed that he understood me clearly and I said, "Thank you very much for your time and consideration, I really appreciate it. Have a great day."

Two weeks later my acceptance letter arrived in the mail from Dean Kennedy welcoming me as a Northeastern University freshman of the class of 1973. In the Air Force I learned that being assertive can pay huge dividends. It got me stationed in Thailand instead of Vietnam and back to Northeastern with full books, tuition, and expenses paid for. Being assertive is a critical element of entrepreneurship.

2
LEARNING HOW TO BECOME A WINNER

Injustices are a part of life and like so many other unfair experiences, it is how you handle them that defines who you are. It is important that each one of us defines who we are and not let others do it for us because they will surely try.

My freshman year in college was better the second time around. Once again, I attended the Burlington Campus of Northeastern University (NU) which was a small suburban campus not far from Route 128, the esteemed technology highway just outside of Boston, MA. I drove up the long tree-lined driveway to get there in my new *1968 Volkswagen Beetle*. During my time there, I worked hard to earn B's and C's and was elected Freshman Class President. There were only 300 students at the campus and I am pretty sure my election success was related to the fact that I was older than the other students, therefore they thought I was wiser. Frankly, I don't recall what the issues of the day were, but leadership and politics intrigued me even though I was raised with the precept that you can't fight city hall.

I majored in education that first year and during the

following summer took the required accounting classes and transferred to the College of Business to major in management. In the fall of my sophomore year I was on the main NU campus in Boston and enjoyed it, despite the 20 plus mile commute and 8:00 a.m. early morning classes. Northeastern University is a private institution that was founded in 1898 and is known worldwide for its cooperative educational program that integrates classroom studies with professional work experience over a five year period. In the late 1960s and 70s NU was a commuter school. Over 90 percent of students lived off campus. Today the opposite is true and their dormitories and campus are first rate and impressive.

One of my classmates, a slight, long-haired guy named Dave Whitney was a straight A student. He was a nice kid and after observing him in a few classes, he didn't seem much smarter than me, but he got straight A's and I struggled to get mostly B's. So, on one autumn day at the beginning of the school year when we were hanging out on the front stairs of the library at the NU quad watching other students play Frisbee, I asked him point blank: "Dave, you don't seem that much smarter than me and you get straight A's and I'm getting B's and C's; what's up with that?" Dave replied, "I am smarter than you, Steve, and I'll tell you exactly why." And he proceeded to do just that in great detail.

"It is because I follow a proven study process," he continued, "and while you're breaking your ass to study and cram for exams, I'm just reviewing my notes and making sure that I thoroughly understand the subject matter." He explained that at the beginning of every school trimester he would get a syllabus to study from every professor or instructor and if they didn't publish one; he demanded it from them; even if it was simply verbal. Then he'd identify the topics and testing dates, take out his calendar and "plan" his study times down to the hour for the entire trimester. It was essentially a road map for a successful academic trip. In retrospect, it was one of the most important days of my life.

After I adopted Dave Whitney's study process, I began getting straight A's too and with each additional trimester I gained more self-confidence. It was an emotional adjustment to change from getting average grades to becoming an exceptional student. I was the youngest of three boys, and my two older brothers were smart. They were in the top curriculum in high school, barely applied themselves, and got good grades while I was the hardworking kid who struggled to get moderate grades and was in the lower curriculum.

Before I met Dave Whitney, I attached myself to the label of "hardworking kid who wasn't all that smart." Learning his academic study process helped me rewrite some of those hard-wired messages in my psyche, transforming how I thought of myself academically. It took a while with occasional battles of self-doubt and arrogant behavior as a defense mechanism, but my self-image got reassured over time by consistent superior academic performance.

I finished my last four years of college earning straight A's. What's more, I had co-operative work experiences that would set me on a path to entrepreneurship. That was the great thing about Northeastern University's cooperative education formula. It was a legitimate opportunity to job-hop and get exposed to different industries, companies, and work environments. You worked for three months, went to school three months, worked six months, went to school six months, and so on. For over 100 years, NU has been a world leader in cooperative education (co-op), the University's cornerstone experiential learning program.

The co-op program was ideal for veterans like me who were a couple of years older than their classmates and already had some real-world work experience. Not only did I have work experience in the U.S. Air Force, but my role was critical to the mission. At eighteen years old I was in charge of munitions control at our active bombing base during the Vietnam War and my performance mattered. Where else can you get that kind of responsibility at eighteen years old? I loved and thrived on being responsible for important work. It felt good to be on top of the food chain.

My first co-op experience was at Ford Motor Company's Boston District Sales Office where my first two three-month stints on the job were spent in administration analyzing data from dealer sales, working for a fellow named Andy St. James. Andy was the model corporate employee and was quite affable. He had a crew cut and wore conservative three-piece suits and wingtip shoes. Andy rated my work with straight A's and said that I was an excellent all-around employee. I was considering a career with the company and imagined myself having a bright future. There were four of us in one good-sized office sitting across from and next to one another. The guys I worked with had a good work ethic, were regular straight-shooters, and I enjoyed hanging out with them at lunch. Good people.

During my third year at NU, I married Peggy who I had met two years earlier. When I returned home from the Air Force I went to the local shopping mall in search of clothes, but lucky for me there was a job available at a shoe store and it would be a perfect summer gig before returning to school in the fall of 1968. Even luckier for me was that I met and became fast friends with Peggy who was working at another mall store that summer.

We began dating two months later in June and it was a wonderful summer for us despite the tumult in America. It was the summer of 1968 after all, a mere two months after the assassination of Martin Luther King, Jr. and Robert Kennedy. The Democratic National Convention was a nightmare. The streets were filled with demonstrators who were fighting with the police and getting beaten with batons and choked by tear gas, while chanting for the television cameras, "the whole world is watching!" There were riots in Chicago, Washington D.C., and other cities, and the anti-war movement was gaining steam. America was in turmoil and President Johnson was not happy.

After returning to classes for a trimester, I decided to return to Ford for my six-month co-op stint and ended up in the Customer Relations Department which, for the most part, was a great experience. I answered customer complaint telephone calls and attempted to solve their problems. It was there where I learned how important listening was and it wasn't so much what you said that counted; it was *how* you said it. In other words, there was a process associated with handling those customer complaints and by listening and understanding the customer you often diffused their issue. In fact, the customer issues were frequently related to discourtesy or personality conflicts at the local dealership, not the actual Ford vehicles. Once again, resolving issues was all about the process. It was satisfying to have a customer call into us really irate and hang up the phone being civil and appreciative. It was enlightening to me and ironic that most customer relations issues had less to do with the vehicle and more to do with the people at a dealership.

By the time I was doing my third co-op with Ford, while I was in my junior year at NU, I was considered a young shining star. I enjoyed my time doing customer service at the Boston district sales office, but that changed when I encountered hate from a local Ford dealer. As I mentioned previously, I learned a great deal by fielding customer complaints, however, one complaint in particular resulted in my having to interact with a racist dealership service manager. I called him and tried to mediate and help the customer when he told me point-blank to mind my own business and that he "would handle things with this nigger in my way."

That service manager's attitude was the exact opposite of the way that I grew up in Auburndale, MA, a small village within Newton, a Boston suburb. The neighbors to our left were Black and those to the right were Irish Catholic and always let my brother and I decorate their Christmas trees. Beyond the four train tracks behind our houses that rattled dishes in our kitchen cabinets when the freight and commuter trains rolled by, what we all had in common was that we were blue-collar working-class people with solid family values. Growing up in the fifties, the neighborhood children were tied together by a mutual love of Little League Baseball and the sports we played on school grounds, in the streets, and in backyards.

Skin color was never an issue for my family. We were raised to be inclusive. In fact, I remember a birthday party for our neighbor next door, Cindy Hill, the little Black girl. Her cousin Candice Hayward was there too and I had a crush on her. During party games we each had a toothpick in our mouth and had to pass round candy life savers with a hole in the middle to each other. It was just 10-year-old kids having fun and chuckling about lips touching lips.

Two stories about race relations when I was younger that come to mind are my dad telling us about his football days back in the thirties when he was chastised by certain teammates for giving a Black teammate a ride home in his car. My dad was one of the few on his football team who had an automobile and wasn't about to let his teammate walk home during a heavy rainstorm, no matter what his skin color was. The other story was when my parents were selling their house in 1959. They had a sale that was about to be closed. The buyers came to our house to sign a purchase and sale agreement and when they saw Cindy Hill, the little Black girl, playing outside next door they called off the deal. Lee Hill, Cindy's mother and our neighbor said to my mother, "Lillian, I'll gladly keep my kids inside so that you can sell your house," and my mother said, "absolutely not! I will not sell to anyone who wouldn't want to live next door to you." Those two powerful lessons have guided me throughout my life and that's why I was so annoyed by that service manager's attitude.

It turned out that my boss, William Entenmann, didn't like the fact that I was advocating for the customer versus the dealer in that situation involving racism and he thought I was being a troublemaker. My position was obvious: the customer should be treated fairly regardless of their skin color. They bought a Ford automobile, and the company should try to solve their problem. That was my job and I took it seriously. Besides, it made me very angry that the Black customer was getting screwed because the service manager of the dealership was a racist bigot and it likely made him feel superior.

As my co-op term was nearing the end and I was preparing to return to classes, Bill Entenmann walked by my desk one day and said matter-of-factly, "you Jew Bastard!"

He was upset with me for being one of those activist Jews who didn't toe the company line. Apparently, I should have ignored the racism at the dealership rather than make a fuss on behalf of the customer and do the right thing. Incidentally, it would have been the right thing for Ford Motor Company too. He followed up by throwing an employee performance review report on my desk. No discussion, no comments, or anything. His demeanor really made me angry. He was a fat, unkempt, and nasty bigot and he was passing judgment on me.

The performance review was clearly biased and negative. Written in pencil and not ink, it was crude, sloppy, smudged, and inconsistent; like Entenmann himself. He accused me of being an inferior employee. This was the polar opposite of the previous two reviews that I had received from Andy St. James and I felt that it was a career-breaker. It certainly was with Ford, but I was more concerned about future co-op jobs and the long-term impact of having such a poor performance review in my college file.

When I reflect on this experience, I remember being marched down to the corner office for a meeting with the District Manager, the Service Manager, William Entenmann, and two other men in the corner office. When I walked into the room the door closed automatically behind me. The District Manager had a button under his desk that closed it using some state-of-the-art electromagnetic device. Apparently, I was supposed to be intimidated, but I wasn't. At this point in my life I had served during the Vietnam War, was a disabled veteran, was married, had adult responsibilities, and had been around powerful leaders before. Nor was I amused. It was a sad display of leadership on the part of Ford Motor Company. Who the hell did they think they were treating me like that?

At one point in the meeting, Entenmann called me "Stroum" loudly and disrespectfully and I said, "my name is Mr. Stroum to you, Mr. Entenmann." They were bullies and effectively fired me by saying that I was unwelcome to return to work there again. I was furious, could feel my pulse rate climbing, but kept my cool and held my temper. That experience really upset me and I thought it would hurt my ability to secure good co-op jobs in the future. After all, who would want to hire someone who bucked the system and had been fired from a leading multi-national automobile company.

I was totally unaware of the antisemitic history of Henry Ford and Ford Motor Company. In 1915 he believed that the "International Jew" was the source of the world's problems which led him to conduct a campaign against Jews in the pages of his newspaper; "The Dearborn Independent." Ford's newspaper articles blamed the Jews for everything from the Bolshevik Revolution and the First World War to bootlegged liquor and cheap movies. He also accused the Jews of conspiring to enslave Christianity and destroy the "Anglo-Saxon" way of life. His articles were later gathered into book form and published under the title: "The International Jew: The World's Foremost Problem." This book was translated into sixteen languages and was to have a profound influence upon the growing Nazi movement in Germany. In fact, Ford's tirades and articles against the Jewish people became so well-known at home and abroad that he was the only American whom Adolf Hitler complimented by name in Mein Kampf.

I knew nothing of this. I also didn't know that Henry Ford also used his leverage as an employer to aggressively try to Americanize immigrants. He was adamantly opposed to labor unions and frequently described them as a global Jewish conspiracy. Although I am Jewish, I was raised in a Christian neighborhood and had never been exposed to extreme antisemitism as a child. After all, back in the fifties we Jews were taught to assimilate just like the Irish and Italians. Although not a formal declaration, it was understood that America was a predominantly Christian country. We even started every day of elementary school with the Pledge of Allegiance to our Flag and The Lord's Prayer, from the New Testament. I remember asking my dad about the prayer and he explained that it was a Christian prayer, but it was no big deal. We weren't offended and nobody made a fuss about it. It was simply the American way back then. Far different from how it is today.

Until the Lowry Air Force Base marching incident in June of 1967, during the Israeli Six Day War, I hadn't personally experienced any serious antisemitism. Our parents also shielded us from it. The holocaust wasn't talked about at home. My parents wanted us to experience the blessings of America. America in the fifties was blessed indeed. We had saved the world from WWII, liberated the concentration camps in Europe, and because of business, technology, and free-enterprise were experiencing a robust economy and improving the quality of life for most citizens. I personally knew nothing about the Jim Crow laws in the South.

Needless to say, I was crushed and angry about my Ford Motor Company experience. I filed a complaint with the Massachusetts Commission Against Discrimination and within months they found that my firing was justified. However, they never interviewed me about my complaint. What a joke! No doubt the Ford lawyers were way too powerful for them, and they were likely intimidated. In reality, I suspect lawyers never got involved. Just the thought of them was likely sufficient to intimidate the administrative staff at the Commission Against Discrimination. Perhaps the claims examiner was antisemitic too. My view of State government workers wasn't very favorable, to say the least.

I was able to get justice, though. A friend of my father's by the name of Joe Kaplan owned Varney Printing in Waltham, MA and was well-connected within the Commonwealth of Massachusetts. He did quite a bit of printing for various state and municipal government offices. In fact, when one of his new printing presses required higher voltage power than was available on his street, he called the mayor of Waltham and within a week a state-of-the-art high-voltage electrical termination was routed directly to his printing business. It even required closing down the street and rerouting the local traffic.

Clearly, Joe Kaplan was a powerful and well-connected guy. In those days, if you got a speeding ticket, you'd call Joe and he'd make it go away. All it would cost you was a carton of Camel cigarettes. I turned sixteen on a Friday and with Joe's influence got my driver's license the following Tuesday, without delay. I passed the written exam, but the driving test was a mere formality.

Upset by the lack of satisfaction I received from the Commission Against Discrimination, I stopped by Joe's office to share the Ford Motor Company story and he leaned back, grabbed his rolodex file with his yellow, nicotine-stained fingers and asked me where this antisemite William Entenmann lived? "Medway," I said. He then lit up a Camel, took a long, deep drag and flipped through the rolodex cards and proceeded to phone the police chief of Medway. After exchanging niceties, he told the Chief that a dear friend's son had been wronged by Entenmann, who lived in his town, and he wanted him "picked up." I wasn't sure what that meant, but soon found out.

From what I later learned, Mr. Entenmann was shocked when the two police officers knocked on his front door at home and explained to him that he was observed leaving the scene of a traffic accident in Boston and they needed to confiscate his driver's license. Entenmann told the officers that he hadn't driven to Boston in three years and surely they were mistaken. The police officers politely apologized and said, "Perhaps there's been a mistake and there will be a hearing next week and you will get your license back then. Not to worry." I understand that his "hearing" was consistently cancelled and finally, after fourteen months, William Entenmann was able to get his license back. In the meantime, his superiors at Ford weren't happy with him and I believe it didn't help his career very much. It may have even cost him his job. I hope it did, but I never really knew. I don't believe that he ever realized that I was the one responsible for the payback either. But, I knew it and that's all that mattered.

Frankly, I would have rather had a fair review of my complaint by the Commonwealth of Massachusetts Commission Against Discrimination. Today, though, having been in business for forty-six plus years and having been involved with politics and State government on several occasions, I understand how things work. The reason I decided to share this story was to reinforce the fact that racial discrimination, sexual harassment, and other injustices are a part of life and like so many other unfair experiences, it is how you handle them that defines who you are. It is important that each one of us defines who we are and not let others do it.

Growing up, my parents told us that we'd be known by

the company we keep. I think it is true and Dave Whitney became one of my best friends in college and he taught me how to be a winner. It is important to associate with and emulate successful people if you want to become a successful person. That's how you learn to win.

William Entenmann might have defined me as a "Jew Bastard," but I defined myself as a "winner" who would ultimately get even with the antisemitic scumbag and receive my well-deserved justice. Thanks to Dave Whitney, I learned how to win using his academic study process and thanks to Joe Kaplan I learned something about how the real-world works, relationships, and the process of living life knowing the importance of friendship and loyalty. I learned how to win and justice prevailed!

3

IF YOU WANT SOMETHING, ASK FOR IT

As Mahatma Gandhi said, "Be the change that you wish to see in the world." In other words, if you want something to happen you must take action and make it happen yourself. Don't wait for someone else to give you what you want, take control of your own life and go after it.

After the horrific Ford Motor Company co-op experience, I was attending classes for six months when an opportunity arose. I was hired as a health insurance claims examiner by The Paul Revere Insurance Company at their home office in Worcester, MA. Looking back, it was no surprise that I was hired because the job was ridiculously easy and the full-time employees there were totally unenthusiastic. Half the time they weren't even working, they were reading the sports pages of *The Boston Globe,* cheating the company out of money. That lackadaisical way of working didn't feel right to me but I maintained a pleasant disposition while I got my work done, knowing that I planned to leave after my three-month co-op term was up. The job was unfulfilling. A policyholder would file a claim for a health issue or disability and we had to verify that they were qualified to receive the benefits. That was it. No telephone interaction and no conversations with people; only paperwork. Ever-growing stacks of paperwork. Mix and match. The same crap every day. There was very little thought involved. I did the work on autopilot, the company got their value, and I lived up to my commitment for three months.

When my co-op term was up, the claims department manager, who was a very nice gentlemen asked me into his office, which was rather formal and well decorated, and said, "Steve, we would love to have you return for your next co-op term," to which I replied, "Thank you very much, I appreciate it, but this type of work is not for me. I need more interaction with people and would rather be involved with sales."

"Well, we've never had a co-op student in sales before," he said. I looked at him and replied, "I'm not your typical co-op student, I'm as old as any entry-level full-time employee in the company, I'm married, I've served in the military, and I'd welcome the opportunity to be considered for a sales position here at The Paul Revere." He said that he'd take it under consideration and let me know.

The following week I heard from him and met with Ken Leard, the manager of the Boston Brokerage office for The Paul Revere and Lou Stanton, the Group Insurance manager. Both meetings were great and I was impressed with both men. Their office was on the 30th floor of The Boston Company Building, One Boston Place; right downtown. I had never been in such an environment before and the thought of working in the city excited me. As it turned out, they were both interested in hiring me. Perhaps it was because I was impressive, or maybe because the co-op budget came from elsewhere in the company and they would have a free employee. They had everything to gain and nothing to lose.

I accepted the job offer from Ken Leard. The main goal of the brokerage office was to recruit, persuade, and support life insurance agents and get them to add The Paul Revere's disability income insurance to their portfolio. The Paul Revere was one of the top providers in the disability market at that time and I was going to provide sales support in the office. They had never had a co-op student before and had no job description or any idea of what they were going to do with me. I would start my job a few months later in June 1971.

Ken was a charming guy and had tremendous product knowledge. Prematurely gray at age forty-three, he was divorced and living at a condominium in Framingham, MA, not far from the small one-bedroom apartment that Peggy and I shared. He had been with the company for fifteen years as an insurance underwriter and decided to try sales after his life-changing divorce. He ran one of the leading offices in the company and reportedly earned about $140,000 a year which was huge money back in the seventies. The median income of a family in 1971 was $10,290.

Ken Leard drove a BMW sedan and offered to pick me up and drive me into the office on my first day of work. Naturally, I was wearing my best conservative business suit, white shirt, and striped tie. I was a little nervous but mostly just excited. After all, I'd be working at a fabulous office building in the heart of Boston. My office was on the thirtieth floor overlooking the Boston Harbor and Logan International Airport. It was a private office and the view was magnificent. It was great being on the telephone and watching sailboats in the harbor and big jets flying in and out of Logan Airport. I was proud of the new situation which I had created for myself simply by asking for it.

A lot of people are afraid to speak up and assert themselves at work. They don't want to risk upsetting their boss or colleagues. Remember, being assertive is different from being aggressive or confrontational. Speak confidently and be respectful. You don't need to use disqualifying language like, "I'm sorry to bother you," and listen carefully to what others are saying in order to understand their perspective. Use "I" statements. For example, "I would like an opportunity to demonstrate my sales ability."

Ken showed me the best route to drive from Framingham and where to park to save a lot of money down by some old, dilapidated buildings which would ultimately be developed into the Faneuil Hall Market Place tourist attraction of today. But, in 1971 all you saw were beggars and parked cars. And if it was raining, you'd see mud. Lots of mud.

Within weeks I was getting bored with the inside sales support, however; I did learn some neat tricks. One time a disability insurance applicant with health issues received a "B" rating which meant that their policy would be more expensive than a standard issue. I called our life insurance agent who sold the policy and explained that his client had received a "D" rating and we weren't happy about it and were going to fight with the home office on his behalf to see if we could get the rating improved. The agent was happy that we were going to try to help him out. Then we'd set the file aside, do nothing, and call the agent back four days later and say, "we called the home office and after doing battle for you we got your applicant's rating changed from D to B which saves your client a lot of money." In reality we did nothing, but the policy was placed and everyone was happy.

This was my first run-in with officially telling a little white lie and the importance of "creating expectations" in the sales process.

I had accompanied a couple of the brokerage supervisors on sales calls and sat quietly, listening and watching, as they made their sales presentations to successful life insurance agents. Paul Revere was a leader in the disability marketplace and worked with the top life insurance agents in the city. I remember one visit to a New York Life Insurance Company duo by the name of Klunan & Rose. Ed Rose was 28 years old and earning about $150,000 per year. Big bucks back then! We chatted and did some business together and I felt every bit his equal at twenty-four years old.

Selling came naturally to me, and I was very good at it. The genesis of my excellence in sales stemmed from the fact that my mother was narcissistic and wanted her three sons to behave the way she wanted us to behave; regardless of what we wanted for ourselves. She saw us as an extension of herself. So, during my formative years I needed to behave in ways that would please her. I was unaware of this, of course, but it became instinctive. I was 'hard-wired' to please people.

My need to make my mother happy was put on steroids by a family crisis when I was eleven years old. It added fuel to the fire of my formative years and the events would impact the rest of my life. I remember it as though they happened yesterday. My brother Jerry, who was seventeen at the time, was angry for many reasons. But the straw that broke the camel's back was that he wanted to attend Newton Technical High School and my mother wanted him to be in a college curriculum. She had visions of him attending MIT because he was very bright and Technical High School was beneath her. He discovered that she went behind his back and called his guidance counselor to plot his future.

After that, Jerry stole our mother's car and ran away from home with his friend, Dave. Jerry was very clever. When he was in New York City he sent my folks a telegram that he was okay, but he had Western Union hold and delay the message for three hours which enabled him and Dave to be far down the highway when the police in NYC were actually looking for them. Unfortunately, they drove off the road during a rare snowstorm and crashed the car in South Carolina.

When my brother Jerry came home from his adventure, he was sitting at the kitchen table talking with my father. One of those light blue metal table tops with a dark blue edge that faded-in atop brown wooden legs, sitting on a yellow linoleum floor. It was a popular décor in 1959. Next to the table was our new automatic washing machine.

While trying to explain something to my father, Jerry raised his hands up toward my father's face. My father, who had an explosive temper, saw this as a sign of disrespect and said, "Don't ever raise your hands to me!" A fist fight ensued. Several punches were thrown and they wrestled and banged against the new washing machine which made a loud bass drum-like noise. It was one of those childhood memories that you recall vividly and when you close your eyes and squint a little, you can see it happen all over again. My brother Jerry escaped and ran out the front door in his stocking feet. He walked several miles shoeless to my aunt's house for refuge.

Meanwhile, my mother grabbed me crying hysterically and held me very tightly and said in a barely understandable combination of crying and shouting, "Don't ever do anything to hurt me!" That injunction was so hard-wired into my psyche that it impacted many major decisions that I made and stayed with me until I was totally rid of it thanks to the many therapy sessions I attended in my early thirties. Can you imagine hearing and feeling that at age eleven? Every damned decision that I made was put through that filter: will it hurt my mother? I even remember dating a girl when I was sixteen years old and the qualifier was, "Would my mother like her?" Unbelievably sad, but true.

Because of my vast experience learning how to please my mother and others, I became adept at figuring out what they wanted from me. That's the essence of selling: listen and observe in order to learn what is necessary to make the sale. While making client sales calls with the brokerage supervisors I was certain I could do the job as well as they did. So, I asked Ken Leard for a meeting and asked him if I could take my insurance exams and go into the field as a brokerage supervisor. He said that he'd have to check with the home office because "they've never done this before." In the meantime, he knew that he'd be getting another source of commissions and overrides that were being paid for by the company's home office co-op budget. He really had everything to gain and nothing to lose.

The answer came back in the affirmative. I was really excited and made arrangements to study for my life and disability income insurance licenses and NASD (National Association of Securities Dealers) stockbroker's license. I managed to get my insurance licenses in only three weeks and convinced Ken to let me go out into the suburbs and make sales calls to life insurance agents by myself. Most of the life insurance agents that his office called on were in Boston and nobody was covering the burbs. It was perfect for me and as luck would have it, I stumbled into a life insurance agent who had a small group of three doctors. He wanted a disability income insurance policy quote for them. A week later he submitted the disability income insurance applications with a heathy deposit amount for the three doctors. It's true, the harder you work, the luckier you get.

Ken always used to say, "at the end of your day make one more sales call." Twenty more calls per month puts statistics in your favor and increases the likelihood of making more sales. Above all else, selling is a numbers game and the more sales calls you make, the greater your likelihood of success. It doesn't matter what you're selling, it is a simple, but smart process that creates another 240 sales opportunities per year.

I really loved working at The Paul Revere Boston Brokerage office and because I was doing a great job for them in sales, they even invited Peggy and me to a sales conference at the Camelback Inn in Scottsdale, Arizona. They had never done that before, but because I really hustled as a contributing member of the team, they took notice, and the perks came. Even when I returned to classes for my final trimester, I was allowed to work with my suburban clients. It provided continuity for the company and was great for me. I arranged most of my classes in the mornings and made sales calls to suburban insurance agents on my way home. It was perfect. The only caveat was that I had to attend classes in a business suit. But that wasn't a big deal; even in 1972.

Ken Leard taught me a great deal and I was hoping to work full-time after graduation in June of 1973. But there was an interesting incident that didn't sit right with him which I would later learn about. He ran a sales contest one month and the prize was that he would take the winner and his spouse or significant other to Anthony's Pier 4 Restaurant in Boston for dinner. It was a beautiful restaurant, right on the Boston Harbor and one of the best in town. Well, I won the sales contest and was very excited. This was a big deal: I worked part-time, and I beat out the full-time employees.

Ken picked us up at our one-bedroom apartment and we were off to Boston. I was a blue-collar kid. What the hell did I know about a prestigious restaurant like Anthony's Pier 4? I had never been there before and it was impressive. Dark wood hallways were adorned with photographs of the Kennedy's, Frank Sinatra, Bob Hope, and other famous politicians and celebrities who had dined there. Everyone was dressed to the max in suits and beautiful dresses. People didn't go out to dinner at fine restaurants in blue jeans back in those days. Once seated, overlooking the water, the atmosphere was spectacular. Fine linen tablecloths and napkins, and waiters and staff in crisp attire dressed the restaurant up even more.

What didn't sit right with Ken was that I ordered an $18 lobster dinner. That was very expensive in those days, and he felt that it was an inappropriate choice. Despite the fact that my sales contributed about $3,600 to his personal income that month, he resented my lobster dinner. In retrospect, what I didn't understand and consider at the time was that he had spent most of his career at the home office as an insurance underwriter and hadn't earned that much money until he was over forty. He paid his dues and felt that I should pay mine too. His frugal background and WASP worldview dictated that I should have been more modest in my menu choice. I probably should have. Interesting that something so trite could end up negatively influencing my future salary negotiations for full-time employment.

I began negotiating with Ken for a full-time position as a Brokerage Supervisor during the spring of 1973. Once again, the "ask for something if you want it" idea manifested itself. In addition to my starting salary, as a bonus I asked for and got five weeks paid vacation in advance to begin working there. I explained to Ken that Peggy and I had promised each other that we would take a week off for every year that I attended college and he agreed to the terms.

So, after driving around and seeing the country and spending a week in San Francisco with a good friend of ours we returned home and I started my full-time job at The Paul Revere Boston Brokerage Office. I was excited to be back and prior to leaving on our trip I had introduced my former classmate Dave Whitney to the company and he had an opportunity to interview at the New York Brokerage office. The manager there was a man named Win Tenack. Dave took the same position as I had taken in Boston. But there was a big difference: Win recognized Dave's need to achieve. Dave graduated first in our College of Business class at Northeastern. What Win Tenack did was create a custom incentive-based pay program especially for Dave so that he would be well-compensated for superior performance. In fact, Dave ultimately spent his entire career at The Paul Revere and ended up managing the New York office where he became the highest compensated Brokerage Manager and employee in the history of the company.

Looking back, I don't know if Win Tenack was more progressive than Ken because he was in New York City or that Ken was simply handcuffed by his own background as a lowly underwriter. In either event, after several months it became clear to me that Dave was making a lot more money than I was for the same sales production. I resented that fact, discussed it with Ken and he wouldn't budge. So, I quit the company to join an insurance agency where I would sell disability income insurance to their clients. I chose to leave Paul Revere because of Ken; not the work. Ironically, if he had chosen to implement an incentive-based program like Dave's he would have made more money and I would probably have had a long-term career with the company too. I really loved The Paul Revere and my job. In retrospect I acted precipitously in resigning. It was a dumb move.

There I was sitting next to the file cabinets at the Krongard Insurance Agency in Newton Center, MA and didn't really have a clue how to mine the data within them. I had no idea how to turn the prospects into customers. I didn't know what steps to take. Should I send direct mail letters to prospects, make phone calls, or go out and see them? I was really stuck, became depressed, and understandably got no guidance from the owner. I sold my way into the agency, got what I asked for, and three weeks later I was fired. What the hell was I thinking?! I was totally embarrassed. A failure.

The days of flying high at The Paul Revere were over. But I had befriended some life insurance agents at a Home Life Insurance Company in Wellesley, MA which I called on and serviced for three years. One agent, by the name of Sam Paris and I became very close friends. I really learned what "closing a sale" was by doing business with him. After calling on him for about nine months, he always saw me and we had pleasant conversations, but he had never placed any orders with me. So, finally, one day I said, "Steve, I've been calling on you now for nine months and you seem to like me and our products, but you've never placed an order with me; what do I have to do to earn your business?" He then told me exactly what I needed to do with respect to getting him a proposal by a certain time along with some other competitive information that would help him make a sale with his client. I did it, and we ended up doing loads of business together and my sales began to spread like wildfire within his office.

Most of the agents there were working with me. In fact, they were so comfortable with me that they gave me my own desk in their office. I learned that closing a sale was being honest by asking for the order and keeping your promises in order to earn the business. In a service business you control the client's expectations so you should always try to deliver a little more than you promised them.

In view of the relationship that I had already established at Home Life in Wellesley, I was recruited to join the agency as a full-time life insurance salesman. Calling on people who didn't want to see me was alien to me. I was accustomed to being an expert who called on a fairly receptive customer base. Selling life insurance was stressful, involved a lot of rejection, and just wasn't very much fun.

My ego was bruised, and it seemed like a really good time to try something totally different. It was 1974 and Peggy and I were married a mere four years. We weren't ready to settle down so I convinced her that we should move to San Francisco. We had a good friend there by the name of Al Ginsburg and visited with him for a week on our five-week journey the year before. Suddenly I was doing something special rather than looking for another job. It was like turning lemons into lemonade and our friends threw us a going away party.

We were leaving for San Francisco from my parent's home in Newton. It was a crisp Tuesday morning in October 1974 and my mother, in her typical fashion came down to the front steps of her house as we were ready to hop into our car and said, "Children, don't forget who you are and where you came from." Then she handed me a business card of a friend's son. His name was Alan Bornstein and he owned

Sanderson Associates, an employment agency in the business district in downtown San Francisco. I thought he might be a worthwhile contact since Peggy and I both needed jobs.

Off we went, driving west in our blue two-seat 1973 MGB Convertible packed with a couple of business suits, blue jeans, tee-shirts, and shorts. Peggy had a couple of nurse's uniforms and together we had a very limited casual wardrobe. The bottom line is that if you want something, go after it. Don't be afraid to take a risk. You never know where it might take you; literally and figuratively.

4

PLANTING THE SEEDS OF CHANGE IN SAN FRANCISCO

Moving to San Francisco and trying new things was important for me. It gave me the courage to take risks and ultimately choose entrepreneurship. Unlike our cross-country trip in 1973 which involved family visits and lots of sightseeing, the drive out to San Francisco this time was a blur. We left Newton, MA on Tuesday morning October 11, 1974, and headed west, driving the northern route on Interstate 90 and stopping along the way to stay at small motels with the exception of one night when we braved sleeping in the car on a secluded Wyoming road. Frankly, I don't recall the small motels where we slept on other nights, but in Wyoming we simply found an area off the main road which was secluded. We cleared the luggage from behind the seats by putting it right outside the car on both sides. Then we put the seats back all the way and slept soundly. We awakened in the morning, put the luggage back behind the seats and hit the road to find the first restaurant to eat breakfast and freshen up. I certainly wouldn't advise doing that today. My, how things have changed in America!

Friday afternoon we arrived in San Francisco and went to our friend Al's apartment at 1801 Beach St. in the Marina District where a note was taped to his doorbell. Handwritten on yellow-lined paper, it said, *San Fransexual welcomes Peg and Steve on October 14, 1974*. We stayed with Al for a few weeks until we found our own apartment in the city. Our bedding was a piece of two-inch-thick foam that was unrolled and put on the floor on his living room. After a couple of weeks searching, we finally found a one-bedroom apartment which was also in the Marina District, a few miles away from Al's place, but not quite as charming a neighborhood.

Initially Peggy and I had planned on taking a couple of months off to play around before getting serious about job hunting. But that was wishful thinking. Neither of us lets moss grow under our feet. In fact, one Saturday I went to a bar up on Union Street, an upscale area, to have a beer, hang out and shoot pool and I recall feeling like it was a total waste of time. It was not relaxing at all. In fact, I felt guilty for doing it. After we began receiving our unemployment checks and getting our new apartment setup, the novelty of moving to San Francisco was wearing off and the reality that "this was our new life" began to set in. And in this new life neither of us had jobs or a purpose and we were beginning to feel very anxious.

Out of my wallet came the business card of Alan Bornstein, President of Sanderson Associates, an employment agency. I phoned him and explained how I got his business card from my mother who was a friend of his mother, and then setup an appointment to meet with him. It would be my initial effort at job hunting and a completely new experience for me. He sounded like a nice guy and very welcoming. Sanderson Associates was a made-up name which sounded protestant and pleasing to the established business community there. It conveyed something different than Bornstein Associates. It reminded me of all of the ethnic actors and celebrities who changed their names to gain greater acceptance in America. Anthony Dominick Benedetto, who left his heart in San Francisco, Americanized his name to Tony Bennett and Kirk Douglas' real name was Issur Danielovich.

Sanderson Associates was in the Business District of downtown San Francisco where the men wore business suits and the women were smartly dressed. It was very similar to Boston. The office buildings crowded out the sun and Al Bornstein's office was on the fifth floor of an old stately brick building. I entered the large brass front doors and walked across the marble floors, generating a muted echo, and took the elevator up, exited to the right and opened the door to his reception area. It was nicely decorated with a conservative feel and I was promptly greeted by a lovely receptionist. All business and very professional, I thought.

Alan was about 30 years old, very genial, had a full beard and receding hairline and at only four years older than me, he owned his own employment agency. He and his wife Cynthia moved to San Francisco about eight years earlier from the blue-collar town of Somerville, MA and started the firm after working for other agencies for a couple of years. After a few minutes, Alan came into the reception area, introduced himself and escorted me to his office which was also nicely appointed. He appeared to be very successful. Once at his desk, I awaited his instructions before sitting and was invited to sit down at a chair just off to the right of his desk.

As we began our conversation with the customary introductions and small talk, his telephone rang. He looked at me and said "Excuse me a minute," picked up the phone and I heard him say, "Hi, how are you doing? No, I'm all set thanks. Is it good stuff? Oh, wait a minute, let me check with someone." He looked at me and said, "Do you want to buy some grass?" I said, "Get me a job and I'll buy some grass." That was my first "official" business transaction in San Francisco!

Al Bornstein and I had a good chemistry and I explained my background in the insurance industry and that I would like to break away into another field if I could. We talked a little more and he walked me down the hall to meet Vince Ferorotti. Even though I was interested in another field, Vince had a great relationship with Fireman's Fund American Life Insurance Company, a wholly owned subsidiary of American Express and felt that he could get me into a good position there. He convinced me to consider a job at a Fireman's Fund office in Walnut Creek which was in the East Bay, past Oakland; about 25 miles from San Francisco and a half hour commute. In retrospect, I was very naïve. They didn't want to help me transition into a new industry because it would have been too much work for them. Besides, I had a great insurance resume and Vince had several insurance contacts. He was also hungry for a commission. It made more sense for him to pick the low-hanging fruit. Live and learn. In every business transaction you really do have to follow the money.

Vince arranged an appointment for me with Cal Farnsworth, the Regional Sales Manager at the Fireman's Fund office in Walnut Creek. The office was in a contemporary redwood building in a very nice suburban setting and location that was beautifully landscaped. We went into Cal's office where he explained the sales position to me. The sales position was similar to my job as a Brokerage Supervisor at The Paul Revere in that it was a wholesale position within the insurance industry. I would be calling on the Fireman's Fund insurance agents who sold property and casualty insurance. They were independent insurance agents whose products included homeowner's insurance, vehicle coverage, business policies of all sorts, and the like. As independent agents, they had a great deal of latitude with respect to what policies they could sell. In effect, they could sell any company's policy. My objective was to persuade those agents to offer Fireman's Fund's life insurance policies to their clients. My job would be to support their efforts and accompany them on sales calls where necessary. I would receive a salary, an expense account, and a new company car.

I accepted the job offer at Fireman's Fund American Life Insurance Company and began working there early in December 1974. In the meantime, Alan Bornstein invited us to his home for Thanksgiving. It was gracious of him, but Peggy and I weren't sure that we had clothes with us that were appropriate and "dressy" enough to wear for the holiday dinner at his home. Nevertheless, we gladly accepted the invitation. Their house was in Pacific Heights, an upscale neighborhood with panoramic views of the Golden Gate Bridge. The home and views were both gorgeous.

When we walked into Alan and Cynthia Bornstein's home the first thing we noticed was a beautiful wall of hanging plants right in front of us and off to the right was a sunken living room, one step down, with a huge bay window and an exquisite view of the Bridge. Wow! The room was large and on the left side was a fireplace which extended into the room with three sides open and there were sofas and chairs along with a large coffee table on the right side. Piled high in a wooden box on the table was the finest marijuana available, sifted, and ready to roll along with the rolling papers, of course!

The dining room had been converted into a bar, buffet, and a dance floor for the occasion. The high-quality stereo system was playing the tunes of the day including Lynyrd Skynyrd's "Sweet Home Alabama" and Billy Preston's "Nothing from Nothing" which were two of my favorites. It was no "traditional" Thanksgiving dinner that's for sure! There wasn't even a dining table set up. Everything was buffet style and there was plenty of food around. So, we proceeded to partake in the marijuana, wine, and food. There were plenty of conversations taking place and during the course of the day there were over 120 people who came to the Bornstein's home to celebrate Thanksgiving. All variations of mankind were represented there and our previous wardrobe concerns were moot. The guests included rabbis, priests, gays, straights, whites, blacks, and Asians from 20 to 85 years old; you name it. It was a totally diverse group of people. Everyone had a blast. Indeed, Peggy and I were very thankful to be included in the most unconventional Thanksgiving dinner we had ever experienced.

What an introduction to San Francisco. It was an amazing contrast to my conservative roots and exposed me to many people with different lifestyles and world views. The Thanksgiving story was such a perfect metaphor for how we can deviate from the conventional family holiday dinner and embrace something completely new and different. It planted seeds of change for Peggy and me.

5

A SALES MANAGER WHO DIDN'T WANT STEAK

The drive from San Francisco to Walnut Creek was an easy commute east against the traffic. That first day I drove our 1973 MGB and it took me only 30 minutes to get there. A straight shot on the Bay Bridge, to the Caldecott Tunnel, to route 24, and a couple of turns into the Fireman's Fund Walnut Creek office building. When I arrived at the office that first day I was treated like family. Cal, my sales manager, was much more laid back than Ken Leard, my manager at The Paul Revere Boston Brokerage office. Originally from New Jersey, Cal had ventured west to California, "the promised land," for a better life. He introduced me to all of the people in the office that I'd be dealing with along with the other property and casualty insurance sales representatives. I was the only Life Sales Representative.

That afternoon we all selected our new company cars. As it happened, the prior year leases all expired right around my start time. We were each getting a new 1975 Oldsmobile Omega which was a compact car. Most of the representatives ordered conservative grey or tan colors, but the car I ordered was bright yellow with a tan interior. I was the sole Life Sales Representative and you could see me coming from a mile away. I liked being the stand-out. I was a competitor and enjoyed winning. That is what I love about sales; it is like a game. There are specific goals and it made me feel good when people recognized my success.

The commute home was also easy and the panoramic view of San Francisco after leaving the Caldecott tunnel was incredibly beautiful. You could see the entire bay area in front of you and the city itself which was often surrounded by fog, especially to the north by the Golden Gate Bridge. San Francisco was always cool, but the temperature increased considerably as you traveled east because the heat in the valley creates thinner air and low pressure which literally sucks the heavier marine air layer over San Francisco. In fact, during the year, the temperature typically varies from 40°F to 83°F in Walnut Creek, but averages only 45°F to 72°F in the city. Because of this, our apartment didn't need air conditioning and we always had the windows wide open. I was shocked that there were no insects.

While I was commuting to the office that first week and becoming familiar with our life insurance products, Peggy was starting her job search. With her creative marketing strategies, she landed a job at the Mount Zion Hospital, as a medical assistant to the Chief of Staff. In fact, they were so impressed with her that they handed her a lab coat and asked if she would like to start working during her first interview. Peggy had gotten a dream job by taking a novel approach. Instead of looking at job advertisements she advertised *herself* at the San Francisco Medical Society office on a bulletin board in the doctors' lounge. Again, it was a great marketing strategy and it worked beautifully.

I always dressed well because I viewed work suits, shirts,

ties, and shoes as a valuable part of the role. If I was an athlete, I'd want the best gear to make me a better player, and if I was an automobile mechanic or carpenter, I'd want the best tools. That's the same way I viewed my business attire. I've always felt that it was important to try and control all of the variables that would impact your success and that it was smart to set yourself up with a wardrobe to help you win the game. The cliché, *you only have one chance to make a good first impression* is absolutely true in the game of business.

After studying the Fireman's Fund American Life Insurance policies that I'd be responsible for getting the independent agencies to sell to their customers, I began to do some analysis of the territory. It turns out that my territory placed forty-ninth out of fifty in the country in sales for the company, a fact that Cal never mentioned. Perhaps I should have asked the question, but it didn't occur to me. Actually, it turned out to be in my favor because up was the only way I could go and up I went!

I approached the job with the same intensity that I employed at The Paul Revere. The sales process was similar, however, the expense account was very generous, and we were expected to befriend the agents over lunch or dinner. I'll never forget how one of my agents, Don Walker responded when I invited him to lunch. After he asked me where I planned on taking him, he asked me how much I thought his lunch would cost. While we had a good rapport, the question threw me off, but I took a guess and estimated it would cost forty dollars. He responded and said, "Steve, I'm busy, can you just send me the check for forty bucks?"

As I sat at the counter at a small diner awaiting my sandwich and soda, I thought about what Don Walker said. I realize that he was only joking, but with comedy there is always a modicum of truth. And the truth was that I felt like a whore for inviting all of these agents to lunch whether I liked them or not. It seemed disingenuous to me, but it was part of the job and I accepted that. Meanwhile, my territory included the entire Bay Area, from San Rafael, to the North of San Francisco, down to San Jose, to the South, and out to Pleasanton in the East Bay which was way out in the country. So, as I did back in Boston, I looked at who the most productive agents were and where they were located. Then I planned my travel around them. I was highly efficient and didn't waste any time. Naturally, I wanted to visit with and meet the best agents first. Prioritizing sales prospects is the foundation for effective selling.

My strategy was working and life insurance applications were starting to pour into the office at a pretty good clip and by mid-February I was beginning to get noticed by people in the home office, just twenty-five miles away on California Street in San Francisco. Only three months into the new job and everything was humming. In fact, I was invited to a meeting at the home office to talk to a group of sales representatives about the concept of prospecting which involves identifying, categorizing, and prioritizing potential customers to call on.

I wasn't comfortable speaking in front of groups, although this was a group of only twenty-five. So, I thought, why not emulate someone who speaks well and "act the part?" That's exactly what I did. I chose to emulate Senator Ted Kennedy from my old home state of Massachusetts. He had a specific intonation and rhythm to his speech. And it worked. I quoted Sam Hayakawa, the semanticist and professor of English who later became a Senator from California. I had one of his books and recall him writing an essay in which he stated, "a cow is not a cow is not a cow." In other words although all were cows, all cows were different. I spun that concept into, "a prospect is not a prospect is not a prospect" and delivered it with the rhythm and intonation of Ted Kennedy. It proved to be a successful approach and I went on to explain how I differentiated, categorized, and prioritized my prospects. "Acting" helped me succeed in this small speech scenario. I shielded my "self" from the scariness associated with public speaking and it worked. Frankly, being successful often includes doing things that aren't particularly fun or pleasant. I always figured that my goals outweighed any unpleasant tasks.

The agents that I worked with in my sales territory liked the fact that I was contributing to their success and I was also having fun being productive. I had brought the life insurance sales total in my territory from forty-ninth place out of fifty in the company up to third place. I even outproduced my predecessor's entire previous year's sales, and I did it in just three months. Achievement felt good and I was proud of what I had accomplished.

My sales manager, Cal Farnsworth, called me into his Walnut Creek office for a private meeting and I was really excited. I figured that I would get a good "pat on the back" and maybe even a bonus or small raise as recognition for my superior, stellar performance. However, instead of congratulating me he said, "You know, Steve, in life there are people who need to eat steak to be happy and there are other people who are satisfied eating pork-and-beans. Around here pork-and-beans are just fine. Do you get what I mean?" Wow! I did get what he meant and I was amazed by what I had just heard and was numb with disbelief.

By the time I drove home to the city that evening I was so angry that I decided to barely work for the next several weeks. I'd make a few phone calls to agents each morning and then go down to the Marina Green for a jog and sunbathing. Cal's comment made me feel both justified and confused. His idea of "the promised land" was a cushy job in Walnut Creek and I naively thought that sales success was the objective of everyone in business, especially in a major corporation.

Then one day about five weeks after my meeting with Cal, I was in the San Francisco home office for another meeting and the vice president of brokerage sales, Dick Wolf, approached me, put his hand on my right shoulder and congratulated me for leading the company in sales for the past month. At that point anger, frustration, and inexperience ruled the situation and I said, "Shame on you, I haven't worked for over a month and I'm leading *your* company in sales." At that point he asked me to join him in his office for a private conversation. He was very bright and empathetic. So, I shared my experiences with him and said that I couldn't continue working for Cal and wanted to come into the home office and create the company's national sales training program because it was clear that I knew what I was doing since I had outperformed every other territory while not working even part-time.

We talked about such a position and Dick Wolf said to me, "What would you do if we didn't promote you into the home office." I said, "then I'll resign and go to Safeco, I'm sure they would be interested in what I could contribute to their sales program." Safeco Insurance was Fireman's Fund's largest competitor. Two weeks later, Dick promoted me to "Assistant Director Life Marketing Training Development," to create the company's first national sales training program for life insurance sales representatives.

Moving to the home office was an absolute culture shock. I had always been a field salesman and an expert calling on someone who I could help with their job. In short, I had freedom. I had the company car, the expense account, and was bringing value to my customers because I knew more about the topic that they were interested in than they did. I made things happen for them and it felt good. The home office didn't provide any of those rewards for me. Seated out in the middle of a large room with everyone else was humiliating. There were no partitions and listening to giggling girls sitting in front of me talking on the phone was totally distracting.

After a few weeks, my new boss, Richard Purtle, who was soft-spoken and very perceptive could sense that I needed some "sales action" to recharge my batteries so he asked me if I would like to fly down to their American Express office in Phoenix, Arizona to sell life insurance to their office employees. I welcomed the opportunity to get away and was looking forward to traveling with a fellow Life Sale Rep named Sonny Wilhelm.

On the way down to Phoenix Sonny and I strategized about our approach and decided that we would circulate a sign-up sheet for the employees to talk briefly with us about their life insurance and financial planning needs. We figured it wouldn't be hard to convince young office types to take a break from their mundane routines, even if they had to listen to our pitch. For our sales approach, we created an informal setting in a small side office with coffee and plenty of ash trays to set our prospects at ease.

We'd start with small talk, then segue into to our rehearsed questions designed to get them to close a deal with us in under twenty minutes. Are you saving money? Unsurprisingly, the answer was usually no. Would you like to save money if you could? Unsurprisingly, the answer was always yes.

This enables you, as a salesman, to control the prospect. Open-ended questions are to gather information and closed-end questions are to get affirmation. The next question was, "Could you save twenty dollars a month, a mere five bucks a week?" Their answer was invariably, "Yes, of course." Then, I'd begin filling out a life insurance application by asking their first and last name, date of birth, etc. I would explain that this savings program also provides a life insurance benefit, so that if you die your beneficiary can get some money. "Would you like your mom to be your beneficiary if something happened to you?" The answer was typically "yes," and I'd get a signature and wrap up the brief meeting. Virtually everyone we met with ended up buying life insurance. Sonny and I did this all day long for three days in a row. I knew that our approach was sketchy at best and unethical at worst, but that didn't matter because the home office loved the results that we were getting. The Phoenix mission was a resounding success.

After the Phoenix visit I returned to my desk to continue working on my National Sales Training Program which merely formalized what I had done myself in real-time for several months as the Walnut Creek Life Sales Representative. By this point, I had grown stagnant and I wanted to figure out what the hell I wanted to do and where I fit into the workspace. So, I took the opportunity to get vocational counseling at the University of California, Berkeley. A major part of their program involved taking the Strong-Campbell Interest Inventory Test which helped individuals identify their work personality by exploring their interests in six broad areas: realistic, artistic, investigative, social, enterprising, and conventional. The results revealed your areas of interest as well as what professionals you identified with the most.

My Strong-Campbell results were art, writing, merchandising, sales, and business management, with merchandising and sales being off the chart at the high end. I clearly had very similar interests to those of an advertising executive and no other occupation even came close. Mathematics, which is a big part of the insurance industry was, low on my interest scale. No surprise there.

I created the National Sales Training Program within three months and presented it to management at a major sales meeting at Silverado Country Club in Napa. The manicured lawns and landscaping were foreign to me, but they were beautiful. The colorful plantings integrated with the stately white buildings were breathtaking. It was a totally new scene for a blue-collar kid.

As I approached the lectern to make my presentation to management, I remember walking down an aisle and looking behind the scenes at a television where Johnny Bench from the Cincinnati Reds was catching, and the Boston Red Sox were at the plate. It was the 1975 World Series and I would've much rather been watching the game. My presentation turned out to be a disaster. I failed to line up my alliances, which I didn't know how to do in a corporate setting because I was always a field salesman. Politics wasn't my strong suit and that was my biggest error. I was up there all alone with no supporters and not getting a positive response. I should have created some allies and shared my program with them. On top of all this, the program held everyone accountable and I had learned from past experience that accountability, excellence, and high-achievement weren't part of the corporate culture at Fireman's Fund American Life Insurance Company at that time. It was more like chill-out and just do enough to get by and get your kicks outside of work.

I was down in the dumps again and began utilizing the company library to research other companies and jobs I might like to pursue. One afternoon I just had to leave the office which wasn't typically allowed, but I couldn't breathe as a captive in the large room full of mediocrity and needed some fresh air. In fact, in 1975 at the Fireman's Fund home office each door had an armed guard standing there because there had been a period of unrest as a result of the assassination of Mayor George Moscone and Supervisor Harvey Milk by former Supervisor Dan White in November. As I was leaving the office and lighting up a cigarette, I began walking away and the guard said, "Where are you going?" And I said, "To the bar down the street" to which he replied, "Halt!" I laughed and said, "Go ahead shoot me in the back." After a beer and a couple of cigarettes I cooled off and returned to the office.

As destiny would have it, one night during that period, our friend, Don Bornstein was coming to our apartment in San Francisco for dinner from the south bay and on the train up to the city he bumped into someone who we both knew. When asked where he was going, Don told him that he was going to see me and mentioned my achievements and frustration at Fireman's Fund. Then the guy told Don about a business opportunity in San Mateo that I might be interested in.

As Peggy, Don and I sat at dinner that night, I shared my frustrations over the management at Fireman's Fund. I knew that as a VP of a major retail chain, Don understood the difference between a good and bad manager. Good managers focused on bringing out the best in their subordinates, and bad managers, like Cal Farnsworth, didn't care about their subordinates' growth.

A day later I received a phone call from a guy named

Mike Gerber. He was very glib and gave me an overview of his company and a new company they started called "Newsmaker," outlining a potential opportunity for me. He explained that he was partner in a communications company called "Cuniform, Inc., which creates marketing plans for small companies and can also implement the plan recommendations for them. The very clever company name was derived from cuneiform which was one of the earliest known systems of writing. While many prospects didn't need a full marketing plan, they could all use product publicity because it is the most cost-effective and versatile form of communications. Hence, the establishment of Newsmaker. "We make news about our clients' products which results in free exposure in trade and business publications for them." That exposure was worth from three to five times the value of paid advertising, claimed an article in *Advertising Age Magazine*. My interest was piqued, and we set up a date to meet later in the week.

Cuniform was in a San Mateo office building that was clean and sleek looking, with floor-to-ceiling windows, giving off a vibe of efficiency and success. What differentiated Newsmaker was their business model. In lieu of a retainer, where a client would contract to pay a specific fee for PR (public relations) services over a designated period of time, like other agencies that wanted cash-flow predictability, Newsmaker had a one-page contract that outlined the publicity services provided for a very reasonable fee of $375. The company's strategy was to have higher volume with a lower fee. Mike Gerber explained that our direct sales job was to identify a company to call on, telephone the president to make an appointment to meet, close the sale for publicity services, and get a check on the spot or setup another meeting for the purpose of starting a project. Then a writer would call and set up a meeting to conduct an interview to learn about the products and company and execute the terms of the agreement.

The meeting with the managers that day resulted in a job offer. I saw a lot of promise in the role and was excited about the potential client list I could build. After all, virtually every small company in the hundreds of industrial parks in the Bay Area were prospects, regardless of industry.

A few days later, I scheduled a follow-up meeting to learn more about the role. This offered me some time to think about it and discuss it with Peggy. When I went back, I immediately recognized how different the environment was compared to the companies I had previously worked for. The leaders seemed to be in control of their own destiny and that inspired me. I wanted to emulate them.

They offered me the job as General Manager of Newsmaker which was actually an appeal to my ego. It was really a direct sales and sales management job. The compensation was straight commission of $130 for personal sales and overrides of $20 commission on sales made by my sales team members plus a car allowance of $130 per month. There was plenty of incentive to hustle and recruit good people and a lot of opportunity to grow and learn from the impressive leaders. The idea of being in a real entrepreneurial situation that would allow me to get paid what I'm worth was exciting, however; the idea of only earning commission was a bit frightening.

I went home and weighed the options, agonizing over the decision. I knew that I wanted to get out of the insurance industry and into my own business. Now was the chance to do that, however, I knew that it would be taking a risk. Straight commission with no guarantee! If ever I was going to make a move and take the risk, this would be the time.

Peggy had a good paying job and we had no children. Still, it was hard to step up and put my ass directly on the line. I remember sitting on the living room rug in our apartment discussing this with Peggy and I had such a headache that I put my head on her lap and began crying like a baby. What should I do? What if I failed again?

6

A TASTE OF ENTREPRENEURSHIP GONE SOUR

Deciding to work on straight commission was the scariest thing I had done to date in my life. Being assertive and talking myself into new situations in the past were steps up the ladder. This time, however, there was a real risk that I would fall off and get hurt. The only way to avoid dealing with this reality was to work hard. I didn't realize, though, that hard work could become a compulsion.

My first day at Newsmaker was supposed to be January 2, 1976, however; I couldn't wait to dig in and get started. I had already gone to a nice men's shop downtown and invested in two Yves St. Laurent suits that were tailored handsomely and fit me like a glove. A few new dress shirts, ties, and shoes completed my business uniform. I looked and felt every bit as successful as I wished to become.

When I arrived at the Cuniform-Newsmaker office a week before Christmas, Mike Gerber said, "What are you doing here? We can't officially put you on the books until January." I said, "Mike, I'm not looking for money, I just want to get to work!" The sales pitch materials included a nicely prepared presentation book of press clippings and the one-page publicity services contract for $375. One dollar in 1976 was equivalent in purchasing power to about $5.58 in 2023. So, by today's standards, the services would cost about $2,100.

Consistency is critical to achieving sales goals. Sales is both an art and a science. Art relates to your work ethic and preparation and science relates to numbers. The more sales calls you make, the greater the probability you will make sales, regardless of your skill level. Having a good work ethic is essential because it sets the foundation for consistent effort and dedication to achieving goals. It means being reliable, responsible, and diligent in your work, and helps to build trust and respect with colleagues, clients, and partners. With a strong work ethic you are more likely to take ownership of your responsibilities and be proactive in problem-solving, and consistently deliver high-quality results.

I was passionate about Newsmaker and passion is the fuel that drives the motivation and sustained effort required to be consistent. When you are passionate about your work, you are more likely to be engaged, energized, and committed to achieving your goals. In the entrepreneurial setting, passion can also inspire creativity and innovation because you are also more likely to think outside the box when pursuing something you truly care about. So, if you have a good work ethic and passion, they can help you achieve your goals and become successful.

When I first met the founder of Cuniform, an eccentric man named Ace Remas, it all became clear to me why I was not inspired by the other managers. Ace set a good example and he wasn't afraid to try new things. In fact, he went up against a bunch of biotech executives before biotechnology took off, and sealed a marketing plan thanks to his extreme confidence and fearlessness.

Ace was a dream boss for someone like me, who was motivated and driven. When I brought a new idea to him, he would say, "Don't think about it; do it." As a firm believer in the experience itself and moving away from the fear of failure, Ace propelled me to reach higher and become fearless. Those evaluations of the experience would be made independently much later because he believed that they would interfere with executing the task. He taught me that the fear of failure would negatively impact your behavior and inhibit your performance. Therefore, he thought, get rid of it. Become free of the fear of failure. It cannot help you. Ace believed that you should just do the best that you can in the short term and don't be dissuaded by worrying about the outcome. That said, he sure loved productivity and achievement; almost at all costs.

San Francisco in the mid-seventies was all about self-awareness and the Human Potential Movement. Young people often migrated there to "find themselves" or to get a fresh start. Myself included. Popular during that time was the EST program which was a form of Large Group Awareness Training. We had salespeople who had participated in the program and found it worthwhile. Founded by Werner Erhard (born John Paul Rosenberg), who lectured and wrote extensively about self-improvement, EST stood for "Erhard Seminar Training." The seminar's objective was to change a person's lifestyle so that they could eliminate or change situations that they had been tolerating, and to achieve this by implementing the ideas of transformation, personal responsibility, accountability, and possibility. The seminar was a four-day, 60-hour self-help program given to groups of 250 people at a time. It was very intensive and each day would contain 15–20 hours of instruction.

In a very real sense, Newsmaker was a new-age type of company. We were taking a new approach to an age-old business model and worked with similar intensity to EST. In the traditional advertising and public relations business, a single account executive handled the solicitation and execution of a client relationship and there were typically only a handful of clients. Payment was always in the form of a retainer, which is an agreement to work on a continuing basis for a defined number of hours per month over a long period of time. Since an agency typically worked with a limited number of clients, the retainer provided payment predictability.

A long-term retainer involved more money than a simple, one-time $375 fee and, therefore, was a much bigger decision for a prospective client to make. What Newsmaker did was to create a new business model similar in concept to the life insurance business model, making us unique in the industry. Being disruptive and standing out is fun. It is also what leads to success for a lot of companies. That's one reason why I was so comfortable with the Newsmaker idea. In the life insurance business, you had one insurance salesperson who sold life insurance, disability income insurance, health insurance, and pensions. That person didn't have to possess the skills necessary to execute those insurance and pension programs, but they needed to understand the key provisions of the various policies in order to sell them to prospective customers. Sales were made, of course, by identifying and solving a prospect's financial problems using the various insurance policies. In short, you don't have to know how to manufacture a product to sell it. Likewise, Newsmaker salespeople didn't have to be public relations specialists.

So, you can see the value proposition we had at Newsmaker. For a small one-time fee we would get news published about your product in the news sections of the media where your customers were reading and paying attention to in the first place. Product publicity is a very versatile marketing tool and much more cost-effective and believable than paid advertising and we knew what editors were looking for. Another practical aspect of our new business model was that it was less expensive to hire salesmen than account executives and our writers didn't require extensive marketing skills. What's more, by working on a low-cost project basis we didn't need client retainers because we had cash-flow volume produced by several salespeople and could have an unlimited number of accounts.

We were all young. I was twenty-seven, Ace was thirty-six, and Mike Gerber was the old man at forty. Ace and Mike were fearless and I wanted to be like them. Professional selling is not for everyone. To be successful in sales you need to realize that there is a process and that the word "no" from a prospect is merely a detail. You are typically rejected seventy percent of the time in sales. That's why it is important to look at selling as a game. An all-star baseball player fails to get a hit seven out of every ten at-bats.

Mike was the best salesman I have ever met. I'll never forget the time I shadowed him on a sales call. It took him only seconds to build a rapport with the client, but it was how he presented the information that really wowed me. In clear and concise language he spoke about how publicity could benefit the customer's company. And then he laid it all out for them, continuing in a matter-of-fact tone as he explained what our services were and what they cost. After each point, he would check in with the client, and say, "Do you see how that works or do you see what I mean?" He would get agreement before proceeding from point-to-point, all the while engaging the prospective customer. Then he would continue and again get affirmation with each point because there was no sense in moving forward if the prospect didn't understand and agree to what you've just discussed. When Mike got to the end of the conversation and asked for the order, then the real selling began.

Mike Gerber would say, "Well, you said that you understood what publicity was and what it could do, and agreed that it would benefit your company, exactly what is it that is preventing us from working together today?" The prospect would reply, for example, "My product isn't quite ready." Mike would then implement what I call the "if-statement." He'd say, "May I ask you a question? If your product were ready today, would we get started?"

If yes, then he'd say, "Great, when will it be ready?" If no, then the same process would begin all over again until he got the order, asked for another appointment to bring back some ideas and discuss it further, or was asked to leave. That last option didn't happen very often. It was always important to get permission to ask a question because it engaged the prospect. What was great about this selling process, or sales track, was that you could listen and observe the prospect's body language and determine whether or not they were being truthful. Most were not being truthful, but also felt uncomfortable saying, "no."

What made Mike so successful in direct sales was his ability to establish rapport and build trust with a prospect. He also understood their needs and wants and tailored his pitch to those needs by amplifying the benefits of our service and how they could help him achieve his goals. Finally, Mike was able to overcome objections by addressing them in a way that reassured the prospect. These ingredients to sales success are even more important today because of the bombardment of messages that prospects receive from social media and friends.

The fascinating thing about direct sales is the inherent bias in the meeting: I don't want to buy versus I want you to buy. That's the prospect-salesman dynamic and why it is so important in direct selling to get a referral. It helps eliminate the bias. Believability and likeability are the two keys to making a sale. Regardless of what you are selling, it always boils down to "do I believe this person is being honest and can they be trusted?" Naturally there has to be a fit for your product or service. You need to solve a problem or provide a benefit that the prospective client believes he or she needs. But, if they don't believe or like you; nothing will get them to place an order. Just think of how many times you've gone into a retail store and the salesperson was pushy or obnoxious. You said, "I'm just looking, thank you" and they persisted in following you like a puppy dog and questioning you. So, you just turned around and walked out of the store. Even if you knew exactly what you wanted, you left empty handed; damned if you'd buy anything from that idiot!

When I did a brief stint working for Home Life Insurance Company in Wellesley, MA I learned how to develop referrals. There aren't too many people who long to hear from a life insurance agent, so referrals are key. As Sam Hayakawa the semanticist would have said, "a referral is not a referral, is not a referral." The optimum referral is a recommendation from a customer and I learned how to gather those while on calls at other businesses in the same industrial complex. I would enter each meeting with an index card listing five other companies in the prospective customer's industrial park or office building. At the conclusion of our meeting, I would take it out of my pocket and with reference to the first company I'd ask, "can you help me out for a minute? The answer was usually yes and I'd continue, "are you familiar with this particular company?" If so, then I'd ask more about them and who the president was. Then I'd continue down my list of companies. Everyone wants to be helpful and the index card created an expectation.

By doing the index card routine at the end of every meeting, I'd establish a backlog of companies to call for an appointment. If I had no further details, I would call them and say, "Hi, I was speaking with so-and-so at XYZ company right next door to you and your name came up in conversation. (I brought it up, of course). My name is Steve Stroum from Newsmaker and we specialize in getting news published about small companies like yours. I would like to come by to learn more about what you do and determine if it is newsworthy. Would next Monday at 10 a.m. work for you or would Tuesday at 1 p.m. be better? If there was resistance, it was usually softened by saying, "I can assure you that at the very least you will find our meeting informative, and that your time will have been well spent."

Since Mike Gerber had managed forty salesmen at one time, I knew that I would learn a lot from him, however; I didn't discount the fact that I too, had a lot to contribute to Newsmaker. I created training plans and documents that the salespeople could follow, which allowed me to ultimately be in control of their interactions with customers. In turn, they brought in more sales, and I made more commissions. Knowing that salespeople are independent to a fault, and they are in sales for a reason...to avoid being held accountable at a nine to five salary job, I put as much effort into training them for success as I could, and while it was laborious, it was well worth it.

When I officially started working at Newsmaker in January 1976, the first thing I did was increase the price from $375 to $395. The prospect was likely already thinking $400, so I figured the twenty bucks wasn't going to matter. I began pitching two weeks later. This is when the telephone cold-calling began and if the conversation went as planned, I'd close the call by setting up a future appointment. It was during my second week that I made my first sale. Coming back to the office with a check for $395 from a total stranger who trusted me enough to hire me on the spot was exciting and validating. It was a victory in the game of sales which often begins as a competition between a buyer and a seller. Winning is exhilarating for me and receiving accolades from Ace and Mike was incredible. It felt great to be a winner in the rough-and-tumble real world of entrepreneurship and I really enjoyed the recognition from these two men who I so desperately wanted to emulate. It was a far cry from Cal Farnsworth of Fireman's Fund American Life Insurance Company. I felt at home in that winning Cuniform-Newsmaker environment and I was having fun.

Effective selling involves a great deal of repetition and that's what I did for the next several weeks. At the end of the appointment setting day, around 5:30 or 6:00 p.m Mike and I would sit down across from each other in the conference room and refine the sales presentation. We'd discuss what I did, refine the sales pitch and he'd type on an IBM Selectric® typewriter. That practice was repeated weekly for a few weeks until we were satisfied that the sales presentation was more than adequate and easier to teach to our new salespeople. I remember Mike mentioning to me that he wanted to write a book someday about what entrepreneurs need to do to become successful. He would ultimately go on to write numerous best-selling business books including *The E-Myth Revisited which* is a must read for any entrepreneur, and several other versions for specific markets and professions.

I genuinely enjoyed working with salespeople and I made it a point to take Mike's advice, swallowing every morsel he had to offer. He would say, "You have to take these salespeople by the hand and hold it, then slap it, and then hold it at the same time." It was important to be strong and supportive.

By the end of February, the sales were beginning to roll in and I was starting to make some serious money in commissions and overrides and naturally Ace and Mike made a deal with me. On March 4, 1976 I signed an agreement, without an attorney, to own one-third of Newsmaker and I agreed that all income paid to me, including my car lease, were advances against my share of the net profits of the company. At this point, I was also going to receive a fixed salary of $600 per week which worked out to $31,200 (equivalent to $174,000 in 2023) annually, plus the nice car. So, even though it wasn't likely that I was going to receive any monies beyond my salary and lease as applied to the net profits, I figured that it was cheap tuition for what I was learning and the overall opportunity that I had.

I was satisfied with the new business arrangement and was excited that Newsmaker was getting its own two-room office across the courtyard and moving in a positive direction. But my excitement for the company quickly hit a wall when, a few weeks later, Ace asked if he could borrow some money from me to meet cash flow requirements. I had $3,000 in savings that I let him borrow and he prepared a straightforward on-demand promissory note. Naively, I didn't even want to consider that he wouldn't repay the loan or that he was using me. Peggy and I had socialized with Ace and Mike and at this point, the lines between my work life and personal life were non-existent.

It was springtime and I was working at a torrid pace. My typical workday was from seven in the morning until somewhere between nine o'clock at night and midnight. I was a workaholic. Reflecting back, I either had a lot of passion or was damned afraid to take the time to think objectively about my situation. Perhaps it was a little of each. If not for Ace and Mike being right beside me in terms of putting in long hours, I'd have been suspicious of their motives. That was the effort needed to be successful, I thought. That's what entrepreneurs did. The reality, however, is that a workaholic is someone who is addicted to their work and has an intense and compulsive need to work excessively and continuously. Workaholics often prioritize work above all other aspects of their life, including family, friends, and self-care.

The action that goes along with helping others and building something is what I treasure. I became consumed by this and in turn consumed by the work I did for Newsmaker. To provide more efficiency, Mike suggested we hire someone to set up appointments so our sales team could stay in the field. While I was dubious of the suggestion at first, I deferred to Mike's expertise, and we hired a woman named Fran. Back in the mid-seventies there were a lot of small manufacturers because China's economy hadn't opened up until 1979 when the U.S. and China reestablished diplomatic relations and signed a bilateral trade agreement that ignited the rapid growth of trade between the two nations.

While Fran did telephone a lot of small businesses and

speak directly with the presidents, she failed to provide them with the proper expectations and the clients were told they were getting a "free publicity evaluation." Needless to say, the prospective client was disappointed when I showed up prepared for a sales meeting. Too often, they didn't even remember setting up an appointment with Newsmaker. It was beyond frustrating and a huge waste of time.

By early June I was feeling totally burned out and really needed a vacation. But, having to terminate Fran and the experiment with her that hurt our sales momentum was a problem that required lots of energy to solve. I needed to recruit and hire new salespeople while I was out making sales calls myself to fund the company. I was exhausted and stressed. I had lost twenty pounds and was smoking two packs of cigarettes a day. In fact, I had previously mentioned to Mike and Ace at the outset that Peggy and I had planned to go back to Boston over the Fourth of July holiday, nearly two years since we moved to San Francisco, and the trip was etched in stone.

Newsmaker was all-consuming and the much more experienced Ace and Mike were pulling my strings and keeping me motivated and running at full speed ahead. I knew they didn't like the fact that I was leaving for a week. Perhaps it was because I would be out of their control? I began to wonder, were they really sincere partners? Whatever the case, Peggy and I decided to take our vacation to see everyone back home and enjoy the bicentennial July 4th celebration in Boston. She would stay for two weeks, and I'd return after one week because there was lots of work to do building Newsmaker to the next plateau and I felt uncomfortable being away any longer.

We stayed with my folks while we were at home. I decompressed and it was good to eat breakfast, lunch, and dinner. Alongside crowds of people, we watched the bicentennial fireworks in Boston from the MIT side of the Charles River on the lawn by Memorial Drive in Cambridge. The fireworks display was ignited from a barge in the river adjacent to the Hatch Memorial Shell, an outdoor concert venue on the Charles River Esplanade in the Back Bay section of Boston which was built in 1939–1940 and had wonderful acoustics and was a great setting for a concert. In those days, all sorts of boats and canoes would be in the water enjoying the music and festivities. After nine-eleven that changed. Boats were no longer allowed too close to the Esplanade during holiday festivities.

My folks also put on quite a party for us at their home complete with a professionally painted banner on the front of the house that read, "Welcome home Peggy and Steve." They invited about seventy-five or a hundred people including cousins and friends. We had a great time and shared stories that were atypical, like the party we attended in Marin County, north of San Francisco, where the hostess greeted us at the door wearing nothing but a scarf around her neck!

After a week, I kissed Peggy and my mom and dad goodbye at Logan International Airport in Boston and boarded a plane back to San Francisco. I had a great visit with them and felt like I recharged my batteries. I was ready to return to my beloved Newsmaker. The night that I arrived home I was surprised to receive a phone call from Mike Gerber telling me to meet him at the airport the following morning at nine for a consulting gig in LA. He told me he'd tell me all about it on the plane.

The next day, Mike and I visited an electronics manufacturing firm on the outskirts of the sprawling City of Angels and met with the president and marketing vice president.

This was all part of a Cuniform consulting deal. Ace and Mike had managed to get control over a substantial budget for a group of doctors who invested in different small companies. They had the authority to spend a few million dollars on their behalf. As it turned out, the meeting was essentially a fact-finding mission. I enjoyed the experience and always liked touring manufacturing facilities.

Aboard the airplane on the way back to San Francisco, Mike revealed the real reason why he wanted me with him. They wanted me to sell for Cuniform and start another business with them, while another colleague, Stan, took over Newsmaker. Stan had just joined Cuniform and went on a couple of sales calls with me before I left for vacation. Apparently, he was evaluating me. Stan was a slick dude, kind of a con man, and I didn't know him very well. He had a Hollywood-style bachelor pad with a closet in his bedroom that was converted into an aviary with beautiful white birds flying around and soft lights into the background for full effect. Mike Gerber's news felt like a punch in the gut, so unexpected that it sent a ripple of confusing emotions through me. What happened to our partnership agreement?

Their proposition was for me to run my ass off and starve myself again building another new business from scratch. I had been run ragged for a full six months and finally thought the pressure would be off a little when I returned to my San Francisco home and I could live a little more "normal" lifestyle. I felt as though I had paid the price and earned the right to a more normal situation.

I didn't even ask what the business plan was and simply said, "Mike, that wasn't our agreement, I'm really going to have to take a few days and think this over." Later that night I spoke with Peggy on the phone and shared the news. She could instantly tell that I was totally dejected. But I was rested, had my head on straight, and despite being shocked, angry, and disappointed, I was in a position to think more clearly than when I was exhausted. And "think" I would do.

One of the things that occurred to me is that my business agreement was bogus. Even though I thought at the time that Ace and Mike were really friends, it was wishful thinking. From that day on I never signed another business document without my lawyer reviewing it. Unfortunately, however, after this experience I still mixed up my business and personal life and it ended up costing me dearly, financially and emotionally.

7

WHERE DO I GO FROM HERE WITH MY LIFE?

We've all been in a situation where we've been caught off guard and losing Newsmaker was like losing my first love. Whether you experienced this in a relationship, academics or the workforce, the feeling of being underappreciated can lead to confusion, emotional turbulence and a questioning of one's own value.

After Ace and Mike presented me with a dead-end proposition that would require me to give up my life, I was heartbroken. Newsmaker was like a child to me and I had trusted the leaders. What's more, being totally practical, if I were to start another business, why would I put myself in a junior position again with limited control of my future? So, I resigned and worked another two weeks to wrap things up properly. I was taught to be the bigger person when it came to doing the right thing. As another layer of betrayal, Ace refused to repay the $3,000 I loaned him until I signed a non-compete agreement. It was clearly a way of him controlling me until my last minute on staff and beyond.

I wanted to leverage what I'd learned and find a good job. I began responding to help wanted advertisements for sales managers and scheduled several job interviews. I was a sales professional and knew that losing my job was like losing a sale and I had to move ahead and schedule job interviews. One memorable interview was for a facsimile (FAX) machine company. Although it's hard to believe today, in our booming technological era where we have seamless global connectivity, the fax machine was new and exciting back then. These bulky one-hundred-pound machines cost $18,000 which is why they were only used by Fortune 500 companies. This was during the days it took six minutes to transmit a single page of an urgent document, but it was a major technological advance as far as communication in the workforce was concerned.

I had what I thought was a successful interview with the regional sales manager and was invited back for a meeting with the vice president of sales that evening. During dinner that night I found myself more interested in the job as each second passed and part of me already felt like I was part of the team. So, as you can imagine, I was filled with disappointment when the sales manager called me back to inform me that I simply didn't have enough experience and I was denied the position. Losing that opportunity always bothered me because I spent three hours drinking wine with the management team. I thought that it was a sure thing for me to be selected for the position. Otherwise, why would they have entertained me for so long?

You know, it took me about twenty-five years to figure out the real reason I lost the FAX machine opportunity. It came to me in my sleep at about 3:00 a.m. one night. Bubbling up from a deep memory, it occurred to me that if I had just ordered a diet coke rather than wine and had the wisdom to leave after about half an hour, I might have been hired. Staying and drinking for three hours on a job interview was not the appropriate behavior. My inexperience and immaturity cost me the job opportunity. I should have recognized that this was a business interview and not a social event.

Now it was August 1976 and I wasn't making any progress getting a new position. I was also mystified by why I was so driven to succeed. I knew that a balanced life was more desirable, but I was driven to the point where it dominated my life and became more important than eating and sleeping. Regrettably, at the time it was even more important than my relationship with Peggy. Fortunately, she understood me and stuck with me while I worked things out. Thank goodness for that bicentennial trip back home to Boston. Even though I knew a balanced life was what I should've been striving for, I found it to be challenging for me to attain. I couldn't get there. It seemed to veer away from my natural tendency. I had to figure out why I was driven, as though there was a gene or switch within my brain that would instantly straighten things out for me. Unlike ambition which is influenced by external factors, being driven is often rooted in internal desires and they are frequently subconscious.

Determined to get some answers, figure out my next move, and get it right, I purchased the book, *Where Do I go From Here With My Life?* by John Crystal and Richard Bolles. It was an oversized 257-page paperback and essentially a training manual that helps people in occupational decision-making, job-hunting, and the analysis of education, skills, and values. It accomplishes these things by having you answer multiple questions through various exercises and write a series of essays about when you were enjoying life: what were the activities involved; what skills or special talents were employed; what kinds of tasks were involved; and what kinds of accomplishments were being done?

The goals of the book were to enable you to list and understand your top skill clusters, learn what you want to accomplish before you die, identify what is your life's mission, what needs doing in the world, what are you trying to become, and what's unique about you. After a series of essays, it distills all the information in a meaningful way that results in a large sheet of paper that details your job objective in a clear and concise format.

I was highly motivated and excited to work on this project and I was determined to discover what it is that I should be dedicating my working hours to. In fact, it became my full time job. I would get up every morning, make coffee, eat breakfast, have a second and third cup of coffee, light up a cigarette, and get to work. There was no slacking. The book was my life and would get me the answers that I needed to move ahead and make progress. It was mid-August 1976 and I was dedicated to the task at hand. The process of answering the book's questions and writing essays became my passion. Driven to succeed, there was no manager or supervisor pushing me. I owned this totally and there was no turning back. It is precisely this attitude that is necessary for entrepreneurship. You need to take responsibility for where you are going by better understanding where you've been.

It was right about that time that I received a phone call at home from Dennis Lone, the creative director at Cuniform who doubled as a fabulous technical writer for us at Newsmaker. Dennis realized that I had been treated unfairly and gotten screwed by my two partners, Ace and Mike, and he decided to quit too, having no desire to work alongside unethical colleagues. He informed me that he wanted to venture out on his own and he asked me if I would teach him how to sell.

That was many years ago but I can still see Dennis Lone in my mind's eye. He was a teddy bear of a man, a big guy with a full beard and gentle manner. He asked me to meet him at a tavern in Mountain View, California which was about a 45-minute drive south of San Francisco. Surely, I could break away from *Where Do I Go From Here With My Life* for an afternoon to help an old friend.

We met at the tavern mid-day and ordered a couple of beers and snacks. I recall it was dark inside and there was a distinct smell. Not a musty smell, but not fresh either. If anything, there was a hint of Aqua Velva after shave in this blue-collar establishment. After the obligatory small talk, Dennis began asking me open-ended questions: information gathering. That was the first sign of a good writer, I thought. You see, I had a secret agenda: I wanted to learn how to write the press releases for which I had created the sales presentation. In some sense, Dennis and I were teaching each other in that meeting, sharing our talents.

I've always had a love-hate relationship with selling. I could do it very well, but it was almost too easy for me. Years later, in the early 1980s with the help of a great therapist, I would figure out that it was because I learned my selling skills by making my mother happy. The poor woman was narcissistic and my brothers and I received her love when we behaved the way she wanted. That instinctive "pleasing behavior" became a hard-wired skill. So, it wasn't that selling was too easy; it was that it brought up bad feelings of a mother-child relationship that wasn't truly unconditional. What's worse is that those bad feelings were on a subconscious level. I didn't know why I felt bad. Making people happy and satisfying their needs or solving their problems in order to get rewarded by making a sale felt simultaneously good and bad, but I never understood why until later. Nevertheless, I have experienced a lot of bittersweet victories because of those refined capabilities.

Dennis Lone continued asking his questions for about two and a half hours and picked up the tab on our beers and snacks. All the while, I watched how he skillfully used open-ended and closed-ended questions to learn about how to construct a sales presentation and how to validate his information. He learned that in sales you need to explain to someone who you are, what you do, how it can help them, how you do it, and what it costs. At every phase of the "sales pitch," you need to get affirmation because if someone doesn't feel good about who you are, they will be uncomfortable and not pay full attention to your explanation of what you do. I think you can appreciate what happens then. The prospect begins waffling and objecting because of this "feeling." Often, he or she won't know it on a conscious level. They just don't feel right. Ultimately it all boils down to "trust."

As our time together was closing in on a few hours, I asked Dennis about his writing formula for preparing product news releases. It would ultimately become the basis for my own style. He told me that it was important to explain what a product is, what it does, how it does it, where you get it, and what it costs. He told me to avoid advertising and superlatives at all costs. "Keep to the facts," he added. "Editors don't want fluff. It offends them because it is super clear that you're looking for free press. Of course, you are seeking editorial coverage, but you get it by providing the editor with a solid piece of copy that helps them craft a publication. That's the service you give them. After a while they'll recognize that you can help them." Once I was comfortable understanding Dennis' writing formula and thought process for preparing news releases, I finished my beer, made certain the last of the snacks were devoured, and we were out the door of the tavern and into the street full of parked cars.

Having exited the tavern like a Groundhog on February second, I remember vividly how bright a day it was. Four o'clock in the afternoon in Mountain View, California was very sunny. Reflections from chrome and glass showered us from all angles. Dennis Lone stood outside and asked me how much he owed me for consulting time. I lit up another cigarette and said, "Dennis, we're more than even, trust me, you don't owe me a dime because you just gave me a writing formula that is going to make me a millionaire. I'm going to move back home to Boston and start my own Newsmaker."

He laughed and put his big right foot up on the bumper of a truck. It was as much a scoff as a laugh. I think he wrote my response off as the sales enthusiasm of a cocky 27-year-old and pulled out his checkbook and a pen. After trying for a while to reinforce the fact that the trade in information we made was fair he said, "I insist." "Okay, make it fifty bucks," I said, and he handed me a check. My regret to this day is that I cashed that check. I should have kept it in a frame because I didn't need the fifty dollars at the time and the formula indeed became the basis for building a very successful business providing publicity services to small- and medium-size companies and becoming independently wealthy and free while doing it.

The next morning, I was back to work on *Where Do I Go From Here With My Life*? making good progress in terms of understanding who I was and where I fit vocationally. On September 9, 1976, I completed my 18" by 24" sheet of paper with my top skill clusters identified in a large circle in the center of the page surrounded by 12 satellite circles with topics including:

- What needs doing
- Ultimate life goal
- Personal traits or qualities
- Philosophy of Life
- Ideal job specifications
- Distasteful working conditions
- Preferred people environments
- Five most important achievements up until now
- What I would like to accomplish
- Starting salary
- Potential targets of interest in terms of companies or organizations.

It is interesting to note that in the "What needs doing" circle I listed the following:

1. More considerate interpersonal behavior
2. Equitable taxes and law enforcement
3. Growth of the small businessman and enhancement of free enterprise and competition
4. People need to be more responsible for their own actions
5. More vocational training

All of this flowed to the right side of the page where I wrote "My Primary Functional Goal" and "My Primary Organizational Goal," followed by a "Specific Immediate Objective."

It was scary committing a specific immediate objective to paper. But the process made me comfortable. This is what I wrote: "Marketing or sales management position with a growth oriented organization possessing strong qualitative goals where successful experience recruiting, training and motivating sales personnel and staff members, proven skills in selling intangibles to senior executives and other opinion molders plus unusual perception in human relations, the ability to write promotional schemes, training programs, sales presentations and effective public speaking talents can be utilized to the fullest advantage preferably where a background in instruction and an interest in human resource development can also be additional assets."

Peggy and I were now approaching two years living in San Francisco and the book raised questions about where you might want to live and offered a structure with a listing of 38 factors and a column of likes versus dislikes. They included weather, topography, proximity to family and friends, cost of living, and much more. Despite the fact that we had previously driven around looking for houses in the Bay Area, we discussed each of the 38 factors and proceeded with our check marks of likes and dislikes for Boston versus San Francisco. Boston won 18 to 8 in the "likes" column. We had decided to move back home, hugged each other, and it felt great. It felt right.

The book also offered complete instructions on how to pursue a job search, resume writing, creating a list of contacts to network with, how to approach them, and ultimately how to set up job interviews. I was going to the business library in San Francisco and prospecting for accounts back in the Boston area to either work for or put on the books as my first clients. I actually began a dual track of searching for companies to work for and for prospects to call on for my own business called "Sales Development Associates" which would essentially become "Newsmaker

East." The company names and contact information were written on 3" by 5" index cards and kept in alphabetical order. It was late September, 1976 and we were thinking about moving back to Boston by mid-October.

Finishing the book and making a decision that Peggy and I were comfortable with was important. Not just for the obvious reasons, but I knew that most people would never have persisted. It was tedious work and I had to be brutally honest and trust myself. I was distinct for having done it. After the horrific Newsmaker disappointment, completing the book's exercises and actually having a plan reinforced that I was on the right track. I was optimistic about the future. Peggy and I arrived home, almost two years to the day after we left in 1974, to a note on my parents' kitchen table that my mother was in the hospital with pneumonia.

8
EMBARKING ON AN ENTREPRENEURIAL JOURNEY

It didn't take us long to get used to living in Boston again. Peggy and I were proud of the accomplishments we'd made in San Francisco and we knew our next employers would have big shoes to fill. In the two years we spent on the West Coast, we both doubled our incomes and learned a ton about life. We worked a lot, but we also played. There were visits to ghost towns and hikes to Mt. Tamalpais, north of San Francisco, with gorgeous views of the city blanketed with cotton-like fog banks, visits to the Santa Cruz mountains, Reno, Nevada, Napa Valley Wineries, and camping out beneath the towering redwoods north of San Francisco.

The first job interview that I had after our move back to the East Coast was with a company called American Career Planning Services at the Prudential Center tower in Boston. The owner was Walter Cameron, a really nice man in his mid-fifties who started the company to help people with their career development. He was looking for a sales manager to hire and develop a sales force, something that I had experience in doing.

Walter Cameron had a small but nicely decorated office on the 45th floor of the Prudential Center tower and we had a terrific conversation. I could tell that he liked me a lot but was concerned about my lack of experience which doomed me again. That said, Walter asked me what I planned to do next, and I said, "I may be starting my own business because, although I lack experience, I know what I've done before and I know that I can do it again." He sincerely wished me the best of luck. I thanked him and asked, "if I do start my company, may I call you?" "Of course, he replied" and we shook hands.

The one thing about starting a company in San Francisco was that if I failed, I could always go back to Boston because it was simply part of the general west coast experience. Now I'm home and starting my own company. Like a prize fighter entering the ring, the thought of failure never occurred to me. I wouldn't allow it because failing was simply not an option. There was no "plan B" Besides, deep down inside, I really always wanted to be my own boss.

I remember my Uncle Sam, my father's younger brother, visiting us for a few days when I was a young kid. He was a small businessman and owned his own automotive and electronics manufacturer's representative firms in Seattle, Washington where he met his wife and settled after being stationed there in the Army post WWII. Sam Stroum was a big influence in my early life. My mother idolized his professionalism and financial success. He would travel to the East coast to visit the principal companies he represented and when he did, visited with us at our home in Auburndale, not far from the emerging technology center around Route 128, west of Boston.

Uncle Sam was larger than life, especially to a six-year-old boy. I remember him standing next to a step ladder with one foot on the step and his impressive black alligator shoes gleaming. He was an imposing figure who was handsome, charismatic, and always looked very sharp. When I lived in San Francisco, Sam had some business there and invited me to lunch. I was just getting started with Newsmaker at that time and recall how wonderful and generous he was. He made me feel special. I really wanted to emulate him and had a visceral need to get into business for myself.

After the American Career Planning Services rejection, it became clear that I wasn't going to be getting a sales management job. What's more, I really didn't want to work for someone else. So, it was now time to become an entrepreneur. I recreated Newsmaker in New England and named the business Sales Development Associates. The name represented the benefit of making news which is making sales rather than just the feature making news itself. Ironically, that was the essence of the sales presentation that Mike Gerber and I collaborated on. I opened a bank account right down the street from my folks' house at the Shawmut Bank and deposited $300. I was in business for myself and now just needed to get some accounts and make some money. It was exciting and scary at the same time.

And so my career as an entrepreneur began. My parents offered us my old high school bedroom as office space. It was a tiny room, but enough to get started. We had a telephone installed with our own Sales Development Associates phone number. It was a rotary-style phone and now we just had to make it ring! When we got a phone call, Peggy would answer "good morning, Sales Development Associates, may I help you?" If the call was for me, in order to seem high-tech and professional, she clicked the rotary dial to make it appear as though the call was being transferred, and then she'd hand me the phone.

Next, I contacted an old high school friend who was in the printing business and learned about a graphic designer who I subsequently hired to create our logo, stationery, and business cards. At about the same time I was taking care of the graphic designs, I struck a deal with my first salesman who was the brother-in-law of one of my old Paul Revere office mates. He had experience in direct straight commission sales, selling vacuum cleaners door-to-door. He was hired on the promise that he would become our sales manager. But he never recruited and hired anyone. He was really just a salesman with a fancy title.

I also created our sales materials which included a telephone sales presentation complete with typical objections and rebuttals that salespeople would likely hear, procedures for appointment setting, the field sales presentation itself, and typical objections and rebuttals that would arise during the presentation. They would ultimately be printed on our new stationery and put into a nice blue binder. My experience at Fireman's Fund creating their National Sales Training Program was paying dividends for me. Naturally, I adopted the Newsmaker materials that Mike Gerber and I worked so diligently preparing. In addition to providing invaluable knowledge and training to the salespeople, the professionally prepared sales materials gave them a sense of security. They had a road map to follow in the land of potential sales.

The telephone presentation was simple and effective. After introducing myself, I'd describe to prospective clients how I could help them. Since I was in the business of getting news published for small- and medium-sized companies, I made it clear that I could help them get successful editorial placement so they wouldn't have to waste money on paid advertising. Editorial exposure was worth considerably more than paid advertising. Then, I'd set up an appointment to meet with them.

When I first saw our logo design which was a dark blue arrow pointed upward to the right with Sales Development Associates inside in white letters on three lines, it felt like my dream was coming true.

The company I conceptualized and named in my kitchen in San Francisco was becoming a reality. The blue arrow was positioned on the right side of the business card with our name and title under it and on the left side of the card was our address and telephone number. Because I was a firm believer in the importance of first impressions, I made sure I had the best quality business cards.

I clearly remember those early sales calls and swear that we made a lot of sales via our prospects' thumbs. They often rubbed the card between their thumb and forefinger and felt the raised printing as we talked. The cards were exquisite and made our company look polished and professional. I was able to get everything printed for $125 and then I was ready to call Walter Cameron at American Career Planning Services. It was a bright early winter day in Boston. The skies were clear and I recall how excited I was driving into the underground parking garage at the Prudential Center, with the tires squealing as I turned corners on the painted floor.

I scheduled the meeting for 1:00 p.m. and gave Peggy Walter's phone number and asked her to call me at about 1:15 p.m. "Why?" she asked. "Because I want to look busy and create the illusion that my services are in demand," I replied. Peggy was my assistant and was quite competent. She had far more important responsibilities in the medical field and was a quick study. When we entered Walter's office, I introduced my salesman, Len Landstrom, and began a conversation about the weather and starting Sales Development Associates. Then his telephone rang. Walter was a one-man company and answered the phone himself.

When he handed the phone to me, he was within listening distance and I play-acted, "Well, just tell him that I'll be back later this afternoon and I will give him a call. Explain to him that I'm in an important meeting right now." So, I apologized for the choreographed interruption, and it was back to my sales presentation about product publicity, emphasizing that publicity is news and news is a powerful equalizer. News is the only way that a small company can look as big as General Motors. "With news coverage," I explained, "you can't tell the size of a company."

After discussing what publicity is, I began pointing out what publicity could do for American Career Planning Services. Then Walter stopped me and said, "Listen, I've already spent a good deal of money on advertising." I asked, "How much, Walter?" and he replied, I'm not General Electric, I've spent $40,000 which is a lot of money for me." I countered with, "Well, then you can't afford not to spend another $395 to see whether we can help, can you?"

Walter agreed with me and then I filled out the Publicity Order form and asked for his autograph. As we approached the elevator Len and I were trying to maintain our composure. When we got on the elevator we were so excited that I accidentally hit the number thirty-eight and we were propelled to that floor. Since we both had to use the restroom, we got off the elevator and wandered around the halls until we found it. After leaving the men's room we noticed a sign right across the hall that read, "Associated Industries of Massachusetts." Curiously, we entered the office and ended up purchasing a *Directory of Massachusetts Manufacturers* for $15.75. When we returned to our tiny bedroom office, everything we needed to tap into local businesses was right in front of us in that directory, including the company name, president, address, phone number, etc. Hitting the button for floor thirty-eight turned out to be one lucky push. We immediately began making cold calls, determined to add to the one client we had just scored.

Next on the agenda was to deposit the check and buy a typewriter. I made our first sale as a writer who had never written a press release and as a writer who didn't even own a typewriter. That was chutzpah! I recalled my speech at Fireman's Fund where I emulated Ted Kennedy and remembered how effective it was. It was a "fake it till you make it" prescription for success, I also read a book, *Winning Through Intimidation* in which the author described how he made the jump from a struggling real estate agent to an all-star commercial realtor earning ten times as much income with essentially the same job description by making certain changes. One of his changes was to create an exceptional business card that included a photograph of the earth from Apollo and another was that he would meet with out-of-town prospective customers at conference rooms in airports and have catered luncheons. My plan was working and our second sale came later in the month. We were excited and looking forward to hitting the ground running in January 1977.

I didn't have a formal marketing plan for Sales Development Associates other than my well-documented procedures for setting and scheduling appointments and making sales presentations. I also created sales report forms which summarized the meetings, next action steps, and indicated which meeting it was. It would let me know where my salespeople, referred to as account executives, needed help. There were only two acceptable options resulting from a sales presentation: a sale or another appointment to get started on a project. Of course, they didn't always happen that way and there was always more work to be done, but those were the goals.

Starting this business wasn't without a great deal of stress and fear. To reassure myself, I created a specific set of goals and the specific behaviors that were necessary to achieve them. The goals were for my own sales program, not for others, because if I didn't make things happen there would never be others. With deference to my old classmate at Northeastern University, Dave Whitney, who introduced me to the process and specific activities that were required to succeed academically, I listed my goals on one sheet of paper. There were five steps needed to earn $3,000 per month income. I had to sell 24 orders per month, or six orders per week, which would require that I set 15 appointments per week or three per day. My approach would be to get two referrals a day and set two appointments per day. Given my follow up meetings and other duties I'd be too busy to worry about failing. Besides, based upon my previous experience, that process would *assure* my success, even though it would mean working hefty hours seven days a week. Also listed on the sheet was that eight orders per week equaled 32 orders per month or $4,000 in income.

I believed it was essential to control the variables if I wanted to have any type of success. That included my attire and our sales presentation. In the 1970s nobody wanted to do business with someone who didn't present themselves well. Learning our sales presentation word-for-word was critical because it allowed us to listen and observe the prospective client's attitude and body language throughout our conversation. A scripted sales presentation is akin to taking the train versus driving a car. When you're on the train you can observe everything around you and concentrate more easily because you are not worried about driving and dodging traffic. On the other hand, if you're in the driver's seat you need to concentrate on the road and miss a lot of what's going on elsewhere. The presentation is a script and you're playing a role that lets you listen and observe your prospect's responses, both verbal and nonverbal.

Controlling the sales presentation is especially critical when selling an intangible business service because the prospect's decision is ultimately based upon whether or not he or she trusts you. In other words, you can have the best service in the world and a wonderful track record, but if the prospect doesn't trust you or like you; then you are not going to make the sale. People are people! We are all influenced by emotional and rational factors. Relationships matter.

There's an old expression in professional sales circles: people buy emotionally and then justify rationally. Engineers especially see themselves as logical, rational, and unaffected by color, scent, and subliminal messages. They come from a "cause and effect" world where troubleshooting always begins at the power source. Vance Packard, the American journalist and social critic wrote in his classic

1957 book, *The Hidden Persuaders* about how the automobile industry learned to put beautiful convertible automobiles on display in their showrooms to attract potential customers. Then the majority of those customers who they attracted would purchase sedans. Today, automotive marketers typically display shiny red convertibles in showrooms and the most popular cars on the road are white or silver sedans.

In January 1977 Len Landstrom and I hit the ground running. We partitioned our weekly appointment book pages so that we were in a specific city in the morning and then that same city the following afternoon. We arranged the cities geographically so that we drove during lunch hour. This would allow us to have two or three appointments in the morning and three in the afternoon in different cities. It also gave the prospects a simple choice to make because you didn't want them to wonder *if* they would see you, but *when* they would see you.

I didn't believe in fumbling and wondering when you could see someone while you were talking on the phone. It was much more efficient to simply fill in the blanks based upon geography. Effective selling requires discipline. Discipline involves scheduling as well as presenting. A sales manager of straight-commission salespeople needs to sell them on the importance of following the aforementioned process. There was always the need to reinforce that being efficient trumped being busy.

Selling is like playing football. Tom Brady spent hours studying his opponent, watching films, strategizing, and practicing in preparation for one-hour on a Sunday afternoon. Prioritizing prospects and geographical territory management are essential elements of being a successful salesperson. Being familiar with your prospect's business and the issues they face is important too. The bottom line is that you want to put yourself into a position to make the most sales by controlling the variables that will impact the sales call. All entrepreneurs must learn how to be professional salespeople regardless of industry. If you're a photographer, for example, you won't be taking many pictures unless you can get yourself hired. As Dennis Lone concluded, a great writer needs to learn how to sell if he is going to succeed in business as a writer.

Len and I were busy on the phone setting up meetings. My brother Rich had given me a couple of referrals and I was able to schedule meetings and actually start projects. Having referrals was a bonus because there was already a sufficient amount of credibility established which made us more believable. After we set up several appointments, we arranged three to five meeting times with ourselves for alternating mornings and afternoons to make phone calls. My policy was to never spend more than an hour on the phone during one session because your efficacy deteriorates rapidly. Often, I would stand up when speaking on the telephone, in order to project positive energy. Again, it takes discipline to trust the process. Sometimes we'd strike out and other times we'd make five appointments in a row. The temptation, of course, was to set up a meeting during the self-appointed telephone session time if that's when the prospect wanted to meet. When you did that, though, the prospect was controlling you and their time became more important than yours. It is a costly mistake and you are better off setting up the meeting for the following week. It accomplished two things: kept you in control of your schedule and created the impression that you were busy, both of which are helpful in sales.

Our progress was slower than I had expected during

January and we only made a total of seven sales. That expectation of greater progress was probably typical of all entrepreneurs who are very optimistic by nature. Len made four sales and I made three, plus I did all of the copywriting, media list research, and vendor selection. Going in to see Len's clients as the copywriter allowed me to learn how well they understood what we did, evaluate how effective he was at selling, and subsequently help him improve. During February we had nine sales and Len made eight of them. Again, I was copywriting and researching media lists. Even though I had Dennis Lone's writing formula, I wasn't as fast as I would have liked. Furthermore, we didn't have automated label printing equipment in those days. Peggy was the label typist and she did it days and evenings. In between she'd answer the phone. All the while she never took a paycheck from the company. Obviously, I shared mine with her.

On January 14, 1977, Peggy answered the phone, and it was Margaret Brennan from SMA Controls in Needham, MA and she very abruptly asked which bank we used. Peggy thought quickly, opened the desk drawer and saw the deposit slip from Shawmut Bank. "Shawmut Bank," she replied and later that afternoon Len brought in a check from SMA for $395. Incidentally, 46 years later I am still working for the company. Today, though, it is Margaret's son, Matthew, who is the president and the company is now called Esco Tool. As an aside, we developed their company logo back in 1978 and it sits proudly atop of their building today. We also designed their product catalogs and other marketing materials and have worked together monthly doing product publicity releases through all these years.

At Sales Development Associates, we all kept plowing ahead. Peggy and I moved into an apartment in Framingham, MA, but the three of us kept working out of the small spare bedroom at my folks' house in Newton. Life was incredibly busy but we were thriving and we loved every second of the satisfaction we received from growing our business.

By mid-March I had begun looking for office space. We sold fifteen orders for the month and had good appointment-setting activity going forward. Things were moving in the right direction and several of our new clients expressed an interest in placing more orders with us which was an excellent sign. I wanted a prestigious address, so I looked in Wellesley, MA. It was and remains an affluent town and conveys the message of success if you lived or worked there. Folks in eastern Massachusetts knew that and it was important for what I was trying to accomplish. A nicely appointed office in a prestigious location would also help with recruiting. Sales Development Associates was ready for take-off!

9

LEARN ON THE FLY AND FAKE IT TILL YOU MAKE IT

I rented a three hundred square foot office suite that miraculously had space for three separate offices. The suite, located on the third floor of a building in Wellesley, MA, consisted of my office, an office to be shared by salespeople and writers, and the reception area which had a desk and two separate tables. Our telephone appointment setting presentations now included, "Sales Development Associates from Wellesley." Even if it only made our salespeople feel better, the addition of "Wellesley" was important. The building itself was a contemporary bright tan brick building, on a well-landscaped plot of land, and located next to a residence in a quiet commercial part of town. Next door was the Linden Deli which made phenomenal sandwiches and still does today.

We occupied Suite 306 on Monday, April 4, 1977, but I didn't sign the lease until April 7th when the company was officially incorporated. There was already a company called Sales Development Associates, Inc. elsewhere in Massachusetts, so we couldn't use that name. They were in a different business entirely, importing China. Although we couldn't incorporate under that name, we could still do business as Sales Development Associates. I had to think quickly and come up with a corporate name. So, I took the last three letters of my first name, *ven* and my middle name *Mark*, combined them and came up with *The Venmark Corporation*, and on that day I became the only shareholder. The following Monday I visited a cousin of mine at Offices Unlimited, Inc. in Boston and invested in desks, chairs, tables, and file cabinets for the entire office suite.

We had only 11 sales in April. Len had six and I had five. I wasn't too happy that he only had six sales and I had five while seeing a lawyer, buying furniture, visiting clients, writing and researching media lists, coordinating photographers, dealing with telephones and office supplies, and starting the recruiting process. Clearly, he didn't possess the skills that I thought he did in the beginning. But, after all, he was selling vacuum cleaners door-to-door at homes, so I shouldn't have been too surprised. Something else that became clear is that we couldn't depend on the clients to provide us with suitable photographs in a timely manner. And the longer it took to produce a project because of the photo, the longer it would take to make the next sale with that client because it typically took 60 to 90 days before they started to see results in the trade and business publications. Each publication had an editorial schedule, and it typically took that long to compile and print it.

So, the challenge was that I had to find a photographer who was willing to work on a project basis by coming into my office one day per week and picking up products to photograph back at their studio. That was unusual because most photographers had a daily or hourly rate. My appeal to them was that they could shoot our product shots at their convenience and if someone broke an appointment with them, for example, they could still use the time productively by doing our work. Back then, most product shots were black & white, although sometimes full color was taken, but it was considerably more expensive because media submissions back then required 4" x 5" color chromes which were essentially large positive slides. If larger machinery and equipment was the news release topic, then it required an onsite photographer at their facility.

For the month of May, Len had 11 sales and I had two. I hired four account executives and their first day of training began the day after Memorial Day, 1977. That Tuesday morning, Sandy Noonan, Henry Michaels, and two other people began our training program. That first day I explained everything to them about our sales presentation, the rationale, etc. and why it was important for them to learn it word-for-word. The analogy that I gave them was that of traveling down the rails on a train versus driving a car down the highway. With the former you can observe and focus on the environment and with the latter you cannot. So, it was important to be able to focus on your prospect and listen to their concerns. That's where the sale is made. Naturally, it was acceptable to paraphrase for personal comfort, but not rewrite it. The next morning, we would begin role plays and in the afternoon discuss the telephone sales presentation which would be in front of them when they dialed. We called it "smiling and dialing."

Sandy had previously worked in an administrative position at a bank and was a 29-year-old woman who wanted an opportunity to get into sales. She was unafraid of straight commissions and knew that she would need to find an entry-level position to make the switch from administration to sales. She really understood what Sales Development Associates was all about and she was smart, enthusiastic, and attractive. On Thursday, their third day, Sandy and Henry began setting up appointments. By Friday morning, Sandy had set two appointments. She was a natural!

The two other account executives I hired had dropped out by Thursday. Believe it or not, our structured approach was too demanding for them. They didn't even possess the self-discipline required to learn our sales presentation. One of them sat across from me and attempted to give his sales presentation and it became obvious that he was reading it from his briefcase to the side of him. So, I said, "excuse me, I need to go to the bathroom, I'll be right back," and left my office. But, when I returned, instead of going back behind my desk, I sat down next to him and asked him to continue role playing his presentation. He got all befuddled and we agreed that he would be better off employed elsewhere. If you don't have the self-discipline to learn your sales presentation, then you aren't going to be successful as a salesperson.

At the end of that Thursday, Sandy came into my office and started to cry. Sobbing mercilessly, she explained that she had never sold before and was petrified to go out on a sales appointment by herself the next morning. My schedule wouldn't allow me to go with her, but what I did do, however, was give her one of my best pep talks ever. I said, "Sandy, I'd like you to imagine something for me." "Okay," she said as her whimpering began to subside. "Stop and imagine that you've been selling for 10 years and that you had personally sold over 1,000 accounts! How would you feel then? Would you be scared?" She replied, "No, of course not, I'd feel confident and just go out and sell them." I said, "Of course you would! Feel the confidence and remember that you know more about publicity than your prospect does. And when you go out tomorrow morning to make those sales calls, I want you to imagine that you've been selling for 10 years and that you have over 1,000 accounts, and behave accordingly. Just go about your business and remember, you know more about product publicity than they do. You're going to do just fine. Go out there and have fun, Sandy."

Sandy went out that Friday morning and made what we call a *one call close*. It was her first appointment and she nailed it, pulling in a check for $395. She went on to set up a second appointment for the following week. We went to that meeting together on Tuesday and made the sale. It was great because she also got to watch me conduct a writing interview and saw how thorough it was. I typically asked hard questions that the client never saw coming. Being exposed to various technologies and spending time scanning trade publications for ideas allowed me to conceptualize new uses for existing products in different markets. And, frankly, my curiosity helped me do it very well. I really enjoyed the process and still do today.

Incidentally, I took the writing very seriously because that would ultimately prove to be what clients were buying. Frankly, that first press release I wrote for Walter Cameron at American Career Planning Services was awful compared to my fiftieth one. Practice makes perfect in whatever you do. The more reps you do, the better you get. Consequently, I rewrote it and redistributed it for him at my own expense. He never knew it, but I felt better about providing him with a better product release. Walter Cameron believed in me, and I wanted to be sure that he got my best work and the best value that I could provide for him. It is good karma: what goes around comes around.

The month of June 1977 was a break-out month for us. In addition to Sandy and Harvey Michaels I hired a salesman by the name of Dan Bowman. He was a little eccentric, but clearly understood what Sales Development Associates was all about and really wanted to be a part of it. He was an excellent salesman. We sold 23 orders that month.

I held our sales meetings on Monday at 5:00 p.m., so if anyone had a problem we addressed and corrected it right away and I could rally the troops and fire them up for the week. In direct selling, enthusiasm is infectious. It worked beautifully and our team got along well. I never understood why companies held their sales meetings on Friday afternoon and didn't take advantage of propelling the team into an enthusiastic and productive work week rather than into a relaxing weekend. Another reason Friday meetings were bad was because if you had to chew out a salesman you didn't want them to be stewing about it over the weekend. That was never productive. In fact, it wasn't unusual for me to take the team out for a few beers on Friday afternoon to set a positive tone for the weekend.

Henry Michaels was lagging behind Dan and Sandy. He only had two sales for the month of June and I was getting concerned. After our sales meeting, I was leaning out my office window smoking a cigarette and just happened to look down and saw that Henry was walking down the street towards the Volkswagen dealership. The next morning, he was in the office and I asked him if he was having his car serviced the day before. He said, "No, I don't own a car." I was totally blown away and expressed this. "What the hell were you thinking when you applied for this job? How were you going to visit clients?" He said, "By taking the T (MBTA mass transit)," to which I replied, "I don't know of too many industrial parks along the T lines. Henry, I'm sorry, but I have to let you go." He wasn't surprised, nor was it a surprise that his two sales were to companies located in the city of

Boston. Again, direct commission salespeople frequently came with a back-story. I never knew why he didn't drive, and it didn't matter anymore. I suspected that he may have had his driver's license revoked. From then on, though, I always checked on the vehicle status of future recruits. A simple, "What kind of car do you drive?" was sufficient and could shine some light on the potential employee's values. If they owned a new BMW they would likely be willing to hustle and work hard to make those payments.

It was right around this time that one of our clients, Bill Kahn, the owner and president of Digital Laboratories, Inc. in Watertown, MA, had invented a word processor for one of his customers. Bill was an MIT graduate in electrical engineering and a prolific inventor. In fact, he invented the pocket calculator and sold it to Hewlett-Packard. His word processor had a one-line display that hovered over the keyboard and was mounted on a swinging arm that was attached to the side of the printer and stored data on cassette tapes that were read in a modified Radio Shack cassette tape player.

The word processor had a typewriter-style keyboard and was integrated with a DEC (Digital Equipment Corporation) high-speed digital printer. It was perfect for our copy writing situation because we wrote copy and then visited the client for approval. Because there were almost always changes needed, it was easier to make those changes if the copy was stored on tape. So, I agreed to rent one of his machines for $300 per month. At the same time, he was hiring us monthly for $395 and it worked out well for both of us. Sales Development Associates was right on top of the emerging technologies at that time. We literally had one of the first word processors in the world.

During July 1977 we started to get a few repeat orders

and I could see that we were on a solid trajectory and that it was time for me to think about hiring a writer. Fast! So, I thought, who better to hire than a trade press editor? That led me to contact Charlie Fox who was the editor of a major electronics manufacturing magazine which was based less than 10 miles away. He had a master's degree in science communication and was soft-spoken. Perfect, I thought. But he was so soft-spoken that he asked if he could bring his wife in to meet me. Perhaps that should have been a red flag, but I was desperate for a good writer to take the load off me. I would still edit his copy and make certain that we were producing the best possible product news releases for our clients, but having someone else write the first draft would free up a lot of time for me.

Charlie and his wife, Mary, came to our office at the end of a workday and I remember Peggy having her one-line computer display reading, "Welcome Mary and Charlie!" Their response was tepid, at best. The two seemed to be suspicious about us and the meeting started off slowly but ended well. A week later, Charlie Fox was on our team with the title, Creative Director.

Charlie Fox was a great press release writer, but since his experience had only involved writing for one industry, his focus was too narrow. One of the things that I discovered for myself was that product publicity could be an effective tool for finding new applications for products and new markets. But to do that type of press release writing, you needed to take a broader view of a product's features and benefits and think about what other markets besides the current market might be applicable. That was not only useful for clients, but it was very useful for editors who were looking for new ideas to bring to their readership. That creative marketing approach benefited everyone. I once made a presentation to a civic group where I told them that the difference between a press release and a publicist is analogous to the difference between a racecar and the racecar driver. A press release is the vehicle, and the publicist is the driver.

During the winter we settled in as a team. Despite being interrupted for a week by the *Blizzard of '78*, we managed to do well. The Blizzard of '78 brought 27.1 inches of snow to Boston over two days. This came right after the city gained 21 inches on Jan. 20, 1978, making it a record breaker of snow dumped on the city. One member of the Sales Development Associates team got stuck on Route 128 and had to go to a hotel for four days with his girlfriend. It's a good thing his wife never found out! Sandy Noonan even made a sales call from her home on cross country skis.

For the first three months of 1978 we booked 103 publicity orders plus several photography sales. In addition to our standard $395 North American Publicity Order, I created a $795 Western European Publicity Order which also began to get sales traction. I saw that our brand was starting to take hold because of our repeat orders and it made sense to expand our service offerings. We were starting to get two sales for every one call too. I was also working with a graphic designer because I personally wanted to develop brochures for clients. However, there were too many subjective variables such as color, taste in typography, writing style, and other opinions of people inside a company to control and, therefore, to predict our profitability which is why I didn't want to develop a standard packaged product. What's more, I didn't want the sales team to lose their focus on what made us special: our product publicity packages and the extreme control we exercised over the entire writing and distribution process.

Our packaged publicity services distinguished Sales

Development Associates. Unlike conventional advertising agencies or public relations firms, we weren't responsible for an entire marketing program and bound by exclusivity. Our niche was publicity which was overlooked by advertising agencies because they didn't view it as a profit center. Consequently, they had their junior staffers handling it by default and they did a subpar job. The staffers were more interested in impressing their bosses than serving editors. It is important for small businesses to find a niche such as providing custom services not available in a big company. Small businesses cannot compete with large corporations on price; they must be distinct or add value

By mid-1978, we were starting to outgrow Suite 306. In fact, at one point, there were eight people working from the tiny 300 sq. ft. space. We had a sign-in sheet with specific times that each person could be in the office and use the phones. And by all means, there was no loitering allowed. It was the most efficient work situation that I ever experienced. No wasted time and maximum productivity.

In January 1979 I signed another lease for two additional offices in Suite 106 on the first floor. It gave us some breathing room, but I could clearly see the drop in efficiency which, I suppose, was to be expected, being housed on separate floors. Reflecting on the move, though, it was interesting to note that I had hired another writer by the name of Richie Thomas and a fellow named John Kenmore to replace Len, who had resigned, never having progressed enough to claim greater involvement in the business. Richie was a Northeastern University graduate too and had a degree in journalism. He was in his early twenties and very sharp, dedicated, and personable. John was referred to me by my old friend from Home Life Insurance, Sam Paris. He was in his early forties and more polished than Len. He had the title, Marketing Director, but was really an account executive. Small businesses often anoint their employees with titles they don't deserve in order to play to their egos and recruit them.

Our writers were upstairs, and each had their own desk and workspace with a reasonable amount of privacy. The salespeople were downstairs and occasionally, when returning from a client meeting, I'd poke my head in the door to say hi and see them chatting instead of smiling and dialing. I didn't want anyone setting appointments on the phone longer than an hour at one sitting because it became too frustrating for them, and it hampered their productivity.

With stressful activities like cold calling, it paid to make a game out of it. That's why I created an approach that involved not being on the phone longer than an hour at a time; no matter what the results. The game was to see how many appointments you could make during an hour. Since you only needed three to five, it was typically very attainable. Another trick that I believed strongly in and referenced in an earlier chapter was standing up to speak on the phone. Standing up helped you be alert and project a more positive tone when responding to the inevitable objections from the prospect.

Even if the salespeople had no appointments scheduled after an hour, they were better off going into an industrial park and dropping in on a prospective client they had once been rejected by. They might just get lucky because there was no telling whether something had happened in the prospect's business life that created an opportunity for a sale. Maybe the prospect had just lost an account and suddenly needed to attract new business, or maybe a key vendor had just increased their prices and they needed more business, or perhaps they made a huge sale and had the money to take a gamble and place an order. You never knew unless you stopped by and tried to create a relationship with them.

Relationships have always mattered in selling, regardless of the ever-expanding influences of technology. Salespeople provide a personal touch that technology and the internet cannot replicate. Most importantly, salespeople can offer expertise, problem-solving, and guidance that aren't always available online and make prospective customers aware of new solutions. When asked about customer input in the development of the Ford Model T, Henry Ford famously said, "If I had asked people what they wanted, they would have said faster horses."

Because the traditional advertising business was based upon giving fancy proposals and quotations for a company's entire marketing program, a prospect would occasionally ask for a larger quotation than one of our simple publicity orders. That was usually a red herring and I had to explain the reason why to our salespeople who had a tendency to salivate at the thought of getting a big annual commitment. It was interesting; at that point in time there were clients who gave us over twenty-five thousand dollars in business annually and never would have hired us if we went the traditional route of asking for a large sum such as $25,000. Let's face it, a $395 decision is much easier to make than a $25,000 decision. What's more, as a company got accustomed to using our services repeatedly and benefiting from them, it became an easy habit or pattern to continue for many years.

The beauty of our approach was that we had no competition because of the way traditional agencies functioned in terms of their business model and arrogance. Account executives in advertising agencies were expected to do a lot more than sell. So, they were highly trained and highly compensated. In short, Sales Development Associates' business model was much more efficient. Furthermore, ad agencies devalued product publicity. One of the reasons they did, frankly, was because it was so much more cost-effective than paid advertising. According to an article in *Advertising Age Magazine* from August of 1976 which we used in our sales presentation, publicity was worth from three to five times more than paid advertising. That's why the advertising agencies didn't actively pursue it. What's more, they didn't know how to make money at press release writing and assigned it to their lowliest entry-level employees who typically did a terrible job.

The essence of the Sales Development Associates business model was that there was safety in numbers. One of the problems with traditional advertising agencies was that they could have one or two big clients deplete their resources and control all of their time and assets. On the other hand, Sales Development Associates was clearly different. We had large numbers of companies placing small orders with us and we controlled the workflow and the cash flow. Most importantly our publicity services were objective in the sense that we knew what editors wanted and our one-page writing formula wasn't to be modified. We were writing for editors, not the product's users. Logically, if the editor didn't select our news, then the user or reader would never get to see it. The only reason for a copy approval meeting was to assure that our copy was factually correct. It was all about controlling the writing and copy approval process. I had Charlie Fox create a procedure and presentation for attaining information during a first information gathering interview and the approval session as well, which we used to train new writers.

In fact, because Sales Development Associates was paid in advance, it allowed us to control our entire relationship with the client. We had no accounts receivables staff, no waiting to get paid, sending out invoices repeatedly, and the like. We even explained to prospects in our sales presentation that eliminating those significant expenses allowed us to bring them high-level services for a very reasonable fee. We saw ourselves as a manufacturer who made press releases that resulted in publicity. A client would place an order with a salesperson. It would then get logged into our system and I would send a "thank you letter" over my signature as president of the company. A few days later a writer would call to arrange for an interview, per my letter. Then, during that interview, they arranged a date for a second interview to approve the copy and media list. I would send out a final letter explaining what would happen next in terms of publication, via postal mail.

The client was contacted six times by three different employees of Sales Development Associates within a four-week period; all for $395. The goal was for them to experience a complete relationship with our firm. This CRM (customer relationship management) approach was no coincidence; it reinforced our brand and made it less likely that a salesperson or writer could think about going into competition with us. It is not uncommon for employees in the advertising agency business to try to start their own business by stealing clients. Naturally, as an innovator with a novel business model who was working around the clock, I wanted to prevent that from taking place. Today, of course, there are software programs provided by Salesforce.com, HubSpot, Oracle, and others that focus on CRM.

By mid-April 1978 and after more than 300 product releases, we were starting to get some media recognition and I received a phone call from Drake Lundell, the editor of *ComputerWorld* magazine. Ironically, the magazine was located in Newtonville, a few miles from my folks' house where we had our original Sales Development Associates office. On the phone Drake said, "who are you, I've been receiving all of these press releases from you?" I replied, "I'm Steve Stroum with Sales Development Associates and we specialize in product publicity." Then he said, "Why haven't you called me like every other flack?" And I replied, "Because I'm not like every other flack and I wanted to become recognized for my work." He said, "Well, you have been recognized; would you like to come into my office and meet my staff?" I said, "I'd love to," and we set a date.

When I arrived at the *ComputerWorld* office, we exchanged greetings and Drake Lundell introduced me to his staff by saying, "I'd like you to meet Steve Stroum. He's president of a company called Sales Development Associates and they can introduce us to a lot of companies and products that we otherwise wouldn't know about." It was great to be catered to in that way and to have our work validated. I left there walking on clouds and knew that we were on the right track. When I shared this news with our team, they were thrilled and I'm sure they weaved it into their sales conversations and writing meetings. You have to toot your own horn.

Not long after the *ComputerWorld* experience, Ken Thornley, Regional Sales Manager *for New Equipment Digest* magazine (*NED*) arranged for me to meet with his editor and thirteen others in a marathon two-day visit to Penton Plaza in Cleveland, Ohio. It was an exciting trip because the editors had been publishing our product releases consistently for over a year. *NED* was a large tabloid-style magazine that was filled with new product news. It was one of the most popular industrial publications in America and it wasn't unusual for Sales Development Associates to have a half dozen or more of our clients published in it every month. Clearly we were different. We wrote product news releases that made it easy for editors to select for their pages. They were well written and most importantly had phenomenal photographs that were consistent with the copy. We sent out thousands of press releases every month. In effect, we were marketing to the media and in marketing the three most important elements are: repetition, repetition, and repetition. The media were discovering who we were.

It was a goodwill visit, of course, because editors were taking an interest in us, but my goal was to learn what we could do better in order to improve our service to them. That was essential, because if we didn't serve them, then our clients wouldn't be served. As an aside, getting paid in advance for our service put us in *control* and that was critical for assuring that the editors got high quality news copy and not some puffed up advertisement dressed up as a news release. It is fascinating how some of the smallest details can become important. For example, one editor pointed out that blue paper was difficult to read. And we used blue paper, plus yellow, salmon, buff, and goldenrod primarily to separate stacks of press releases to help prevent any mix ups. We started that because of our space limitations back in Suite 306. Obviously, that practice stopped, and we just stuck with canary, buff, and gold-colored papers because that's what the editors said they liked and were easiest to read.

One of my best experiences at Penton Publishing was meeting Gene Schwind, the editor of *Machine Design* magazine. When I entered his office and introduced myself, he asked me who I was and what I did. I simply picked up his own magazine which I had taken from his lobby while waiting to see him, opened it up to the new product section and showed him four of our product releases on the pages of his very own magazine! I showed him the photograph and copy that we prepared for each one and noted that they were used word-for-word on his pages and that our objective was to become a source of reliable information about products for all industrial and technical publishers.

For added drama and impact, I also had a briefcase with one hundred other product releases that we prepared featuring all types of products and product applications. I took them out and plunked them onto his desk. He was impressed with the voluminous approach and asked a lot of great questions. I explained to Gene that we could write about the same product several different ways because we could focus on different features, benefits, or applications; depending upon our clients marketing goals. Gene Schwind invited me to lunch and we had a great rapport.

Returning home after the meeting at Penton Plaza in Cleveland, OH with all of those editors over two days and sharing the experiences with the team was highly motivating for them and we all felt that Sales Development Associates was something special. We were, and I was thrilled. At this point it was the middle of June, 1978 and the team consisted of Peggy, Charlie, Richie, Sandy, Dan, John, and me. We had interviewed and hired others for both sales and writer positions without lasting success. Besides these employees, there was Leo, our photographer. He had his own studio and visited my office weekly for new assignments. Our business relationship lasted for 26 years, and we are still friends to this day.

Providing photography services became critical for us because it simplified our client's work, made it easier for them to do business with us, and it allowed me to guide the photographer creatively, making sure that the photograph was visually consistent with our sales message. I was no different than a movie director bringing out the best in an actor's performance because I brought out the best in our photographer and as our services evolved this became even more important. In addition, our project workflow went smoother and repeat sales came faster. Even though we were paid in advance and did all of our work, there were still clients who never gave us their products or props for photography even after multiple attempts to procure them.

As Peter F. Drucker, recognized as the dean of America's business and management philosophers by *The Wall Street Journal*, wrote "Entrepreneurship is 'risky' because so few of the so-called entrepreneurs know what they are doing. They lack the methodology. They violate elementary and well-known rules. This is particularly true of high-tech entrepreneurs."

Shortly after returning from my trip to Penton Plaza, one of my clients invited me to address the *American Marketing Association*, Boston Chapter. I prepared a slide presentation and explained what we did, including what publicity was, what it can do for a company and our distinctive business model and how it allows us to work with the smallest of companies; the ones who need publicity the most and know the least about it. My final quote from the presentation was targeted towards high-tech entrepreneurs. *"There is nothing more irrational than investing hundreds of thousands of dollars on capital equipment and tens of thousands of man-hours on the development of your technology and business... and then failing to properly inform the world about your capabilities."*

I was really running ragged again and when I shared that fact with my accountant, Bob Cohen, he invited me to his office to help me get a grip on time management. I was just going, going, and going without taking the time to plan my time effectively. Bob sat me down with a cup of coffee and asked me to list all of the activities that I was involved in on one side of a sheet of paper.

There were quite a few tasks that had crept into my daily, weekly, and monthly routines. Bob then took each task individually and asked me if I would pay someone $100,000 per year to do them. Of course, I said, "no" and then he asked, "Would you pay someone $18,000 to do them?" I said, "Yes," and he replied, "Well, then why are you paying yourself $100,000 per year to do it?" As we went down the entire list of tasks, it became clear that I needed to create a new administrative position and delegate those tasks to someone else. The entire Bob Cohen experience of evaluating tasks and their related costs set the foundation for similar exercises in the future.

In the meantime, Peggy was pregnant, and we hired Janet Bookman, who would ultimately replace her. Within two weeks, Janet announced that she too was pregnant and there was a new joke at the office about my fertile impact on women. The fact that both she and Peggy were pregnant was pure coincidence, of course. Janet would go on to become a key player in the company after giving birth to her daughter, Judy. She was an extremely competent, loyal, and well-organized person.

Amidst all of the growth and challenges of that time, I was playing around with "Venmark Creations," a company division selling a Wine Sak, which was a slim canvas bag that I designed for carrying a bottle of wine. It also had a pocket on the side to hold a corkscrew, and a thin rope sling arrangement that closed tightly when you slung it over your shoulder. My invention was inspired by my memory of breaking a bottle of wine while climbing up Mount Tamalpais, North of San Francisco. It slipped out of a backpack. Our second client, Boston Hand Print was making them for us. We were also selling Wine Saks directly as a result of our own publicity releases. I learned a lot about consumer product marketing and media relations from that process.

A highly credible wine publication that was based in Boston called me about the Wine Sak and invited me to bring one to their office to examine. So, I purchased a bottle of wine, put it in the Wine Sak, slung it over my shoulder and visited them. The big takeaway lesson was to listen to the editor when they say they can't accept the bottle of wine because it violates their publisher's rules regarding accepting gifts. I insisted they keep the wine along with the Wine Sak and we never got any publicity from them. It was a huge faux pas.

Another product I invented for Venmark Creations was Photo-Needle Art. Put simply, a customer would send us a photograph and we would have it printed on a needlepoint mesh so that they could create needlepoint art from the picture. Photo-Needle Art never got off the ground, but we did make a few sales. One customer actually came to our office in Wellesley who was buying one for his wife. His name was Joe Iandiorio and he was a patent attorney from neighboring Waltham, MA.

Joe was in his late thirties and had been a solo practitioner with one assistant, for about 10 years. He decided that he wanted to grow his law practice and right around that time, advertising had become legal for lawyers, but Joe thought it was "tacky" and didn't want to advertise. But he was receptive to the idea of publicity to get exposure, establish his credibility, and build his brand. Joe wanted to expand his practice and get involved with State politics. I also wanted to get involved in politics, so I made a deal with Joe. He would purchase black and white portrait photographs from our photographer, Leo, to use for press releases and I would duplicate them and keep them on hand. I then advised him to arrange to give speeches to various civic and professional groups and send me a copy of his speeches. Then I would write and distribute a press release about each one and he would get lots of free publicity.

As a result, Joe Iandiorio was published in *The Boston Globe, Boston Herald, Bay State Business World, Inc Magazine* and many other publications. In short, our plan worked spectacularly well and within a year Joe was appointed Chairman of the Commonwealth of Massachusetts Small Business Task Force by the Secretary of Economic Affairs for the State. There were 50 members of the task force and Joe made me one of them. My strategy for getting involved in politics was working and, naturally, I was able to get publicity for myself and Sales Development Associates too, which helped build our own business.

As Sales Development Associates continued making new and repeat sales and getting lots of publicity for our clients through the remainder of 1978, it became abundantly clear that recruiting new employees was the most challenging function for a small business; especially for an underfunded startup like ours. Usually you don't have the time, knowledge, testing capabilities, and resources to do it properly. Small businesses cannot afford a human resources professional or to staff an HR department. We were no different. I was so busy that it hampered my decision-making; especially when it came to hiring. I was engaged in too much wishful thinking as opposed to critical analysis. Frequently, my hiring mistakes resulted in one step forward and two or more steps back. As they say, "it is hard to drain the swamp when you're up to your ass in alligators!"

I was up to my ass in a business that was growing out of control. If I had an opportunity to do it over, I would have hired an experienced management consultant to help me acquire the right people and I'd have borrowed money to finance our growth and taken the pressure off myself so I could make better decisions.

10

GROWING PAINS, TUMULT, AND CRITICAL DECISIONS

Between Christmas and New Years of 1979, I invented the Press Pak©, which was a product that we prepared for our clients. The Press Pak© included previous product announcements and a company history and biography of key employees, all compiled neatly into a large white envelope emblazoned with the client's company name and logo and ours too. It was a low-cost press kit for trade shows and a great way to leverage the previous work that we had done. Editors who attended trade shows liked them because they provided background information for an exhibitor and included photos and publicity releases that they could use. It made their research jobs easier and, as always, our writing was concise and to the point, without fluff, and simple for them to use. Years later we veered away from the envelopes and moved everything to CDs to keep up with the changing times.

What was really neat about our Press Pak© was that it could be sold by our salespeople. Although there were several components involved, the salesperson could price it out on the spot with a simple ordering matrix and then ask for the order and payment. It let them check off the Press Pak© contents and quantity and was another convenient service package that our sales team had to sell in addition to North American Publicity Orders and Western European Publicity Orders with addenda for various other regions such as Central and South America and the Far East.

I was also creating other products which we eventually introduced including 1-, 2-, 4-, 6-, and 8-page newsletters that had a product section which consisted of our previous work. Our clients saved money by getting more value from their previous expenditures and we saved time too. Traditional agencies wouldn't routinely leverage previous work. Instead, they would find a reason to do new projects. On the other hand, we encouraged our clients to use our photography and copy for other marketing purposes such as trade show booth backgrounds and brochures, and they appreciated it.

There were so many new things happening at this point in time; one of them being the acquisition of our second computer system. It was a used system that I purchased from a manufacturer's representative of one of our clients. It was a Radio Shack TRS80 Model II Computer with three custom made seven-inch floppy disk drives added on for data storage and a high-speed printer. The system was all bundled and used a more universal operating system (software) called CPM, rather than Radio Shack's TRSDOS operating system. It cost $9,000 back then, used, and paid for itself in three months.

Another new experience for Sales Development Associates was hiring a co-op student from Northeastern University. I recall how wonderful the program was for me and thought that it would be great to participate and employ a smart student. That smart student was named

Kathy and she helped set up the computerization of our production log and taught it to Janet Bookman who was our production manager. I used titles that were found in industry because we were essentially a manufacturer of news releases and I wanted our employees to relate to our clients, most of which were small manufacturers. As an aside, we referred to news releases as "product announcements" in order to differentiate and position our company as the leader in the field. Other people prepared lowly news releases, while we prepared *product announcements* and there was a real difference.

Differentiating yourself from competitors is important because it increases the perceived value of the services you provide. Clients are willing to pay more for services that they perceive as unique or superior. In addition, differentiation can help you build brand recognition and establish a unique identity in the marketplace. This is especially important with service industries because perceived value dictates what you can charge for those services. More on this in Chapter Sixteen.

Publicity was our only business. We never purchased advertising or required retainers like traditional creative agencies, and never prepared fancy proposals. Our business model was more akin to that of a manufacturer. Our salespeople sold our products and they were, in turn, manufactured by our writers and administrative team. It was similar to insurance policies where the sales staff sold them and the underwriters, actuaries, and inside team produced them.

I divided up Massachusetts, Rhode Island, and Southern New Hampshire into five sales territories. Even if there were unassigned territories, it was important that our salespeople remain focused and build their client relationships and referrals within a specific territory. It also fostered their familiarity with the territory geographically which saved them a lot of travel time. That said, the sales team did share leads with each other. Sales were driving everything that we were doing. It necessitated the hiring of additional writers, getting more automated equipment for labeling and applying postage to envelopes, and the ultimate move and consolidation into larger office space from our third floor and first floor offices.

The two largest circulation industrial publications at the time were *New Equipment Digest* and *Industrial Equipment News* and we often had a dozen or more clients published in each monthly issue. In addition to making those clients very happy, the publications became great sales tools and gave us tremendous credibility. After all, these were the two largest industrial publications in the country at the time and when you added up the New England companies that had free product publicity in them, we were far and away the clear winner.

Interestingly, advertising agencies didn't help their clients take full advantage of product publicity because it was so much more cost-effective than paid advertising. Just ask yourself why you read a publication? The answer is obvious, for the news, information, entertainment, and editorial content. That's why publicity is so much more effective than paid advertising which has to draw you away from the content, the reason why you're reading the publication in the first place.

We continued to grow and hired more writers and salespeople throughout 1979. I assisted with inside training, while Charlie Fox, Creative Director, (really the head writer), and John Kenmore, Marketing Director, (really the head salesman), could provide training in the field. Each new hire was costly in that we had to train them, pay their automobile expenses, provide medical benefits, absorb their additional time on our telephones, and other office expenses, all of which added up quickly.

I was desperately looking for someone who I could trust to help me build the company. I was becoming exhausted, maybe even burnt out, and in a strange way, disinterested. It wasn't unusual for my work days to be 14-16 hours long. Reflecting back, I think it was more important to me to *do and create*, rather than *sustain and maintain*. At any rate, my older brother Rich was interested in joining Sales Development Associates and I thought that it would be great. He could be my right-hand man and I could trust him. His background was in the computer business as an operations manager and he was getting tired of it. But, by early 1979, Sales Development Associates was earning a lot of money and I could make him a good offer that included a nice salary and automobile allowance, plus medical insurance. I did convince him, however, to keep the stock that he had in his previous company, CLSI, which computerized libraries throughout North America. One can't predict the future and it didn't make sense to let the stock go, in my view. Fortunately he took my advice.

My brother Rich became vice president of Sales Development Associates and his training began in sales and writing. All the while, he also refined our internal systems to help keep our production and distribution of product releases highly efficient. In addition to learning the business, making sales would be an important way of funding his salary. I recall that he brought in a company called Algorithmics to develop operational software for Sales Development Associates from top-to-bottom including order entry, writing, media distribution, production, and so forth. There weren't standard agency software packages on the market at that time. Ours would be custom-made just for us, or so I thought.

In the process of learning about our business in order to prepare a proposal, Algorithmics would become privy to our entire proprietary business model and system. Frankly, undressing in front of them in that way concerned me a great deal and I'll never forget the day that they brought us a proposal for the custom software they were going to develop for us. It was going to cost a pretty penny and they had the audacity to provide us with a contract whereby they would own the software and then lease it back to us. Oh yes, the contract also gave them the right to market our software to others. I didn't build Sales Development Associates so that they could sell the idea and operational software to someone else and create competitors for us. So, I took the proposal from their president and ripped it up in front of them before I threw them out of our office. I was livid and didn't hold back my feelings.

Right around the same time, our production manager and Janet Bookman's husband, Ralph, was looking for a new sales job and ended up working for my brother Jerry in Norwood, MA at his Aamco Transmissions franchise. Ralph would sell the shop's transmission rebuilding services wholesale to other automotive repair shops. Around the same time, Dan Bowman, one of our salespeople needed to purchase a used car and my brother Jerry had one for sale. Relationships were becoming incestuous at that time. Business and personal boundaries were totally blurred.

Our team was growing rapidly and it seemed like we were adding salesman monthly. The business was such that you knew within a few weeks whether someone was going to work out and in straight commission sales it is not unusual to have a lot of turnover. It was getting very tedious and I was exhausted. That said, terminating employees wasn't cost-effective or pleasant for anyone. We also added another writer and had three full-time account executives. Fortunately, my brother and I could handle any writing overflow, so that was a good safety valve. But I was still editing all the copy. On March 24, 1979 I hired one of my old brokerage supervisor friends from The Paul Revere Insurance Company, Bernie James, to join our sales team as an account executive. Frankly, I don't recall whether he was just tired of the insurance business or was really impressed with Sales Development Associates.

As spring arrived, we were growing sales nicely and our team was bonding. We were getting a lot of repeat business and media recognition too. Everything was moving ahead well and I really wanted to stabilize the sales force. The decision to hire my brother was beginning to show some troublesome signs. Not from him, but from his wife Jackie who was the dominant influence in their relationship. I knew her since I was nine years old. She and Rich were coming to our house one evening and I had recently purchased a new Porsche and installed a new stereo system in my house earlier that day. Well, as Jackie entered our home she noticed the car in the driveway and heard our stereo system. Then she said, "I guess you really are *rich*, aren't you?!" It was said in a very sarcastic way that made Peggy and me extremely uncomfortable. We'd have rather heard, "Hey, great sound system and a beautiful car too!" It would have been nice if she was happy for us, but her comment came out cloaked in jealousy.

Spring turned into summer and we decided to have a company picnic at Ashland State Park which was about a thirty-minute drive west of Wellesley. The park had over 470 acres including a 157-acre reservoir. Tall pine trees and great scenery too. All of our employees, their spouses or significant others, and their children were invited. All told there would be about 18 adults and a handful of kids with food and drinks and loads of fun to be had. The park had an area with picnic tables under shady pine trees, not far from the water. We staked out our tables and a couple of barbecue grills for the burgers and hot dogs, and were ready for a relaxing day of fun games, swimming, and bonding.

It was a beautiful June day. Ralph Bookman, Janet's husband, who used to work for a sporting goods store decided to bring custom made Sales Development Associates T-shirts for everyone. They were white with blue trim and our blue arrow logo over the left breast area and looked awesome! Everyone put on their shirts and showed great company pride while they tossed Frisbees, played ball, and frolicked. One person, however, refused to wear a T-shirt and it was my brother Rich's wife, Jackie! Needless to say, I was embarrassed that my brother, the vice president of my company, couldn't persuade his wife to play a supportive role and wear the T-shirt for the benefit of our company and employees. Not only was I embarrassed, but I was very angry and worried about the impact of her behavior on the other employees. She was clearly dissing me, everyone knew it, and it was a damned unpleasant feeling.

Throughout our fast growth period in 1979 and the early eighties, I was performing other marketing tasks for certain clients. I'd created a simple three-fold two color brochure template and single-page sales flyers and data sheets that were fun to create and design. It reminded me that I was the class artist back in the fourth grade at the Williams Elementary School and rather than building on those skills and my love of art, my mother discouraged it. She was afraid that I would become an unproductive, creative nonconformist bohemian. In her mind, she wanted me to become a wealthy businessman like my Uncle Sam Stroum who owned several companies in Seattle, WA.

The additional marketing work that I performed kept me interested and challenged while the other employees were doing their jobs. I was also giving speeches at various business and civic clubs and that was always good for business. Frankly though, I had to push myself to do it because public speaking didn't come natural to me. Nevertheless, once I got started in front of a crowd, I usually pulled it off pretty well. It was also during that time that my work for Joe Iandiorio, the patent attorney with political aspirations began paying off. That's when he became Chairman of the Commonwealth of Massachusetts Small Business Task Force and invited me to become one of their 50 members.

The most interesting marketing work that I did was with Charleswater Products, Inc. and the founder and president, George Berbeco. He was building his static control materials company very rapidly and was using product publicity as a way of generating sales leads and then using those leads as bait to attract and support distributors and representatives around the country and ultimately the world. George also used publicity as a market research tool. In other words, rather than building a lot of products and putting them into inventory as was customary, he would first hire us to do a product announcement and determine the interest of the media and market. If the response was sufficient, then he would make the product. If not, he wouldn't pursue it; all the while saving thousands of dollars by not creating an inventory first. Initially he kept this approach a secret from me for fear I might not play along. George always liked to travel close to the edge and was a very clever marketer and businessman.

George founded Charleswater Products, Inc. as a static control company after attending an electronics trade show in California and noticed that 3M Company was the only firm involved with static control at the time and they had a complete catalog of products for use in electronics assembly areas. Electrostatic charges, of course, can destroy electronic devices and in those days the industry was young and electronics assembly and manufacturing facilities were becoming popular. One of George's best and most creative ploys happened while he was exhibiting at a trade show in Houston, TX and he managed to get himself invited as a guest speaker. George had a master's degree from MIT in chemical engineering which was obviously prestigious. He hired me to publicize his upcoming speaking event. When he prepared his biography, he included that he was the president of the second largest static control products firm in the country. Of course, he was because there was only 3M and Charleswater at that time. One was huge and the other traded on that identification. Brilliant marketing ploy!

The show proved to be a success for George who was able to attract several customers, distributors, and manufacturer's representatives around the country. Working closely at that time, George and I would go out to lunch monthly and smoke quality Dominican cigars afterwards at our favorite restaurants. I loved being a part of his company and seeing the direct impact that my ideas had on his business. I named products and created advertisements for him and they were making a significant impact. Within a couple of years, other companies began selling static control materials and Charleswater's products were becoming commodity items. Naturally, that caused price erosion because all static control products were essentially the same.

George and I were having lunch at the Newton Marriott,

seated by a window overlooking the Charles River, when we were discussing ways to position Charleswater as the leader of the static control industry. That's where I came up with the tag line, "Technically Superior," to help him differentiate Charleswater from the competition and position them as the best in the business. George was quite pleased with my creation. I later created full-page advertisements for the leading electronics trade publications that just used the center section of an entire page with an outstanding product photograph. It also included and a brief product description followed by the Charleswater logo and the 'technically superior' tag line. George invested quite a bit of money into their advertising program and it was extremely successful.

What's more, the advertisements leveraged our previous product publicity work for Charleswater Products by using the excellent product photography and it saved him lots of money. Traditional advertising agencies never would have done that because they'd have required a new photo shoot. I really wanted to provide George with the most value and save him money if I could. It was actually in our mutual best interest and it ultimately created more work for Sales Development Associates.

The holiday season of 1979 was memorable for many reasons. Sales Development Associates was growing and hiring new people and in December we had a total of 97 publicity orders, 33 new clients, and 64 repeat orders. Selling in December was great because you could drop in on clients and wish them a Merry Christmas while building relationships. Because of the season, people were more receptive to being interrupted in that way. They were laid back, feeling the friendliness of the holidays, and less cynical than they were during other times of the year. More importantly, they often had money to spend to avoid paying more income taxes. That's why our repeat orders were so high at the end of the year. I loved doing business in December.

We were also consolidating our offices from Suite 306 and 106 into Suite's 105 and 105A which were connected and became one big 1,550 square foot office space. We had a conference room, an office for my brother, offices for salespeople to make their phone calls from, a large writer's office which housed three writers, a computer office where Janet Bookman ran operations from, a nice reception area, and a very good-sized walk-in storage closet. One wall in the conference room featured a dozen framed magazine covers hung with pride. Naturally, I had a nice corner office and there was a separate room for the coffee maker and postage machine. The move would take place early in January and I purchased more office furniture for delivery during the first week. It included new desks, chairs, tables, filing cabinets, and shelves which were top quality, of course.

The one thing that I learned from my previous experience at The Paul Revere and Newsmaker was that a really nice Christmas party paid dividends. The employees and spouses or dates would talk about the party for weeks. I arranged for our party to take place at the Newton Marriott Hotel and it was a beautifully catered affair. As appetizers and drinks were passed around, our employees and their spouses or significant others chatted, milled around, got reacquainted, and also met other new hires. Then we sat for dinner and I gave a brief speech and toast to everyone about how thrilled I was with our team's performance and how proud I was of our growth.

My toast was well-received by everyone. Then I was totally surprised by the toasts that came back my way. It seemed like everyone wanted to thank me for their opportunity. John Kenmore presented me with a gorgeous framed print of a seagull flying with the inscription, "They can because they think they can." I was really grateful and humbled by the way the employees toasted me and Sales Development Associates. They were enthusiastic and shared their own stories. It was fantastic and the wine was flowing. Afterwards, my sister-in-law, Jackie, walked directly up to me, got right into my face and said loudly, "They think you're Jesus Christ!" Peggy was standing next to me and neither of us could believe what we had just heard. The sarcasm, venom, and the tone of her voice were embarrassing and hurtful, and it became abundantly clear that there was really going to be trouble ahead for me.

By early January, we were officially all moved in to Suite 105. After a couple of days in the field visiting clients, I came into the office suite and walked down the hall to my office which was the last door on the left. As I turned the corner from the reception area, I spotted my brother leaning back in his chair with his feet up on his desk, not appearing to be working very hard. He only made five sales for the entire month of January. Nevertheless, as a team we had 103 orders in January and the year was off to a good start.

The greeting card that I received from my mother at the office for our company move into larger space caught me totally off guard. Her inscription on the inside was, *"To all of you at SDA, congratulations. Love, Mom Stroum."* Perhaps it was a thoughtful gesture, but to me it revealed her narcissism and "love" was too deeply personal for a business setting.

We had increased our fees nominally at the start of 1980 and in retrospect; we shouldn't have been so conservative. We went up $50 per order and should have made it $100. I was also beginning to feel the pressure of overhead as we were now providing medical benefits and paying for office furniture, software development, and other growth associated expenses. We had three full-time writers now who all received automobile allowances and two salespeople in training who drove up our telephone bills without results. After a few months, I concluded that obtaining more office space than we needed was not resulting in an increase in productivity. In fact, during the month of April, I had to loan the company $30,000 to meet payroll and expenses.

I was feeling the pressure big-time and not having fun anymore. In the beginning, I never felt "pressure," but now the long hours and personnel issues, especially my brother Rich's lack of productivity and communication with me, were really troubling. I needed a break. So, I took a four-day weekend and went to Florida to meet my buddy Al from San Francisco who was visiting his folks in Delray Beach, FL where my folks also lived. Al was one of my oldest and best friends. He was a smart guy, had a Master's Degree in management, and I respected his opinions. Al also knew Rich and Jackie very well. So, when discussing the Jackie incidents with him he suggested that I take her to lunch and have an open conversation about my concerns. In other words, get everything out on the table and deal with it directly. I thought it was good advice and a great idea.

When I returned from Florida, I invited Jackie to lunch at the Pillar House Restaurant, a Wellesley, MA institution. It was one of those old-fashioned restaurants where men had to wear sports jackets and if you didn't have one on, they loaned you one. I always wondered how many bodies one of those loaned sports jackets had been on. Jackie and I talked about family, business, and a host of other topics. What really shocked me though was when she made it clear to me that she believed in "sibling rivalry" and thought that it was a good thing. I couldn't believe it, but I knew that she had a conflicted relationship with her only sister. Clearly, there could be no winners in a sibling rivalry; only losers. That was really disturbing to me because Jackie and I used to be very close. When my brother Rich first went overseas to Thailand in the U.S. Air Force, before I enlisted, I would take her out to dinner and then spend time together with her at my folks' house. There were never any problems. As I said, I've known her since I was nine years old and she was like a sister to me. Her jealousy had become a terrible thing.

Well, the pressure mounted at work with respect to meeting our financial obligations and my brother's lack of productivity and virtually zero communication with me bothered me tremendously. The vibes were clear and my sixth sense was that we had a very serious problem that needed to be addressed and I had to take the initiative to resolve it. Hoping to get a better grip on my situation, I talked with my mother about having to terminate Rich. Her reply was very revealing and upsetting, to say the least. She said, "What do you expect, he's just like your father?" Surely she couldn't have thought too highly of my father. Of course, that in itself was troubling.

Early in June I was going to arrange a lunch meeting to discuss Rich's future with the company and his termination. After all, I had lent the company a lot of money and was looking at a situation where I had to make a business decision: it was either the survival of my company, my dream and life's work, or terminate my brother. One had to go. Ironically, before I had the opportunity to set a date for that fateful lunch, Rich returned from having lunch with his former boss at CLSI, his old company, and came to my office to inform me that he was resigning because he no longer enjoyed the work and he was going back to his old job. Fortunately for him, I had insisted that he keep his stock in that company and as it turned out, the company was sold a year later and the money from the value of his stock was enough to change his life at the time. He bought a brand-new Corvette sports car and his wife, Jackie, was very impressed and loved to show it off.

Later that evening I asked Rich to come over to my house for a conversation. I was troubled and needed to talk with him. I felt totally let down and was disappointed. So, he came over and I asked him how long he had been unhappy working at Sales Development Associates with me and he said, "For six months." I said, "You've been unhappy for six months and never said a word to me! Why didn't you say anything to me?" His reply was, "Jackie wouldn't let me." Everything added up to me then: sibling rivalry nearly destroyed Sales Development Associates. That was the end of our relationship for many years after that. It was ironic that I hired my bother Rich because I wanted someone who I could trust, and in the end, I couldn't trust him to be candid with me.

11

BLURRED LINES: BUSINESS AND PERSONAL

It became clear that business and personal boundaries had become a huge problem for me. I was living my dream and the excitement was unbelievable. We had one of the most prestigious accounting firms in the area working for us and not billing us very much. They assumed that we would expand nationally, or even globally, and they were willing to make an investment in terms of their time and effort in order to grow with us. Sales Development Associates was a hot, fast-growing company.

In less than five years, we already had more than 2,000 companies who had hired us at least once and a terrific repeat business ratio. What's more, I had just come to grips with making the single biggest hiring mistake that small businesspeople make which is hiring family and friends. Despite having a bachelor of science degree in management, I had violated the first rule of management which is: define the position you are seeking to fill very clearly, create a formal job description including expectations and achievement benchmarks, and annotate the skill-set and other criteria necessary to fill the position. In other words, clearly know who you are hiring and define what you expect that person to accomplish.

Looking back with the clarity of hindsight, I can see that the desire to hire someone I trusted was due to the lack of trust I had with myself. I didn't trust my own skills to hire someone off the street to fill a position. It was interesting that I hired Sandy, Dan, John, Janet, Charlie, Richie, Greg Jones, and Sue Patterson who were working out well, but I failed to fire others who weren't worth keeping. Consequently, I began to doubt myself. So, I hired my brother Rich. Under the pressure of a fast-growing business which was getting more tedious than creative for me, I made the erroneous assumption that my brother would be as motivated and dedicated to Sales Development Associates as I was. I also assumed he would be a loyal employee.

Oh, I have lots of salespeople stories from the early days. One incredible story was about Ted Foote. He was a character. The consummate formal WASP. He loved Sales Development Associates and everything we stood for, but after failing to make very many sales over the first month or so, I began spending more time training him on how to sell our product publicity services. That went on in vain for two months with very few sales to show for it. So, I really came down hard on him in one meeting and his defensive response which he delivered with a "How dare you question me" attitude, was, "I have an undergraduate degree from Yale and a Harvard MBA!" I simply said, "Then you ought to be smart enough to learn from me since I'm the founder and president of this company and the creator of our products and sales materials!" Ted Foote was fired a week later. He never got it, though, because for several years he used me as a job reference. His higher education protected his ego and prevented him from learning the truth about himself.

Hiring salespeople was especially challenging. For example, one of my client's inside salesmen was a fellow named Howard Norman. As a client of ours, he had experienced first-hand what we were all about at Sales Development Associates. He enjoyed the process of getting publicity for his company, the resulting sales leads, and benefited tremendously from the exposure that we got for his employer. After several product announcements with us over time, Howard asked for an interview for a sales position. So, I thought, who better than a former client who knew first-hand what we did? He would be "believable," which, of course, is the most important character trait of a sales person. So, I hired him and I was initially enthusiastic about adding him to the company.

Howard talked a great game and for a while I bought into it. After several weeks, however, he hadn't made a single sale. It was interesting, though, that on his weekly sales report, he added that he was in conversations with the economic development section of the mayor's office in Fall River, MA and had several meetings scheduled. Well, after a couple of more blank weeks I decided to telephone the mayor's office. It turns out, they had no idea who Howard Norman or Sales Development Associates were. When I confronted Howard he had no explanation for what he did. Who would have thought that someone who had been a client and asked for the job would totally fabricate such a story? Obviously, I fired him.

It was December 1980 and I was not feeling very good about life. The stress of building Sales Development Associates was contributing to my exhaustion and my exhaustion was contributing to my stress. And my stress was causing me to become depressed. I wasn't happy and felt trapped. But, since I was experiencing very clear success, it didn't make much sense to me. One of the books that I purchased to help me understand what I was feeling at that time was titled *Overcoming the Fear of Success* by Martha Friedman. She had a history of creating roadblocks for herself until she was 56 years old and I feared that I was on the same track. I mean, our rise was meteoric and there were many factors affecting my view of the business. I had a love-hate relationship with sales and was surely tired of sales management.

It was the creative side of the business that intrigued me. Creating more services to sell with our packaged approach, along with the accompanying sales presentations, creating brochures, marketing strategies, publicity announcements, and advertisements, and sales consulting for clients was what I enjoyed the most. That's what I liked spending most of my time doing. At that point, Janet Bookman, our production manager was handling day-to-day affairs and she was doing a fantastic job of making sure that all of our orders were being produced efficiently.

In retrospect, 1981 was probably the most intense year of my business and personal life. I say both because of their total intertwinement. It was clearly unhealthy and I had begun seeing a therapist, on December 29, 1980. He was referred by my old friend Sam Paris' therapist, Saul Goldman. He was 56 years old, Jewish, and became the legitimately strong father figure that I really needed. He told me that when he was 50 years old, he realized that he was working at the wrong job as an engineer and was married to the wrong woman and needed to make some major changes. So, that's when he got divorced and attended Harvard where he earned his Master' Degree in Public Health and then became a therapist.

I found the process of therapy to be fascinating. In the beginning I saw my therapist three times a week because I was really quite depressed and it was a challenge to just get out of bed and function on a daily basis, but after a couple of weeks I settled into a weekly routine. He was located in Providence, RI near Brown University, where I had several clients and worked until later in the afternoon when I had my 4:00 p.m. therapy session with him. The timing worked out well and making the hour trek back home let everything from our session sink in and percolate within my psyche.

My therapist was excellent at exposing layers of ideas in an orderly fashion so that their meaning could be understood viscerally. He explained that the process of therapy was like peeling an onion. Each layer that you peeled and exposed allowed you to assimilate a lesson from the previous layer. But you could never skip layers and it was a long, tedious, and rewarding process that involved questioning everything. And I mean everything; especially work and marriage. Frankly, I learned a tremendous amount from therapy. My therapist's professionalism and discipline helped me have revelations about my "self" and life in general. He understood my ego and told me the chair that I was sitting in during therapy was also occupied at other times by some of the most influential political and corporate leaders in the State of Rhode Island. Knowing that I wasn't alone and was one of several winners getting therapy, made me feel better. He was a godsend and there were many weeks when our hour-long sessions saved me from total misery and collapse.

At one point during the summer, my depression was so severe that I had a panic attack while driving from a therapy session in Providence, RI to Cape Cod where Peggy and I had rented a cottage in a remote salt marsh in the town of Wellfleet. While on the highway, I got a vision that I would arrive at the cottage to find Peggy and Marc bludgeoned to death. I saw blood everywhere and was convinced they were slaughtered! My heart raced and I was perspiring profusely and really scared. My Porsche kept driving faster and faster, breaking traffic laws until I arrived at the cottage and quickly saw that everything was okay. Oh, I was so happy to see them alive and well that day! Marc was only two and a half years old and he was a bright, handsome little boy. On another afternoon I drove west on the Massachusetts Turnpike to clear my head and had my Porsche hitting 95 miles per hour when I thought about how easy it would be to steer into a bridge abutment and end it all. Nobody would know it wasn't a mere auto accident. It was a fleeting thought and thankfully the last of its kind. I was very depressed and had hit rock bottom that day.

I began to question my interest in the further development of our sales force and also began to understand why success had created problems for me. In her book *Overcoming the Fear of Success*, Martha Friedman described her "Family Olympics" paradigm which is a metaphor that refers to the way in which families can unintentionally create an environment that promotes competition and undermines support among family members. She was categorized and labeled a certain way as it related to her siblings and parents. And the reason that she didn't excel and become a doctor until she was 56 years old was because she allowed the paradigm to govern her life. The family forces to keep you in place are extremely powerful and when you permit yourself to grow beyond them, it creates a lot of friction from all of the affected family members.

My parents were a problem and so were my brothers who were always smarter than I was academically. They were in Curriculum I, the top group in high school, and I was in Curriculum II for those who weren't quite as smart. That was my label: not as bright as my brothers, but a hard worker nevertheless. I had bought into that until I met David Whitney, my Northeastern University savior who taught me how to study properly. It turned out that I was as smart as my two brothers and I upset the applecart in my family by becoming successful so fast. Much more successful than they were.

Therapy brought out painful, but relevant, memories. For example, I recalled my trip to Orlando, Florida to visit my oldest brother Jerry, whom I idolized, when I was 15 years old. He was 22 years old and married to an alcoholic woman six years older than him. She had a son, Johnny, who was nine years old. At fifteen, I was totally unaware of her alcoholism. His house was on the outskirts of Orlando which was a small city back then. It was before Disney took over Central Florida and their house was in a rural setting. What happened there was a major misunderstanding. I was sitting in my brother's living room and looked over at the kitchen table and said to his wife, Delores, "hey, Dee, we ought to take a picture of your kitchen and send it to my mother." Well, that comment made her mad! Apparently, the other side of the kitchen, which I couldn't see, was piled high with dirty dishes and was a total mess. She thought that I was dissing her and I had no idea what her problem was. Well, when my brother Jerry got home from work later that night, the shit hit the fan!

Delores was crying hysterically, or drunkenly, and Jerry

was dangerously angry. While screaming and yelling, he literally chased me down the hallway until I escaped into a bedroom where I was playing with Johnny and locked the door. Jerry was actually threatening to kill me and poked a screwdriver through the door several times trying to open it and get at me. I told him to stop or I would hurt Johnny. I was totally terrified. I didn't know what else to say or do and told him to leave me alone and I would go home. He finally stopped trying to pry the door open and I packed my suitcase and slipped out the back door without saying goodbye. I walked across his dark back yard through a field full of snakes, and out to the main road which was really a rural country road. I came across a 7-Eleven and met a guy who offered me a ride to the Trailways bus terminal. I arrived there around 9:00 p.m., in a sketchy section of town, and the next bus going north wasn't leaving until 7:30 a.m. the next morning.

So, I called my folks and explained what happened. My mother's response was, "What did *you* do to upset Jerry?" The position that I, the clear victim, was somehow responsible for being kicked out of his house in the dark of night was echoed by my brother Rich who got on the extension phone. It was an amazing display of "Family Olympics." The oldest son, Jerry, could do no wrong even though he and his wife were both drunkards and literally physically attacked me that night at their home in Orlando, FL. Naturally, that horrible experience of being threatened by my brother Jerry, who would have stabbed me with that screwdriver in a fit of rage, was my fault. Nobody believed me and I felt totally isolated.

Therapy brought out other memories which gave me a new level of understanding. My father's, "you're stupid just like your brothers, you can't use your hands, you can't do anything right, and you're a quitter," were put into perspective. They were the labels that prevented me from doing certain things; not the reality of my capabilities and talents that were on full display every day at Sales Development Associates. Not the reality of starting a business with $300 that now employed 12 full-time people who were all making a terrific living. All those revelations, as a result of therapy and keeping a daily journal, helped me get a much clearer idea of what were personal issues and what were business issues.

When my father visited my office and belittled me in front of my employees on April 29, 1981 it was a clear example of him trying to lift himself up by putting me down. It was his way of winning (tongue in cheek) at the Family Olympics. Coincidentally, I had a childhood memory of him telling me when I became a catcher in little league baseball that he was a catcher too as a kid and I wasn't as good as he was. What an unfortunate, insecure man. I had to ask him to stay away from my office because of his behavior. My mother told me that I hurt him, which was nonsense. My father was unable to support us emotionally and she acknowledged it. What I learned from that experience was that there are two ways to rise up: one by putting others down, or two, by growing and actually lifting yourself up. I preferred doing the latter and it upset the applecart in terms of my family.

Further evidence of the boundaries between my personal and business life being crossed up came to light when our salesman, John Kenmore, phoned me and told me that it took him over a half an hour to get the courage to call me. Previously, he had told Janet that he was home and that he was okay and I shouldn't worry about him. Clearly, that wasn't appropriate behavior or conversation for an employee phoning his supervisor. What had happened was that in my own fog and frustration, I had become more authoritarian in my management style with him and apparently it mimicked his ultra-strict father, so he had regressed and projected his personal issues onto me. Our relationship had become a blurred mess.

As therapy continued, I also understood my mother more clearly. Especially the inappropriate greeting card she sent congratulating all employees on the new office with the closing, "Love, Mom Stroum." So, as I had done with my sister-in-law Jackie, I took my mother to lunch at the Pillar House Restaurant which was her favorite eating place. Established in 1952, it was very well known. She was trying to play too large a role in my life and I very compassionately needed to explain to her that it was inappropriate. The room where we were having lunch together was the porch. Surrounded by colonial style windows, it was decorated with fresh cut flowers. Bright and sunny, it was a beautiful place.

What I did at the table, which worked very well, was to take out my pen and draw a Venn diagram with a large circle on a napkin with two large stick figures and a small one inside. I explained to my mother that this was Peggy, me and Marc; my family. Then I drew a smaller circle to the side which overlapped my larger circle and said to her, "Mom this circle represents you and Dad. You see, at this point in my life, this is where you fit in. You're no longer part of the larger circle. This is where our two respective families intersect, but it doesn't diminish our relationship, it just puts into perspective that I am your *adult* son and I have my own life and family now." She cried a little, but fully understood what I was saying. I knew from her tears and facial expression that she understood and was proud of the way I talked with her about the situation with love, empathy, and compassion; not anger.

As I was dealing with my personal issues, business was great and I was appointed as one of 18 members to the Commonwealth of Massachusetts *Advisory Council on Small Business* by Governor Edward King in April, 1981. That honor resulted from my relationship with Joe Iandiorio, Recall that he came to my office in 1977 and I agreed to prepare publicity releases for him gratis in exchange for a future political opportunity should he become successful as a result of our collaboration.

The speeches that Joe Iandiorio made and the subsequent newspaper and magazine articles that were published helped build his brand, leading him to become a member of the Board of Directors of the Massachusetts High Technology Corporation, a private-public partnership to assist in the process of technology commercialization. It ultimately became the model organization for other states too. As Chairman of the Massachusetts Task Force, Joe was responsible for assembling the *Advisory Council on Small Business* which would be an 18-member team working directly with Edward J. King, the Governor of Massachusetts.

The day of the swearing in ceremony to the *Advisory Council on Small Business* was exciting. It was a bright, sunny day and Peggy and I drove into the Massachusetts State House where I and 17 other members were sworn into office for a four-year political appointment by the Governor. We took official photographs, had a grand time, and it felt good. I was proud. For contrast, at a meeting the following week, I was approached by a gentleman who asked, "Are you Steve Stroum?" I replied, "yes" and he said, "I wanted to meet you." I told him that I was flattered and he said, "Don't be flattered, I'd just like to know what you have on Joe?" "What do you mean?" I asked. He continued, "Your name was number 18 on the list of appointees and every time someone removed your name Joe replaced it. So, what do you have on Joe?" I was blown away by this guy. Tact was certainly not his strong suit.

The gentleman's attitude implied that I had something scurrilous on Joe. All I had was the experience of helping him get notoriety as a patent attorney and become recognized as a technology leader by Massachusetts political leaders. We had a very simple arrangement: Joe would schedule speeches and send the dates and information to me; I had his practice background, biography and photographs and would then prepare press releases and get him loads of publicity every time he gave a speech. He had tremendous exposure in all major Massachusetts newspapers and it reinforced his expertise and brand.

Ironically, another honor and recognition of my business success was also happening. I was being nominated by Joe Grignaffini, my office landlord, a Rotarian, to become a member of the International Rotary Foundation Group Study Exchange Team and tour South Korea for six weeks as a goodwill ambassador. Rotary International is a global humanitarian service organization that brings together business and professional leaders in order to provide community service, promote integrity, and advance goodwill, peace, and understanding around the world. In the 1980s, Rotary was a significant organization in the U.S., but was really huge in South Korea where small businesses were burgeoning.

The Rotary Foundation's Group Study Exchange program was a unique cultural and vocational exchange opportunity for successful business and professional men and women between 25 and 40 years of age. The program provided travel grants for teams to exchange visits between paired areas of different countries. Our program would be six weeks long to experience South Korea's culture and institutions, observe how each group member's vocations are practiced abroad, develop personal and professional relationships, and exchange ideas.

It was early in July, 1981 when Joe Grignaffini called me and said, "Hey Steve, do you want to go to Korea for six weeks?" "No," I replied. Then paused and said, "Yes, of course, Joe!" Joe told me that I would have to be interviewed by a panel, followed by a family-style dinner which Peggy could attend and other meetings as part of the selection process. Then we made arrangements for me to be away with respect to work, passports, travel clothes and the like.

I was selected as one of five members and was extremely excited. Candidly, I couldn't wait to get away from Sales Development Associates. Frankly, part of my decision was based on my desire to escape because I wasn't really enjoying work at all. Naturally, my "public face" was all about the opportunity that the Group Study Exchange was offering me. And I was really excited, but underneath I was happy to have a "legitimate reason" to escape from work. The alternative was to quit work and that was totally unacceptable. By taking advantage of this professional service opportunity, if the business failed, it wouldn't be my fault, I reasoned. As part of the process of preparing for the trip, I took Janet Bookman to my attorney's office and we created a comprehensive, 26-page document detailing her power of attorney for The Venmark Corporation and Sales Development Associates while I was gone. Janet was an effective and loyal employee and I trusted her completely.

It was amazing. I was falling apart personally and in therapy weekly, yet these honors and wonderful opportunities were still coming my way. They did help give me the strength to persevere, and so did my acting ability. Undressed I felt a bit fraudulent, but that is what depression does to you. My business success was real and helped to shore up my self-esteem. It was a battle though, to be honest.

On my final day at the office prior to leaving for Korea, Charlie Fox, my Creative Director and chief writer, hugged me and actually began to cry real tears and said, "I will miss you terribly. You're more like a brother to me than my own brother. I want you to have a great trip. Don't worry about a thing: my mother-in-law will babysit and take care of Marc while you're away, and my wife Mary will take care of Peggy. Naturally, I will look out for your best interests here." So, we hugged again and said our goodbyes for a full eight weeks, not six, because Peggy was flying out to meet me in Maui, Hawaii for two weeks and a well-deserved vacation for her. For those two weeks, Charlie's mother-in-law moved into our house to care for Marc who was only two and a half years old at the time.

September 23, 1981 was the day we left for South Korea, via New York and Tokyo, Japan. Peggy drove me to the airport and she and Marc walked me to the gate where my Rotary colleagues were. Everyone was saying goodbye to their loved ones. Those were the days before the TSA and Homeland Security disallowed it. It was a beautiful autumn day and Peggy and I had mixed emotions. We were very excited for my upcoming journey, but would miss each other terribly. We'd been married 11 years and we had never been separated for this long.

When our flight from Boston landed in New York, a sign at the international terminal read, "Egg Rolls and Knishes," and it was clear to me that we were on an international journey. I knew somehow that the trip would change my life, but I wasn't quite sure why or how it would happen. I was prepared, though and kept a daily journal that forced me into making contemporaneous entries in three distinct areas: personal, cultural, and professional. Korea would be a fascinating experience.

12

HONOR IN KOREA AND BETRAYAL BACK HOME

The six weeks of touring South Korea were so intense that it took a couple of years to internalize all of the lessons learned. Imagine pouring a thick, creamy liquid into the top of a funnel at a rate much faster than it can flow from the bottom spout. There was no possible way that you could absorb and understand all there was to see, hear, smell, and touch without stirring it up occasionally. And I did stir it up frequently because I was committed to making an address to any Rotary Club in Massachusetts that wanted to hear my presentation for a full year after the trip. I recall making over 30 slide-show presentations and it was the least I could do for such an incredible life-altering experience.

Our first two days of the trip were spent in Tokyo where ordering breakfast was no easy task. Seated in a quaint little restaurant with tables and chairs considerably smaller than we Americans were accustomed to, made me feel like a seven-foot-tall basketball player. Outside the restaurant, by the front door, were life-like plastic models of the food on the menu which helped us decide what to order. Somehow the waitress understood what I wanted and my breakfast was served. It came in a basket; two pieces of one-inch-thick toast, butter and jam, two chunks of pineapple, a hard-boiled egg, hot coffee, and a toothpick that would last the day.

After leaving the restaurant, we were off to tour the city. A group of uniformed school children passed by with radiant smiles and I reached for my camera. By the time I took aim, half of them were in competition for my shutter. Tokyo provided an effective cultural bridge to Korea because it allowed us to become accustomed to being visitors in an Eastern land. The people were uncommonly gracious by American standards and the city was immaculate and orderly.

It was early afternoon when we arrived at Kimpo International Airport, Seoul, South Korea. Our small, but congenial welcoming party greeted us with signs and then showed us to their subcompact cars in a parking lot full of small cars with names and styles that we'd never seen before. Then we were shoe-horned into the cars and off for the five-and-a-half-hour drive to Gwangju, a city of about 800,000 people in the southwest part of the country.

The first thing I noticed as we took a right turn out of the airport parking lot was a guard post. Out front was a young Korean soldier, armed and standing tall. Behind him was a shed surrounded by sand bags protecting an intimidating 50 mm machine gun. At the time I wondered whether this level of security was good or bad and whether there was a possibility of bloodshed while we were there. The highway to Gwangju was nearly a straight line. Eight lanes wide, there were sections on standby for use as landing strips for military aircraft, complete with 55-gallon drums full of kerosene that were ready to become markers for those pilots in case there was an invasion by North Korea. It was a stark contrast to the rice paddies, quaint villages, and foothills that bordered the highways.

We stopped twice at roadside restaurants during the trip. Equipped with large parking spaces for buses, they were considerably different from the Cracker Barrels, Howard Johnson's, or Stouffers that dotted the highways back in America. There was an open-air section in front and a stale air section that consisted of smelly restrooms located off to the side. Also hanging on the wall in the front were rolls of toilet tissue. Guests would tear off a piece, depending on how much they needed, before going to the bathroom. Obviously, you had to know your own digestive system, that's for sure! Inside there was a sparse dining area with old fashioned Formica® top tables lined up in rows. Food was served family-style and after one bite I wished I was at a firehouse. Fond of spicy Mexican and Chinese food, I had never tasted anything as hot as kimchi, which is Korean spiced cabbage. I didn't like it at all.

We arrived at the Gwangju Tourist Hotel at about 10:45 p.m. after an exhausting day of travel. The accommodations were quite different from the luxury hotel that we stayed at in Tokyo. After a brief visit to the disco and a relaxing bottle of beer we went to sleep. Out of the 800,000 people in Gwangju, we were told that there were only 45 Caucasians at the time. At first it was exciting to be stared at and attract the many children we came across. Kids would approach us and twist the hair on our arms and feel our beards. Four out of five of us had full beards which was unusual for young men. We wondered why so many Koreans were shocked by our beards and we learned that growing a beard as a young man in Korea showed a lack of respect toward your elders. At that time in Korea men typically didn't grow full beards until they were 60 years of age, and both men and woman died their hair jet black until they reached that age.

Our first full day in Gwangju was very exciting. We met the mayor, presented him with a silver Paul Revere Bowl on behalf of Governor Edward J. King of Massachusetts, and then attended a press conference. This scenario was repeated at virtually every meeting we had with dignitaries as the six-week trip unfolded. There was a huge welcome at the Rotary Club and an overwhelming welcome by our first host family. We really felt like celebrities. Rotary International was a big deal in South Korea and it really was an honor to be part of it.

Driving from place to place was quite an experience. Korean drivers use their horns frequently and ignore traffic lanes, signals and the like. Although they seemed hostile and discourteous at first, that wasn't the case. At night the drivers would even shut off their headlights while stopped at traffic signals so that the glare from their headlights wouldn't bother the cars in front of them. It also took a while to catch on, but unlike America, in Korea, if you heard a car's horn it meant don't move, rather than move out of the way. Believe me, I was happy to be chauffeured around.

Back in 1981, Korea was a society of extremes. Extreme colors and extreme tastes. Old and new. East and West. The fruit juices were sweet, the coffee was strong, the food hot and spicy, the signs around cities were extremely colorful, and the advertisements were very animated. Rotarians were generally wealthy and the rest of the population was poor. The average Korean family earned about $1,500 dollars per year. How far could they travel when gasoline cost $4.50 per gallon? But, despite the inequities, everyone seemed to peacefully coexist. That said, the homes in wealthy neighborhoods where we often stayed were surrounded by fences and gates. Streets were full of people, pushcarts, rickshaws, bicycles, motorcycles, and small green taxicabs. There were very few private vehicles.

Another new and powerful experience we had was visiting an orphanage. The children were all toddlers and I distinctly remember the sadness in their eyes as they greeted us. The younger kids slept in cribs and the older children on thick floor mats. Wow, how fortunate my son Marc was to live in America with his mom and dad, I thought, and wondered what would become of those beautiful young children.

The socioeconomic perspective was considerably different from home. In America, being poor symbolized failure and reduced esteem. In Korea and the East, however, material wealth wasn't at the heart of one's value system at that time. Consequently, the rich and poor exhibited a level of mutual respect which was alien to Westerners. Koreans didn't compare themselves to other Koreans and try to "keep up with the Joneses" as we did in America. Their relationship was with the entire "universe." That said, while visiting with the Chief of Police in Kunson, Korea, he shared his views about the future and believed that economic crimes would increase over the next five years and television and materialism were the chief influencing factors. In other words: Western influence.

We had so many wonderful Rotarian host families who wanted nothing more than to please us and make us feel comfortable. One family, for example, learned that hamburgers and French fries were a favorite American meal so they served it to us for breakfast along with whiskey, coca cola, and beer! They didn't realize that, unlike Koreans, Americans had three distinct types of meals per day. In Korea, all meals were essentially the same. One day we were invited to an influential Rotarian's house for breakfast and I instinctively envisioned bacon, eggs, home fried potatoes, toast, and coffee. What was on our breakfast table, though, was a huge family style spread consisting of several small dishes filled with vegetables, fish, seaweed, and live octopus. Yes, live octopus at 8:00 a.m! The table was knee-high and we were seated on the floor.

Our daily activities didn't change very much throughout the trip. Factory tours, meetings with Mayors, important Rotarians, and other civic leaders, big lunches, bigger dinners, visits to temples high above the cities and very little spare time. In fact, the first activity in any new city was a visit to a mountaintop. Surprisingly, 70 percent of the South Korean countryside was mountainous. People adapted because usable space was at a premium. Even gravesites, where the dead were buried standing upright, dotted the mountainsides rather than occupying valuable real estate. The flat shoulders of newly paved roads also doubled as areas used for drying rice.

More than halfway through our trip, one of the Korean Rotarians, a fellow named Philip, which he told me was his Christian name, not his birth name, said in an unfiltered tone, "I can see from your eyes that you are sad and troubled." Surprised by his comment, I said "No, just a little homesick for my wife and son." But I was amazed at how perceptive he was. I thought that I was feeling pretty good and this total stranger from another world saw right through it. That said, I had only made two entries in my daily journal that involved work. I thought that I was doing well and most other entries were positive in nature. I was learning a lot about South Korea, their culture and customs, and myself too.

The trips up to the temples and resort areas were amazing. Aside from being jammed into tiny subcompact cars, the rides were an eyeful. There were rice farmers, families, and machines all toiling awfully hard. People, carts, oxen, cars, and busses all shared the road. Terraced landscapes converted every available square inch of earth into a garden. Depending upon what the plantings were, some were light green, golden brown, or a rich dark green. Majestically, the streams and rivers increased in beauty as we neared the mountaintops where temples, thousands of years old, preserved the identity of a people. Busloads of Koreans pilgrimaged there daily, usually three generations of families.

It was a thrill for me to take my shoes off and step inside a temple and share in a peoples' spirit. On one visit, I crawled down a small stairway to the base of a large gilded Buddha, waited for an older woman to complete her rituals, and touched a 1,300-year-old kettle. How many others have shared that experience over the centuries, I wondered. At that time the neighborhood where I grew up was transformed into the Massachusetts Turnpike 20 years before and the United States of America was little more than 200 years old!

After a few weeks, we all felt the desire to be alone and anonymous. That pointed to perhaps the most poignant difference between the American and Korean cultures at that time. The Koreans were a people and Americans were individuals. Culturally acceptable behaviors on their part, if taken out of context, were violations of our individual rights. For example, one morning at a public bath house, while drying off after bathing, a group of Koreans were staring at us and even though they were in awe of our white, hairy bodies, it was still annoying to be watched so indiscreetly while dripping wet. Another example occurred on the only evening that I had an opportunity to telephone Peggy and Marc. The telephone connection back home was made through an international operator and while I talked to Peggy and Marc, there were nearly a dozen people around me in the room. I had no privacy whatsoever and it wasn't unusual.

One night we slept at the home of a Provincial Governor. There were nine provinces in South Korea. The home was exquisite and the bedroom I was assigned to was magnificent. In fact, the Governor mentioned to me that when President Richard Nixon visited him, he slept in the same bed. I felt honored and slept well that night. Often, though, we slept on a mat, on the floor, or on much smaller beds than we Americans were accustomed to.

One night while asleep on the floor, I had a very strange, but symbolic dream. The scene was a house with a winding staircase and I came home from this trip to see Peggy and Marc there for the first time. The right side of Marc's face was horribly disfigured with a purple port-wine stain birthmark. The vision was very realistic and really startled me. I awoke with labored breathing and banged my knee against the floor while getting up. I forgot that I wasn't in a bed.

The vision was palpable and realistic. It was alarming and shook me to my toes. But I felt that it confirmed my priorities were Peggy and Marc. To me, the symbolism of the dream meant that whether Marc was the handsome child he actually is or severely disfigured that I loved him unconditionally. What he looked like really didn't matter. What mattered was who he was. Also, that my inner peace was more important to me than the material and public success that I enjoyed as president of my own company. It reminded me of my grade-school years when my mother would tell us to be sure to say that my father was a "display manager" when we were asked to tell the class what our fathers did for work. He wasn't a manager at all, but my mother had a need for prestige and felt better if the teachers and other people thought he was.

Status and what other people thought were very important to my mother. My father was really a window trimmer who put seasonal displays into liquor store display windows. Even though he wasn't a professional, he was very talented, did his job well, and took great pride in his work. My mother always wanted us to think highly of our father and she even told us that he was double-promoted from fourth to sixth grade in elementary school because he was very smart, and circumstances later prevented him from attending college. Clearly, she was disappointed by his lack of education and ambition.

Two days later we were off to Mokpo, Korea and, naturally, our first stop was to a temple and monastery high above the city. As we drove up the winding road and approached the monastery grounds, I saw several Buddhist monks working out front. They were pruning the trees and tending to the surrounding gardens. Small in stature, the monks wore nondescript hooded grey robes tied at the waist. After getting closer, one monk turned around to greet me and had the exact same port-wine stain birthmark that I had seen on Marc's face in my dream the night before! Precisely the same in every detail: same location, same color, and same disfigurement. Needless to say, the hair on the back of my neck stood up straight and I was absolutely blown away!

The Buddhist monk was a female from Toronto, Canada.

She looked emaciated, but was very nice and soft spoken, explaining that she had come to the monastery three years before for a brief visit and planned to return home in the coming months. I suspected she had been saying that for quite some time. She spoke to me about the pain and personal growth associated with suffering, and I could surely relate to it. What to make of that dream and the monk? Was it sheer coincidence or divine intervention? I will probably never know, but I've been wondering about it ever since.

The following day we went to a park and each one of us had the honor of planting a tree in our name. It was a touching ceremony followed by another Rotary Club luncheon. We had many similar luncheons throughout the six weeks and were treated like celebrities at each one. As the trip was coming to a close and I began thinking about seeing my lovely Peggy in Hawaii and spending two weeks there, I wrote in my journal, "I know I've come to this realization before, but the clarity with which I see it now is unparalleled. And the realization that I'm referring to dealt with the past. No matter how much I would have liked to have lived it over, it couldn't be done." I believed that I understood my past and felt more secure as a result. I recall writing in my journal, "I know who I am now and how I want to live. I know what's important to me now: I'm confident of that!"

We also had an opportunity to visit two different hospitals in Korea. One was Eastern with a big herb room that had a large wall with several small drawers filled with different types of herbal medicines and large graphic displays showing acupuncture pathways on the body. It was quite interesting, though, that we saw no actual patients and had limited time with staff. On the other hand, the Western hospital we visited was more like what we were accustomed to back home and we had an opportunity to chat with doctors. I noticed that a lot of Koreans smoked cigarettes and I wondered if there was a high incidence of lung cancer. So, I asked a doctor about it and he explained that Korean's don't inhale smoke as we do in America and Europe. Rather, they keep the smoke in their mouth and also swallow it. "Therefore, we have a high incidence of mouth and throat cancer here, not lung cancer," he said. Obviously, whether from the East or West, smoking wasn't good for one's health.

Our trip to the Southeastern tip of Korea emphasized technology rather than culture. Visits to petrochemical refineries, large shipbuilding facilities, and heavy industry took the place of visits to temples, monasteries, and ancient ruins. Clearly, that region was the furthest away from North Korea and, therefore, best suited for industry. The large industrial complexes resembled modern military establishments back home in America. Employee housing consisted of boldly numbered apartment buildings with three room units and clothes strewn over the balconies. Several large corporations in the industrial region provided employee theatres, gymnasiums, swimming pools, and were basically completely self-contained communities.

From that point on in our trip, industrialization and Westernization were the keynotes. We no longer stayed with host families. In Busan, one of the few cities that escaped the ravages of the Korean War, we stayed at the Busan Hotel which was absolutely gorgeous and stately. We also visited the United Nations Cemetery which was sobering. The cemetery contained 2,300 graves of service members from 11 countries; 36 from the United States. Rows of grave markers and a central monument accentuated by dead rose bushes reflected the ugliness of a war past, but unfinished.

Although the United States contributed the greatest number of people to the conflict, 1.7 million, of which 33,739 were battle deaths, most of them were reinterred back home.

A few days later we visited Panmunjom at the demilitarized zone at the 38th parallel. The security, inspections, and tension were overwhelming. As we approached Freedom Bridge and crossed the Imgim River we were in another world. Just an hour and a half drive north of Seoul, a world class city of eight million people and the nerve center of South Korea, there were numerous military tank walls and guard posts. The scene was a far cry from the flowers that we saw planted on the roadsides by school children a few hundred miles to the south.

I could feel the tension at Panmunjom and we were reminded that the Korean War is not over; only an armistice was signed. On July 27, 1953, military commanders from the United States (representing the United Nations Command), the Korean People's Army, and Chinese People's Volunteer Army signed the Korean Armistice Agreement, ending roughly three years of fighting of the 1950-1953 Korean War. What added to our angst was the fact that we each had to sign a military disclaimer that the United States of America would not be responsible for our safety and that our visit to Panmunjom was of our own free will.

Fortunately, while at Panmunjom we had an armed escort with us at all times. "Forever in Front of Them All," the sign read. That's the slogan of the United Nations soldiers guarding the zone. With the military escort in place, we crossed the street and climbed a Pagoda-like tower. Before I could attach a zoom lens to my camera and get a closer look at the North Koreans, their guards had binoculars on me. It was quite intimidating, to say the least.

After a luncheon at the servicemen's club, our first stop was the negotiating room in the blue Quonset Hut that you always see on television news reports, with a table that has a line down the length of it separating North and South Korea. In fact, I took a photograph with half of me in each world and as a North Korean soldier began moving towards me, I moved back quickly. The look on his face surely indicated that he wasn't very happy with me.

"Checkpoint five overlooked the old village of Panmunjom and the Bridge of No Return where the prisoners were exchanged at the end of the Korean War and where the Pueblo crew was returned in 1968," said Private Michael, our young military escort. "Over there," he continued, "Was where two U.S. officers were pruning a tree in 1976 when the North Koreans shot them." Moments later, we were on a bus traveling to that area directly while a military truck with its motor running was ready to block the bridge in case of an incident. It was really tense. Clearly, there was a North Korean threat at that time and it was taken very seriously by the UN Troops (Americans) and South Koreans.

How naïve my generation is, I thought, looking out over the barren landscape that still had loudspeakers spewing propaganda for people in the South to hear. North Korea is a land where individual freedom isn't even a consideration. I said to myself, "even though our freedoms at home don't always match our constitutional blueprint, we can still wear clothes of our choice, move around freely, and speak our minds."

Back in Seoul that evening, we were off to a farewell dinner at the Korea House Restaurant. You can safely walk the streets there at night and ride the subways or visit the sprawling underground shopping mall without hesitation.

How safe would I have felt walking in Boston, a city one-tenth the size of Seoul, at 11:00 p.m.? Another contrast in culture was that high school age students in Korea could be seen planting flowers along the highways and in America they could be seen spray painting symbols, obscenities, and other graffiti on bridges and buildings along the highways. Graffiti art is a form of individual expression in America, a concept which didn't exist and wouldn't be tolerated in Korea.

Most of my thoughts about home on that wonderful trip to Korea were limited to Peggy and Marc. There were very few thoughts about my extended family and the family Olympics, which was a first for me. What's more, I thought very little about Sales Development Associates. Business took a back seat. For the most part, I lived in the moment and was fascinated by the sights and the people who I met. I was being myself in Korea and proud to have been on the trip. No fancy title, no office suite or nice car; just me without the symbols of success. I was homesick and didn't pretend to be otherwise. Despite missing Peggy and Marc terribly and being occasionally sad, I wasn't depressed once while I was on the entire trip where we literally traveled up to mountaintops by tram and then deep into caverns.

In Korea I saw a lot of imitation and very little innovation. I believe incentives drive innovation. Keep in mind, however, that my observation was from 1981. I toured the Hyundai automobile factory when it was only two small buildings. I also recall touring a stone cutting factory where the workers sat on the ground out front and chipped away at the stone by hand using chisels and hammers while there were modern, fully automated CNC (computer numerically controlled) machines imported from Germany on the inside cutting intricate patterns into large slabs of stone. Two distinct industrial and technical eras were represented at a single location. The contrast was fascinating. The workers outside could have been from an earlier century.

The day finally came when our Korean trip ended. Needless to say, I was thrilled to be on my way to Hawaii to see my beloved Peggy. On the plane, I was seated with a lovely couple from Tokyo. They were Americans working a joint venture with a Japanese company. They told me that they had a three-room apartment in Tokyo that cost them $4,000 per month. That's $13,200 in 2023 dollars.

When I arrived in Hawaii, I spent the night at a Holiday Inn and greeted Peggy at the airport the following day for our transfer flight to Maui. It was wonderful to see her and embrace. Her beautiful blonde hair, blue eyes, and reassuring touch were just what I needed, along with some good American food, of course. We rented a Ford Mustang convertible with a torn top and drove to our hotel which was actually a luxurious condominium at Kapalua Beach Resort. On the way there we stopped at a market to buy some food and wine so we could get started on our two-week vacation. I recall that we took some cheese and wine next door to a small cliff overlooking the beach and just talked about everything as we enjoyed the beautiful scenery and turquoise blue waters, and just being together.

While in Maui, we visited Lahaina which is a quaint town with nice restaurants, shops, and art galleries. We also drove through the hills to visit Oheo Gulch (also known as the 7 Sacred Pools) which turned out to be a tourist trap bust. That said, we enjoyed the beach and swimming pool and being on vacation. Peggy shared her experiences while I was away, including her trip with Marc to see family in St. Louis and a trip to see our dear friends Ellen and Michael in Baltimore, MD. She also kept a journal while I was absent and said that she had formed a bond with Janet Bookman from my office who also visited our home and kept her company. The two had created a wonderful friendship.

When I returned to the office and looked at the financial results, I should have turned around and immediately left for another trip. Janet had done a marvelous job and our company's profit for the eight weeks I was away exceeded $22,000. There were other new salespeople at that point who were contributing to our sales, but the job of interviewing and hiring had become very tedious for me. It seemed like we were in the business of hiring and firing salespeople and it wasn't pleasant. That said, I had a cousin who was a leading sales manager for Pitney Bowes, a large multinational corporation, and she told me that she experienced a 25 percent turnover rate with salespeople. In a sense, I didn't feel so bad because even with all of their human resource assets and recruiting filters, they still got it wrong one in four times. Apparently, that is the nature of the beast.

At Sales Development Associates we also had some new writers and administrative help on board back then. In December I began to get a strong sense that Charlie Fox was unhappy. He called me at home one evening and said that he needed more money for automobile expenses and that he wasn't making the money he could have made had he stayed in the magazine business. I sensed that something was up. Then about 10 minutes later he called me again, apologizing profusely for his earlier call. During the following week, he also mentioned to me that John Kenmore had "campaigned against me" while I was in Korea. I never got a clear sense of what he meant by that, but I suspected that maybe John was playing Charlie because he thought that he could influence him. Who really knew what the hell was happening? John was entangled with me and half the time he could have thought that I was his father.

Meanwhile, I received an interesting phone call from Bruce Stenholm, president of National Duraform Company in Newton Upper Falls, the next town over from Wellesley. He was a good client and the company specialized in applying all types of Teflon® coatings and other kinds of plastics onto various fabrications for a host of customers in virtually all industries ranging from aerospace to medical. "Hey, Steve, what's going on over there?" he asked. I replied, "Hi Bruce, what do you mean?" He said, "while you were away in Korea, I received a phone call from Charlie Fox who offered to do my product publicity for half the price that Sales Development Associates charges because he knew all of your costs and overhead." I didn't want to believe it! Frankly, I was so hurt and angry that, I can't recall exactly what I said to Bruce, except that I thanked him profusely and appreciated that he called me. That's the thing about working with small company owners and presidents; they had a real sense of fairness and didn't like underhanded behavior because they certainly wouldn't want it done to them. Accountability and integrity matter a lot to them.

Each step that a small business owner takes along his or her entrepreneurial journey involves "risk," which is the common denominator among all small businesspeople. There are many stories about men and women who started a small business out of necessity because they lost their job and had to take out a second mortgage on their homes and create a business in order to earn a living. They are the real-life risk-takers who never took a college course in entrepreneurship. They are blue-collar entrepreneurs who put it all on the line. I remember asking one of our clients why he went into business for himself and he replied, "Because I am fundamentally unemployable." His answer stopped me in my tracks. He continued, "Yes, I cannot work for anyone else." That answer was brilliant. That is the real-life experience for many small business owners. For whatever reason, they didn't want to work for someone else and didn't believe they had any other choice but to go into business for themselves.

After hugging me, crying real tears and telling me directly, "I will miss you terribly; don't worry about a thing," Charlie Fox tried to steal my business. "You're more like a brother to me than my own brother. I want you to have a great trip. Don't worry about anything; my mother-in-law will babysit and take care of Marc while you're away and my wife, Mary, will take care of Peggy. Naturally, I will look out for your best interests here at Sales Development Associates." He said all of those things and then totally betrayed me. He tried to steal my business with National Duraform and I would later learn that he succeeded with some other companies.

What Charlie Fox did was so egregious that I just couldn't come to grips with it at that time. I'm no angel. I sold life insurance to those poor girls back at American Express in Phoenix with Sonny Wilhelm when I was working at Fireman's Fund American Life and our sales techniques were questionable. Maybe our approach was less than ethical, but the girls still received a life insurance policy that benefited them. This was totally different. Charlie Fox tried to steal my business, after proclaiming his complete loyalty to me. It didn't matter that he gave his word that he would care for my business and I doubled his income in three years. Nothing mattered. I was totally blown away by his betrayal and it really hurt my feelings. It was beyond the pale and I just couldn't cope with it.

After Charlie Fox's betrayal I had difficulty relating to all of my employees. What's more, hiring new people became all muddled at a critical time in Sales Development Associates' tenure as a company. Who could I trust? Frankly, I wasn't even sure that I could trust myself anymore.

13

TWIN LIGHT MANOR AND THE CHANGING TIDES

Once again, I ended up deeply immersed in therapy in Providence, RI. I wasn't enjoying work and I fired John Kenmore who was calling other employees and undermining me. Something had to be done. He was creating too many problems for me. Candidly, we both had issues and our relationship was conflicted beyond repair. But I hadn't dealt with Charlie Fox yet, who I should have fired as soon as I received the phone call from the president of National Duraform, Inc. I felt stuck in the mud and didn't take any action. Obviously, I was very unsure of myself. It was becoming clearer to me that management, despite my college degree in the subject with honors, wasn't something I enjoyed any longer. What I did enjoy was creating marketing materials and programs, but not necessarily implementing or sustaining them.

By mid-February 1982 I really needed a break from Sales Development Associates. I felt liberated in many respects because of my trip to Korea, and that feeling was being threatened. I was depressed and not feeling well, and I definitely wasn't enjoying work. But I was determined to get to the truth about my personal situation. Obviously, I had a lot of unresolved issues that I needed to settle. I was tired of the roller coaster ride that I was on. It was no fun. In the meantime, I had several new salespeople who required training and I had to be a positive influence on them. Also, I really wanted to find a sales manager, but that wasn't progressing well, despite several interviews. I needed to find someone who could do the job, be accountable, and stand up to me.

I wanted to get off of the emotional roller coaster ride that I was on and needed to get away for some serious thinking about business. Peggy found a place for me to escape to for the weekend. It was the Twin Light Manor on the coastal roadway in Gloucester, MA. I arrived there at around 9:15 p.m. on Friday night and it was snowing and raining. When I opened the front door to the inn, warmth enveloped my body. Peggy did well, I thought. The surroundings were quaint and welcoming. Off to the left was a dining room and directly across the hall was the living room which harbored a roaring fireplace, but was a little too formal for my taste. A staircase was on the right side of the room and there were also small tables and chairs around the outside wall.

By the time I completed my brief tour of the downstairs, a young guy in his mid-twenties greeted me and I walked over to the front desk. Actually, it was simply a 10-foot-long Formica® counter which seemed out of character with the charm of the Inn because there were antique tables and mariner accessories on display everywhere else in the space. The front desk, I thought, would have been nicer had it been a large antique wood countertop rather than plastic. "Room 305," the fellow said. "Is it a room with an ocean front view," I asked, and he said, "Yes, it's my favorite room. Climb up to the top of the stairs and go right to the second set of stairs and you're there. I assume you're traveling light," he continued and I replied, "yes" and went out to my car to get my overnight bag, camera bag, and briefcase containing a notebook that was a journal I started in November after my trip, two pens, some packages of peanut butter crackers, a handful of quality Dominican cigars, and a bottle of Merlot wine.

As I walked up the front pathway, I was thinking about bringing Peggy here someday. By the time I reached the second floor and found the smaller stairway to the third floor, I felt as though I was in for a treat. When I opened the door and saw all of the angles and an alcove off to the left, I was struck by the character of the room. Then I studied the big picture window in front of me revealing the black stormy night and I couldn't wait to see the view in the morning.

After snooping around and admiring every nook and cranny of the room, I decided to walk downstairs to the dining room and enjoy a glass of wine. The room was empty and I instinctively chose a corner seat. Surrounded by windows, I could hear the rain flowing through the gutter downspouts outside along with the roar of the ocean across the street. All the while, candles flickered and the fire crackled as I sipped my wine. After soaking in the ambiance and finishing the wine, I went back up to the room and turned on the television to watch the Boston Celtics, then washed up and brushed my teeth, sprawled out on the bed, and faded off to sleep.

I slept like a log and when I woke up in the morning, the first thing I did was pull back the drapes from the large picture window which was framed by two smaller windows on each side that opened. Then I feasted my eyes on the angry ocean right across the street below as the snow fell, propelled by the wind, and disappeared into the water's surface while the waves pummeled the rocky Gloucester shoreline. Each breaker echoed the full strength of Mother Nature. Meanwhile, the fresh white snow clung to the trees and shrubs surrounding the Inn, proudly displaying her majesty.

After a delicious American breakfast of orange juice, eggs, bacon, toast, and coffee, I strolled into the living room where there was a nice fire burning. The living room didn't look so formal this time. The windows were covered with snow and rain droplets, yet somehow the room was warmer than the night before. Before I got to the business of searching for happiness within myself and Sales Development Associates, I had to capture the winter mood and went back up to my room to fetch my coat and camera. Being outdoors in the fresh air and blowing snow was exhilarating.

So far, with the help of Peggy, we had created the right mood for me to be able to reflect and write down my thoughts and feelings. There was a corner chair which I moved over in front of the picture window, pulled the notebook journal from my briefcase, grabbed a pen, and was poised for action. I stared briefly at the ocean pounding against the rocks and reached for a cigar. After opening the right side window a crack, I punched a hole in the end of one of my hand-rolled Dominican cigars, lit it, and took a couple of relaxing puffs. The stage was set.

As I looked out at the stormy seas and hoped for revelations that never came with ease, I began to write and acknowledge that in my business, the involvement with my employees has become much too personal. Dan Bowman let me down by leaving for Cape Cod for three weeks without asking me for permission or even giving me any notice that he was taking a vacation. He just left! I had absolutely no idea where he was or what had become of him and I wanted our sales materials back.

I sent a registered letter to Dan Bowman's home permanently terminating his employment with The Venmark Corporation. I didn't know what else to do, but I certainly couldn't allow him to decide when he wanted to work and when he didn't. He was my best salesman and I had a payroll to meet. Dan really gave me no choice. He hired a lawyer and tried to sue the company to get his job back. No way would I rehire him under those circumstances. Had he called me and apologized for going off the rails, it might have been a different story. I likely would have taken him back had he approached me that way.

It was clear that I was inappropriately entangled with John Kenmore and I was very disappointed by Sandy Noonan. Poor girl got sick mid-October and had to go home to Buffalo, NY for surgery and recovery. But she was supposed to be back to work by Thanksgiving. So, I told her that I'd cover her territory and give her the commissions while she was recuperating. I'd mail them to her parents' home in Buffalo. That was quite generous of me, I thought.

Then Thanksgiving came and went and Sandy told me that she was still ill, had some setbacks, and hoped to return to work before Christmas. She didn't return, however, and said she'd be back right after the New Year. I continued to cover her territory, making sales for her and paying her full commissions. Incidentally, for the 10 weeks that she was away, her commissions were the highest they had ever been for a comparable period of time. Then, on the second of January, Sandy Noonan returned to the office and resigned.

I felt clearly taken advantage of by Sandy Noonan and was shocked, disappointed, and angry. When I asked her, "how could you let me cover your sales territory for all of that time, make all those sales for you and pay you full commissions?" Her reply was, "that was your choice." That statement was from an employee who had never sold before in her life. I had given her an opportunity and trained her in every aspect of sales and territory management, and she had been earning three times what she earned at her previous job. Once again, I was hurt, especially coming so soon after the Charlie Fox betrayal.

On the plus side of employee experiences were Janet Bookman, Richie Thomas, and Sue Patterson. Janet ran the company while I toured South Korea, Richie was my best writer and had been with me for over three years. He was honest, loyal, and as solid as they come. One of our clients, a laboratory equipment manufacturer, offered him a terrific job as Marketing Manager. As a courtesy and out of respect for me, Richie came to my house one evening and asked for my opinion on whether or not he should take the job. Again, he was a terrific employee and I didn't want to lose him. He had asked me for my advice, though, and I honestly felt that he should take the job. It was in his best interest, despite not being in mine. But I had to do the right thing and had no regrets. Richie and I have met for lunch several times since then.

Sue Patterson stopped by our office one day looking for a part-time position as an administrator because she lived close to the office and wanted to be able to prepare lunch for her kids and be home in the afternoon when they came home from school. So, I hired her. She was a terrific employee and about 10 months later when Sandy Noonan quit, she asked for an opportunity to take her position as an Account Executive. At first, I was skeptical, but then she made a strong argument, citing that she had a great deal of fundraising experience as a volunteer and knew that she could be successful as an Account Executive. I believed her and she closed the sale. Sue was right. She became a terrific salesperson and was with us for a couple of years. Then she accepted a job for *Industrial Equipment News*, the aforementioned leading industrial publication, as their salesperson in New England. Although I hated to lose her, it was a compliment to me. Richie and Sue were two former employees who had moved on in a positive way.

The solitude in that quirky Twin Light Manor Inn's room, the setting in front of the big picture window, and my desire for truth enabled me to write on a more human level and face my true self; perhaps for the very first time. Reflecting on what was flowing from my pen to paper, it was less analytical and much more spontaneous. My therapist had a huge impact on me. He always ended a therapy session with a provocative comment or question that got me thinking. Then the onion would peel away, allowing me to see another painful layer of self-awareness. He always set me up to draw a needed conclusion in my self-discovery and personal development. It's incredible how the risk-reward paradigm applies to everything in life. If you don't open yourself up and take the risk, you can't experience real love or true success.

The mystery of my early success and why it caused my depression, rather than elation, was always in the forefront as I thought about my life and business. It was approaching noon now and I uncorked the bottle of wine, opened a package of peanut butter crackers, and relit my cigar which had gone out about an hour before. The weather was clearing, the sun was shining, and the tide was retreating, exposing the beauty of Gloucester's seacoast.

At that point, I felt as though I saw who I was much

more clearly: I was kind, sensitive, caring, considerate, and I was passionate, talented, and smart. As I pondered that further, it reminded me of the book, *On Becoming a Person* by Carl Rogers. He believed that a person's behavior is motivated by self-actualization tendencies to work and achieve the highest level of their potential and achievement. During this process, Rogers asserted, a person forms a structure of "self" or self-concept. A positive self-concept, of course, is associated with feeling good and safe. That's how I wanted to feel.

As I thought more about my situation, I was reminded of all those meetings with editors that I had in Cleveland early on in 1978, and the positive feedback that I received from them. Also, I thought about the letter that I received from Ron Hill, the editorial director of Gordon Publications, Inc. a large industrial publisher.

He wrote, "Dear Steve, I think all of our Editors have a file of the worst news releases. But I don't think any of us ever bother to acknowledge the good ones. These are the ones that move quickly and quietly from the morning's mail almost directly to the magazine. Since I've worked both sides of the desk, I have always been impressed with the News I get from Venmark. To me it stands out above all the rest as the way I would do it if I were sending the stuff out." So, then I went a step further and asked all of our Editors what they think of the material they get from Venmark. The answer was absolutely unanimous, "It's the best stuff we get, consistently! As you know, Steve, that was the main reason why I stopped in to see you last month. I really just wanted to see who was doing all of this great work. Congratulations."

These fine sentiments were repeated by many other highly respected editors. Another letter we received from

Ken Lilienthal, Editor-in-Chief of *Industrial Product Bulletin* read, "I would like to take this opportunity to say one thing: Your press releases are the best-written of the hundreds and hundreds that we receive weekly."

Finally, Russell L. Kratowicz, P.E., Senior Editor of *Plant Services Magazine* wrote, "In short when I see the characteristic 'editor-friendly' Venmark press release, I know it is worthwhile for me to read because I know it contains information that I cannot afford to ignore. The now familiar format means I know exactly where to look for the information I need. That makes my life easier."

I found myself writing about what I had done right and it felt great. I also thought about all of the testimonials and letters that I received from clients thanking us for our work. As I remembered them, I weighed their importance. Clearly, being the best at what I do with respect to creating product announcements that got widely published, and helping our clients achieve their marketing objectives in the most cost-effective way, was far more meaningful to me than selling. It occurred to me that I was an artist and my art was my business and my business was my art.

I felt more pride for having created our product news release writing formula and having it validated than I did from creating the sales presentation and having that validated by actual sales, although that was a close second because of our tremendous level of repeat business. People only hire you repeatedly if you perform well and do what you say you are going to do. That's essential when selling an intangible business service because, as the salesperson, you control the client's expectations. As long as you meet or exceed those expectations, they'll be a client forever.

I'll never forget following up on one of my former salesman's accounts, a company called Sweethart Tool Company, owned by a nice guy named Dave Belson. We had him published in over 30 magazines, including all of the ones important to his business. Dave was a genial guy and when I asked him for another order he said, "I will never do business with Sales Development Associates again." I asked why and he said, "Because your salesman promised me that I'd be published in at least 60 publications." I explained that being in 30 was extraordinary, but that didn't matter to him. The only thing that mattered was his expectation and the fact that he was lied to by one of my sales people.

As I poured another glass of wine and pondered the seacoast, I thought about the genesis of my product news release formula and that meeting with Dennis Lone, the creative director of Cuniform and Newsmaker, at that dingy bar on a sunny afternoon in Santa Clara, CA. Today I was fully appreciating the process that I created. You see, the conventional press release writing formula is based upon an "inverted pyramid" where the most essential information is presented in the opening paragraph, followed by supporting details in descending order of importance. Our formula was totally different.

The Sales Development Associates product publicity writing formula, which I created and refined, consisted of a two-line headline and four very concise paragraphs: 3-4 lines for the first paragraph, 5-6 for the second, 5-6 for the third, and 2-3 for the last paragraph which was simply the price and delivery information, followed by the contact block. The first paragraph was basic and combined with a two-line generic headline identifying the product and a key feature or benefit. This gave an editor enough information to determine whether or not the press release was relevant to them. The second paragraph was about the company's specific product or service, the third paragraph was substantive by quantifying or otherwise supporting claims made in the second, and the last paragraph, as stated above, was for pricing and delivery information. The entire product news release had to fit on a single page of paper.

The discipline of my writing formula was reinforced by Rollo May's assertion that creativity requires limits, in his book, *The Courage to Create*. If you want to design a small product, for example, you must create the size limits first. Then the product must fit those parameters. As described above, we had limits which contributed to our success. Most of the time, our client was the company president and wanted to include all kinds of superlatives and extraneous information about their products and company history. It was an important fact that we were paid in advance because that gave us leverage to complete our work. Occasionally, we had to tell a client, "Look, please let us do the job that you hired us for and if we fail, then don't hire us again. We've been doing this a long time and we're certain that you'll be very pleased with the results."

Our approach was totally different from anything anyone else was doing. You see, in conventional advertising agencies, the lowliest writers were assigned to write press releases because management didn't appreciate their value. Management saw their main job as creating billable hours for preparing advertising materials, brochures, videos, and the like.

The essence of my writing formula was that it made an editor's job easy because each paragraph was autonomous, so that, depending on their publication's space requirements and interest in detail, they could easily edit one of our product news releases to fit their space; without rewriting it. Above all, our photography was exceptional and totally complemented the product news release. If we were claiming "ease of use," for example, then we illustrated that concept in the photograph with a person showing exactly what made the product easy to use. If the product was water-resistant, we might have shown it partly submerged in water or being soaked by a hose. My publicity formula was based upon selling and good selling is problem-solving. I developed our writing and photography approach by listening to Dennis Lone and refined it by listening to Gene Schwind the editor of *Machine Design* magazine, and many other editors.

Above all, we tried to provide photographs that editors would choose for their front covers and we were very successful at it. I doubt that any other firm has had products featured on more front covers of industrial publications than Sales Development Associates. By the end of 1981 we had prepared product news releases for over 2,000 companies, including leading multi-national companies, and surely had more product news published than any other communications firm in America. Advertising agencies typically used left over photos from their more expensive advertisements and brochures for their news releases; whether appropriate or not. Product publicity was an afterthought for them, at best, but for Sales Development Associates, our very existence was based upon product publicity.

Up in that room at the Twin Light Manor Inn I had a salient self-realization. A recognition that I created this monster, Sales Development Associates, and like the angry ocean that I watched transform from a stormy blackness to complete beauty and serenity right before my eyes, I could stop the madness of the revolving door of salespeople and acknowledge that sales management was no longer for me. I couldn't ignore that truth any longer and I really needed to focus on what made me the happiest and most fulfilled. In a sense, like any other employee, I also had the right to change jobs.

The low tide that emerged from the stormy day before, exposing the beautiful rocks to the sunshine, replaced the wind and snow, and echoed exactly how I was feeling about myself and Sales Development Associates. What a metaphor! It was time to put on my running shoes, plus a few layers of clothing and a stocking hat, and go outside and run along the seacoast for a couple of miles.

The run was energetic and I felt great as I reflected and thought about my creative achievements. I really wanted to spend my time on creative pursuits and not sales management. That's the transition that I was seeking. Next was the huge challenge of exactly how I was going to make that happen.

14

LETTING GO AND BECOMING MY OWN PERSON

New people were working for Sales Development Associates and business was just okay during the winter and spring of 1982, our fifth year in business. My personal schedule was filled with publicity sales, writing, consulting, and reluctantly interviewing new salespeople. Charlie Fox had resigned early in May and I was still asking myself why I even allowed him to stay that long after his betrayal. The answer was that I couldn't make the totally appropriate decision to fire him because he was like family and my relationship with him was screwed up; to say the least. I was suffering from depression and, frankly, had a difficult time accepting the reality of what Charlie Fox did to me. I just didn't want to believe it. It was simply beyond the pale! Obviously, I should have fired him after the phone call from Bruce Stenholm at National Duraform telling me that Charlie was trying to steal him away as a client. But, I didn't.

There were other unhappy former employees too. One in particular, Bernie James, who had worked with me at The Paul Revere Insurance Boston Brokerage Office. When he saw that I was having problems, he wrote me a four-page letter reaffirming his friendship and loyalty to me and he shared his enthusiasm for Sales Development Associates. In fact, in that letter, he reaffirmed his loyalty and support to me 17 times! Two days later he quit to take a job back in the insurance business. His sworn loyalty to me and support evaporated within 48 hours. That was another huge disappointment.

Richie Thomas, my former writer, had called Janet Bookman, my production manager and told her that John Kenmore, my former Marketing Director, was conspiring to work with Charlie Fox to compete with Sales Development Associates and me. I appreciated Richie's loyalty. A few months later, I initiated the one and only lawsuit ever in my entire 46-year business career. After several months we settled for a very small amount of money, a fraction of my legal fees to Joe Iandiorio, but I put Fox out of business. Kenmore was off selling real estate in Marblehead, MA. From what I could determine, they took five clients away and I have no idea how many new ones they got. Thieves!

Speaking of Joe Iandiorio, on one balmy autumn day in the 1982, there was a meeting of the Small Business Advisory group at the Boston Park Plaza Hotel. As one of the 18 small business advisors to Governor Edward J. King of Massachusetts, I was in attendance, arrived early, and entered a good-sized ballroom and sat down to observe the "players" before the meeting actually began. Not knowing when I would have a creative idea or a need to make notes, I kept three 3 x 5" index cards in my shirt pocket at the ready. This is what life was like before cell phones and tablets.

As a marketer and student of human behavior, I enjoyed observing the players' interactions with one another. Everyone had an agenda or a "pitch" and some were more discrete than others. In the back of my mind was the comment from a previous meeting: "Don't be flattered, I'd just like to know what you had on Joe." Then I watched someone approach a Vice President of the First National Bank of Boston and their patronization was so obvious it was sickening. I don't know if the banker just played along or if he was actually taken in by this exhibition of bullshit. There was something very offensive about ass-kissing, I thought. It was the stuff that you saw in larger organizations.

After a while I saw Arthur Clark, the Mayor of Waltham, MA, stroll to the front area of the room from the left side. Almost with a cat-like movement, the Bank Vice President approached the mayor before he was a third of the way across the room. He was so zealous in his approach that I thought he was about to plant a big kiss on the mayor's lips, or worse; unzip his fly and perform oral sex. In this world of politics, the "hey look at me" syndrome and the mutual power plays in the name of "public service" made me sick. Perhaps I was naïve to expect anything different or maybe I had become too cynical to play political games anymore.

Almost instinctively I pulled one of those index cards out of my shirt pocket, twisted my Mont Blanc ballpoint pen and wrote down, "What the fuck am I doing here?" I stared at that question for a minute, then got up, walked out of the room into the hotel lobby and bought a cigar and a cup of coffee. I found a comfortable chair, loosened my necktie and sat there watching people. I spent the next hour or so puffing on a fine cigar, sipping coffee, and feeling totally liberated. That was the end of my political career that autumn day at the Boston Park Plaza Hotel.

In the meantime, I was working through deep personal issues with my therapist. Our therapy sessions were magnificent and my personal journal was forming a repetitive pattern that was illustrating my progress on resolving the personal conflicts associated with the several aforementioned unpleasant Sales Development Associates management experiences. Unfortunately, one more betrayal surfaced. I learned that my brother Rich had participated in a reunion party and socialized with Charlie Fox, John Kenmore, Dan Bowman, Bernie James, and other former disgruntled employees. How could he have done that? Why would he be so disloyal to me? I didn't want to believe it.

I confronted my brother about his participation in the reunion party and he didn't think that it was a big deal and he didn't think what Charlie Fox did by trying to steal my business while I was Korea was wrong or unusual either. To this day, I don't understand how my brother Rich could have held that point-of-view and been so insensitive and *disloyal* to me. Despite never having received an apology from my brother, so many years have passed that I've forgiven him. Deep down inside, though, I must admit that I can't trust him unconditionally and it disappoints and saddens me. Richie Thomas and Janet Bookman didn't attend the reunion party of disgruntled former employees and I appreciated their decency and loyalty. Clearly, they did the right thing.

Aside from the nagging employee relations issues, I was having a great time creating publicity campaigns and brochures for clients, writing, editing the work of my other writers and directing my photographer to create the type of images I was looking for; ones that editors and publishers would be proud to put on their publication's front cover. As Stanley Parkhill, Editor of *Compressed Air Magazine* wrote to me, "Perhaps you can use this situation to make a point to your client regarding what can be done by producing a gorgeous photo of a fundamentally plain product."

I was really enjoying my client relationships which were

free from the power-play traps that entangled me with my employees. With clients, there was a clear relationship based upon my helping them achieve their marketing objectives and their appreciation of my work. Like everyone else, I too needed to be appreciated.

I wasn't finished trying to grow Sales Development Associates and had hired a fellow named Harry Leonard to become our sales manager. He was recommended by my accountant and I didn't do enough due-diligence because of that relationship. Reflecting back on that particular hiring, I call it "wish-hiring" because I wanted to believe he was the right guy and I could rely on him and spend my time doing what I liked best. Desperately trying to escape sales management, I did it again. I had convinced myself that he was the right man for the job. About a month later my gut told me that I screwed up. There was a difference this time, though, I wasn't personally involved and I saw the flawed dynamic of wanting to hire someone so badly that I fed them the lines that I wanted to hear. My gut overrode my wishful thinking and I listened to it. A real breakthrough for me. I learned a valuable lesson: referrals are usually to advance the interest of the referrer.

By the end of 1982 it had become clear to me that Harry Leonard was obsessive-compulsive and hated criticism and failure. He was patronizing to me and underneath it all didn't like accountability and as a result of that, he was actually afraid to sell. If you don't try you can't fail. Our salesmen didn't like and respect him and I also had had enough. A big lesson learned: never hire a sales manager who has never sold the product or service before because there is no way that your salesmen will respect them. Unfortunately, I saw several clients make the same mistake over the years. Frankly, my experiences were helping me become more empathetic with clients and even enhanced my relationships with them.

At the end of December 1982, Janet Bookman resigned from Sales Development Associates. She was a great employee for over four years and I'll always be grateful that she stepped up her game and ran the company while I was in Korea and Hawaii. But something unhealthy happened a year after we hired Diane Murray as an administrator and graphic artist. Diane moved into Janet's apartment and became her roommate. As part of my realignment of priorities, though, I had to give Diane a pink slip and let her go. Her service wasn't required any longer. I didn't know for sure, but I suspect that move didn't sit well with Janet whose resignation was sudden, but did include a full month's notice which was very helpful to me. As always, Peggy came into the office and helped in the recruiting and hiring process. After all, it was she who hired Janet four years before and she was exceptional at sizing-up people. Her process after selecting the top job candidates was to have a second interview and lunch with each of them. That's when the rubber hit the road and she found out in a casual setting more about their backgrounds and who they were.

I'll never know, but perhaps Janet saw that the company was no longer growing and her career options were limited. Frankly, I think she also thought that Harry Leonard was more in my favor than she was. That certainly wasn't true, but I could see where she might have gotten that idea. Who knows what he might have told her as part of his play to consolidate power within our small company?

On the topic of growth, it had become clear to me that Sales Development Associates couldn't expand back in the eighties. Our potential for growth beyond New England was limited. The reason was simple and nobody else noticed it.

But the reality was that we had already dominated the major publications with our product news releases at that time. In some months we had four or five clients featured on the front covers and inside feature pages of *Industrial Equipment News, Industrial Product Bulletin, and New Equipment Digest*, the largest circulation trade publications, along with a total of up to 20 other product news releases in each. In fact, it wasn't at all unusual to have the vast majority of product publicity published about companies in Massachusetts, New Hampshire, and Rhode Island originating from Sales Development Associates.

So, if we had offices in other major cities, we'd end up competing with ourselves. And with the addition of each new office, we would harm our own results and lose clients because the industrial media was finite in those days. There were only about 8,000 technical and industrial trade publications back in the eighties. The number of pages available to compete for space and get product publicity was fixed and in some trade magazines we were already responsible for half of their product news. The realization that Sales Development Associates' growth was limited prompted me to think more directly about my future and I was feeling confident about moving on, a topic that I was going to discuss with my therapist.

Being in therapy can become extremely frustrating. You need help and the process cannot be rushed. It takes time. Like baking a cake, it needs to stay in the oven for a specific length of time at a certain temperature. You cannot rush it, no matter what. Nevertheless, you want to know when you're going to be "better" and done with therapy. I asked my therapist that question and he said, "When you no longer want to be the designated patient." Then my hour was over and I had something to ponder for the coming week. My therapist was a strict clock-keeper. In retrospect, it was his way of illustrating the boundary to our relationship. He was professional; one hour at a time. He made me realize that the entire process of self-development was up to me.

My question to my therapist took place after a powerful therapy session the week before. I was having difficulty peeling the onion further. That wonderful metaphor for learning more about yourself as each raw layer of awareness was exposed. Then he decided that it was time to hypnotize me. I had read years before that you remember everything that you see, hear, or learn and the real issue is not remembering something, but recalling it. You can test that by driving somewhere you've been before and forgotten the way without written directions. Relax and trust that your recall will help you get there. When you see the landmarks, it will prompt your recall. You always have the GPS to fall back on.

Being hypnotized was an unbelievable experience. My therapist hypnotized me and while interacting with me as my mother, I regressed to a point in time when I was a six-year-old child and I blurted out, "what will it take to make you happy?!" That statement was transformative. I later learned from a candid conversation with my mother that when I was an infant and toddler, she was very unhappy with her life for many reasons and she used to play with me for hours because I made her happy. I had internalized that it was my responsibility to make her happy. Add to that the injunction that I received when my father and brother had that violent fistfight in our kitchen, when I was 11 years of age, and she grabbed me hysterically and shouted, "never do anything to hurt me," and it became crystal clear why I became confused. Oh, those Family Olympics! They are the most serious and potentially injurious of all games. And, unchecked they can surely last a lifetime.

Alas, I had figured it out: my dramatic and early success at Sales Development Associates was something that my mother wanted and I thought that I did too, but I was doing the job just to please her. It was something I had to do because of early programming. I was *driven* to do it. Of course, it was my choice, but the firmware had been encoded when I was a young child and reinforced throughout my entire life. Even that point in my life when I moved into the larger office suite and she sent that greeting card: "Congratulations to all of you at Sales Development Associates; Love, Mom Stroum."

I resented that card and subconsciously, part of me resented my success too because my mother was getting great pleasure from it. Hence, my self-destructive behavior. Also, throughout my life, whenever I asserted myself and did something that my mother disliked, she would ask me, "Who are you trying to be like?" She never asked me who I wanted to be or what I wanted to do. I may have been behaving like an extension of her because of her narcissism, but I was not going to do it any longer. I was done trying to be like my Uncle Sam, who was an incredibly successful and wealthy businessman. I was now trying to be like myself and it was finally beginning to feel okay.

The dysfunction with my father also became clear to me. I had proved to him that I wasn't "stupid just like my brothers," but it didn't feel right. Unfortunately, his authoritarian behavior that I internalized, ended up trumping my better instincts as a management major. Add to that his bravado to compensate for his weakness and my mother's disappointment in his lack of professional standing and I really had to unlearn a lot of stuff that I had previously internalized. Right after those discoveries and taking a break from seeing my parents for several months, I had a man-to-man in-person conversation with my father and asked him directly, "Dad, do you know who you were talking about all those times that you called me stupid?" He looked at me sheepishly and said, "Yes, I was talking about myself." I fully appreciated his honesty and vulnerability. Then I stepped towards him and we hugged meaningfully. It was a wonderful and loving encounter. We both felt better about ourselves and our relationship.

My working with weak employees to strengthen them was an attempt to strengthen my father, which was obviously a no-win exercise. I also concluded that my superior selling skills were honed by learning how to please my mother in order to be loved. I didn't feel that her love was unconditional because I had to behave a certain way to get it. Her way. I learned how to "win," but the victories felt very shallow. I developed skills at understanding verbal and non-verbal signals from people in order to make sales. That's why, way back in Sam Paris's office at Home Life Insurance Company, I told him that I didn't like sales because it was too easy for me. In hindsight, I didn't like sales because it touched something deep inside of me that I finally understood. I will forever be grateful to my therapist who skillfully used hypnosis to help me discover my SELF.

At my next therapy session, I told my therapist, "I no longer want to be the designated patient and this will be my last session." I finally became fully aware that my issues were mine and that I needed to reprogram myself and eliminate those negative behaviors that I inherited from my parents. They were my behaviors now. I owned them. It was me who I was angry at. *Me and nobody else.* I learned that the essence of my depression was caused by my internal battles and for not forgiving myself. Later I concluded that both of my parents loved me dearly and did the best they could raising my brothers and me. They didn't intentionally cause me harm; even with my mother's excessive narcissistic control and my father's belittling and name calling. They were imperfect human beings who did the best they knew how. But they were my parents. I loved them dearly and we had no unresolved issues at the end. Our relationship was all about love and kindness and today, I miss them both every day.

I was beginning to feel truly confident in myself and I was feeling better about decision-making at Sales Development Associates. If you don't know who you are, it is awfully difficult to make good decisions; if not impossible. There was no doubt that I had more work to do. The process of peeling the onion and exposing the deepest layers would have me making journal entries in my diary for many years to come. With each self-realization, I became less anxious about feeling depressed and better able to understand why it was happening. Most importantly, I was able to correct it. I understood that it is natural to feel happy or sad and that depression results from your internal dissonance. The issues are inside; not outside. In fact, I now think of these issues as challenges rather than problems. It is a much more positive and healthy choice.

My most recent hire during the fall of 1982 was a writer by the name of Paul LaBelle. A tall, thin guy with a beard, he looked somewhat like a college professor and had previously worked in the communications department at Prime Computer, a fairly large company. Paul was an excellent writer and saw how much easier it was to recognize sales opportunities while you were interviewing clients about their products. Not coincidently, the most important aspect of selling is listening. So, he started actually taking orders while on writing interviews with clients and wanted to hone his skills in that area. That was great for our salesmen too because we gave them full commissions when Paul made the sale.

As salespeople resigned or got fired, those accounts became house accounts and contributed to the company's bottom line income. Naturally, Paul would manage those accounts and create a working publicity project schedule with them. Paul was well compensated and I leased him a new company car and gave him occasional bonuses for his contribution to our sales. He actually attended our sales meetings on Monday nights and continued his sales education. He was a terrific employee and was ultimately with me for a little more than three years. I also learned a lot from Paul about writing articles and public relations in general. He was a good man and we've stayed in touch over the years.

One Monday night during the spring of 1983, after a frustrating sales meeting, I took a look at our cash receipts sales journal and saw that between Paul and me, we represented more than half of our company's sales. Then I looked at what Sales Development Associates' income would look like without the unproductive salespeople and the staff required to support them. It had become clear to me that the time had come to downsize. So, unsure of what the real impact of downsizing would be, I went home to Peggy and said, "I've made a decision to downsize the company and we might have to settle for making less money." She simply replied, "I don't care about the money, I just want you to be happy."

The next morning, which I called "Black Tuesday," I let four employees go, including our NU co-op student. I felt bad for her and called Northeastern to let them know. Her term was almost over anyway, so there was no harm done. Paul and I were excited to be working more closely as I coached him on time and sales territory management. He was a great student, worked productively, and I could trust him to ask questions if he needed help. No hand-holding required.

A big difference between Paul and Harry Leonard was that Paul wanted to learn from me and Harry wanted to impress me and, of course, he ultimately failed. As an aside, when Harry returned his company car, he drove it to our home and parked it in the driveway. When I went to readjust the front seat and move it, however, the seat cushion sank to the floor. I got out of the car, opened the back door, leaned in and looked under the seat and saw that it was broken and supported by several pieces of wood. Harry never told me about the seat, but it told me a lot about him.

Indeed, the stars were lining up in my favor and I knew that I was finally on the right track. The next downsizing chore was to speak with my landlord, Joe Grignaffini, to see what I could do about the 1,550 sq.ft. of office space that I had which included Suite 105 and 105A. Obviously, I no longer required a separate conference room and the office in 105A. I hoped there would be office space opening up soon somewhere else in the building where we could move to. Otherwise, I'd be confronted with the hassle and stress associated with finding a new location and moving the business there.

15

WE'VE BEEN TRYING TO GET RID OF YOU

One of my clients, Vance Elkins, owned a company called Enterprise Shafting, Inc. in Pawtucket, RI, which he had purchased a few years before we met. The company manufactured precision machined shafts for all types of motors and mechanical drive systems and employed skilled machine operators. He had become wealthy after inventing a product associated with the golf industry and was a really nice guy who worked closely with a friend of his, a business professor at Brown University, with the goal of creating a utopian small business. Vance was always trying to improve the life of his employees.

Vance even wrote us a letter in which he apologized for doubting the efficacy of what we did. He was referring to what he called the "watered-down copy," which was our intentionally factual and dry copy rather than using advertising-like superlatives. As I explained to him, with editorial or "free" coverage it is the editor who selects the news and if he or she thinks that the product description should include superlatives that is their choice. Frankly, I discovered that the use of advertising-like product descriptions actually offended editors. What they liked was a no bullshit presentation. That's why we were so successful at getting them to select our news releases over others. It was smart marketing.

Ultimately Vance was thoroughly impressed with the results that we achieved for his company in terms of exposure in many important trade magazines along with the hundreds of sales leads that followed. He wrote in his letter, "I consider the program a resounding success," and he became a great client for many years. Hey, there was no shortage of skepticism back in those days. In fact, Vance opined to me once, "Why is it that no matter how nice you try to be with your employees, they always think that you're out to screw them?" He had just implemented a great employee benefits program with a retirement account and the employees thought he was trying to trick them with benefits instead of giving them more weekly pay. Those were the days before too many employee benefits were popular.

I understood Vance Elkins' frustration and had a related experience one afternoon. Straight commission salesmen were a peculiar bunch. One of our salesmen, Deane Gold, was pretty sharp and made some sales early on after starting with Sales Development Associates. That was a good sign because it demonstrated pre-existing selling skills. One day, though, when Deane was in the office using our facilities and telephones to make sales calls, he was using the desk and telephone next to our coffee machine and when I walked in to get a cup of coffee I looked over into his open brief case and noticed that he had his own company business cards in addition to his Sales Development Account Executive cards that we provided. Needless to say, I was upset to see that and walked back into my office.

The above incident with Deane Gold took place during his 4:00 to 5:00 p.m. telephone session and after our administrative staff left for the day, I called him into my office and told him I saw his business cards and I couldn't help but wonder if he was starting his own business while I'm paying his commissions, automobile expenses, and providing him with a telephone. His reply was, "that's the trouble with you, Stroum, you're a suspicious sonofabitch!" I said, "Wait a minute Deane, let me understand. I just caught you stealing from me and you're calling me a suspicious sonofabitch?" "You've got balls!" That was the end of Deane Gold. He left me all of his company issued sales materials right on the spot and was gone.

The incident with Deane was further validation that sales management was no longer for me and that I needed to downsize. When I spoke to Joe Grignaffini, my landlord about deciding to downsize, his partner/brother Lou was in his office with us at the time and said, "We were trying to figure out how to get rid of you." It was said in a light-hearted way, of course, and they went on to explain that Joe wanted my corner office and the office next door, along with my production office, to expand their offices upstairs. His plan was to put a spiral staircase from their office underneath my production office that would go upstairs into my current office which would be expanded into one big office by swallowing up the office next to me. But they hadn't approached me because I had four years remaining on my lease.

It seemed like divine intervention once again. They got to expand upstairs and I got to keep Suite 105 as a smaller office space, redesigned to meet our current and anticipated future requirements, including new carpeting and much lower rent. It was a win-win. There was no need to even change our stationery. What's more, they bought one of my large wooden executive desks and moved it downstairs.

I was thrilled with our new, smaller office suite and the pressure was off. Our North American publicity orders were priced at $595 plus photography at that point in time, and it took the equivalent of two publicity order sales per month to pay our rent and we were still averaging about 40 orders per month. It was the right decision for the time and it worked out great. I reflected on how efficient we were in the beginning when we worked out of half the space in Suite 306 and how much fun we had building Sales Development Associates from a $300 investment into a very worthwhile and profitable small business. Frankly, our business model looked more like a professional practice now, but that was okay with me. It left more time for creative endeavors without the pressure of having to run around making sales just to meet our payroll.

One evening, I was watching television with my five-year-old son Marc when an Atari Computer commercial came on. It showed an unkempt young man getting off a railroad train looking totally dejected. He had flunked out of college because he didn't own a personal computer. The ad's implication, of course, was that an Atari computer would have made the difference between the young man's success and failure. I thought the advertisement was based on an unfounded fear and was totally unethical. Some computer companies, particularly the struggling ones, would have had you believe that you were an inferior parent or neglecting your children if you didn't own a home computer. Those assertions were pure nonsense.

The ad made me angry, so I wanted to fight back. I also wanted the recognition associated with having a large computer company take a shot at me. It would be fun and validate and expand my reputation by putting me on par with Steve Jobs. If Apple Computer, Inc. sued me, for example, I would immediately be viewed by the media as someone worth paying attention to. I wanted to be sued by Apple! In order to protect Sales Development Associates, The Venmark Corporation, and my own assets, I created a new and separate business entity called Crabapple, Inc. which would be an anti-computer club. This was our logo.

The club was a parody which gave me some legal cover. The logo, promotion, and the news release that we carefully crafted conveyed that message too. And the Crabapple Anti-Computer Club struck a nerve with clients and the media because we received a lot of publicity. Ironically, my computer and high-technology clients were the first to join the club for $19 per year and we created a newsletter called *Living and Computing* which included articles that Paul and I researched and wrote or reprinted from other media with attribution to the author about the topic of computers in the home, their impact on children, value for education, and so forth.

The media response to our news release was phenomenal. I was contacted and interviewed by dozens of radio and television networks and stations around the country including Gene Molter from WKOX radio in Boston who called and invited me on his show. My Crabapple telephone was at my home office and one day when I heard it ring, I had just gotten out of the shower and was stark naked. There I was talking to a radio personality in the buff. The following day I heard from KCBS in San Francisco, WBZ in Boston, and WJAR in Providence, RI who scheduled me to come down for a taped television interview. I prepared for that interview by researching early childhood education and the use of computers at schools. It was a new field and there were lots of questions about the role of computers at school and their impact on childhood learning and socialization. It was fascinating to learn about.

Another byproduct of all the news coverage that Crabapple received was the phone calls from old college friends and relatives around the country who heard me on the many syndicated radio talk shows or read the abundant newspaper and magazine articles. My mother even clipped and sent me an article from the *Delray Times,* Florida newspaper. There's no doubt about it, my story would have gone viral today. Other major media that covered Crabapple included *ComputerWorld, Infoworld, The Boston Globe, Boston Herald, The Boston Business Journal, San Francisco Chronicle, The Christian Science Monitor, Omni Magazine, Sales & Marketing Management Magazine, Business and Society Review, USA Today,* and *Inc. Magazine.* As Crabapple took on a life of its own, I was learning and perfecting my interviewing skills.

An interesting experience occurred at my office after my interview with Robin Young from Channel 7 in Boston. She was the very popular prime time news feature reporter who later began hosting and producing a number of primetime specials under her own production company, Young Visions. Extremely talented, she went on to become the "Life" section anchor of *USA Today: The Television Show,* a nationally syndicated news program. She would ultimately receive several Emmy's. Robin Young contacted me to arrange a visit to my office with a camera crew to conduct an interview and learn more about the Crabapple story for her nightly news feature. Before she came, however, Paul LaBelle employed his public relations expertise and slightly rearranged my office to move my framed photographs of Peggy and Marc from my bookshelf to the shelf behind me so that they would be seen by the television viewers.

The interview with Robin Young went very well and what I especially remember was how skilled she was and how she put me at ease. Her technique was interesting, she placed an article that she had seen about Crabapple on my desk and asked me to read a line from it. All the while, the video camera was taping. We wrapped up and it was a fabulous experience for me.

Early the next morning, Robin's Production Coordinator, Rosemary Freitas, called me and said that something had happened to the video and asked if Robin could visit my office again for a re-take. "Unfortunately, that won't work, I said because at 1:00 p.m. today I'm meeting my brother at the Norwood Airport, where he keeps his plane, and we're flying to Provincetown for the weekend." She asked me if Robin could go there to re-tape the interview and I told her I had to check with my brother, Jerry, first.

It was okay with Jerry and she and her crew finished our interview next to my brother's Piper Cherokee aircraft on the small tarmac there at Norwood Airport. I saw her story about us later that evening on the six o'clock news and it turned out great. A couple of days later, Rosemary sent me a lovely note which read, "It is rare that someone goes so completely out of their way to help us shoot a story as you have done. Believe that it is appreciated and I hope to work with you and your organization again someday. Best to you, your family and the 'Crabapples' of which I am one, thanks to you." When dealing with the media it is all about giving, not taking. In business and in life it is great when everyone wins by getting what they want.

In order to be sharp and stay on message during Crabapple telephone interviews, I created a modified sales script on one of my infamous 3 x 5" index cards, kept it with me at all times, and referenced it with every phone conversation. It included five talking points that I wanted to mention in each interview and allowed me to stay on track. Another interesting media contact came from a fellow named Mark Benson who wrote and submitted an article about Crabapple for *US Magazine*. It was nicely written and I was really looking forward to it being published and on the shelves in every supermarket and corner store in the country. He kept telling me that its publication was imminent. Then, at the eleventh hour he called me and said that Warner Communications, who owned *US Magazine* stopped the publication of the Crabapple story because they also owned Atari Computer and didn't want to publish anything that would adversely affect the home computer industry. I understood, but it made me angry. Money talks.

By the way, the Crabapple Anti-Computer Club could attract only about 80 members and was a financial flop. The whole experience had lots of upsides though. Even though I didn't get sued, it illustrated my expertise as a publicist. Beyond that, my sales staff, Paul LaBelle, and our office staff were excited and motivated because the president and founder of their company was making news. I also met interesting people as a result of Crabapple and learned a lot about radio and television public relations that I had never known before. It really was a very worthwhile experience. Far from profitable though, I ended up with a few dozen yellow tee-shirts emblazoned with the Crabapple logo and worm, plus another couple of dozen black shirts with white lettering on the front that said, "Computer Widow" in honor of all the wives who lost their husbands to computer technology at that time. I had sold several of those tee-shirts, but not as many as I had expected.

Another outgrowth of Crabapple's widespread publicity was an invitation to join the advisory panel of the Norbert Weiner Forum at Tufts University to study the impact of technology on society. Weiner was a 1909 Tufts graduate whose pioneering vision of the responsibilities of intellectuals for the proper use of technology was the guiding precept of their project. The Forum was comprised of a small group of academics at Tufts who came together under a grant from CSK, a Japanese software company to study the impact of computers and computer-based technology on society, and to formulate policy recommendations for the wise and humane development of new applications of this technology to help solve society's problems. A parallel investigation was also being conducted by a sister group in Japan at Tokai University.

The first meeting of the Norbert Weiner Forum took place at the International Center at Tufts University and it was a dinner meeting, complete with student wait staff, filet mignon, and delicious accompaniments. The room was on the top floor of the building and was set up with a large U-shaped arrangement of tables around the perimeter. Each table was adorned with a linen tablecloth, the finest dinnerware, silverware, ice water and wine glasses and, of course, bottles of red and white wine.

There were 150 attendees from the "who's who" of technology companies in New England. They included the presidents of Lotus Computer and Wang Laboratories, many other top technology companies and me, creator of the "Crabapple Anti-Computer Club, a parody organization to poke fun at the early foibles of computer advertising. As the president of Sales Development Associates, I had worked with many small and some larger high-tech firms, including Wang Laboratories, Apollo Computer, and Digital Equipment Corporation (DEC).

Although I don't recall the specifics, I do remember that the presentations that evening were fascinating and I was looking forward to participating in future meetings. It was exciting to be part of a forum which would ultimately contribute to our greater understanding of the impact of technology on society. I felt like I was part of something on the cutting edge and apex of the business world where technology and academia met and that it would be a worthwhile endeavor. I was proud to be involved.

A few months later, the next meeting took place, but it wasn't at the main dining room at the International Center at Tufts University. It was at a smaller room a few floors down. This time there were about thirty attendees, cheese and crackers and fruit and wine instead of a multi-course dinner. We filled our own plates and we sat at nondescript tables and talked about the impact of technology on society. Somewhat of a let-down from the previous experience, it was a nice evening nevertheless.

Then, several months later, the time came for another meeting of the Norbert Weiner Forum and it was a real shocker. I was at my office in Wellesley working feverishly to meet deadlines for clients and earn a living, struggling with the day-to-day responsibilities of running a small business that was less than seven years old at the time, and making ends meet when I looked up at the clock and realized that I had to leave for the Tufts University campus in Medford, MA. The 45-minute drive was a nuisance at rush hour. But I thought the Forum was a valid reason to hassle with the traffic.

When I arrived at the University, I learned that this time the meeting was at Professor Daniel Dennett's office. Believe me, it was a long way from the International Center; literally and figuratively. It was six-thirty in the evening and, having battled route 128, route 2, and route 16, which were high-traffic roadways, I was anxious for a meeting that would justify my time and the major pain-in-the-ass to get there during rush hour traffic. Much to my dismay, however, there were only 12 attendees, none of which were high-level participants, and the food this time was a dozen Dunkin' Donuts and coffee! What a comedown from that first meeting only nine months earlier and I was really, really angry.

So, after a few minutes, I asked Professor Daniel Dennett what happened. With a smirk he said, "We used up our budget." I responded in a harsh tone, "you what?!" I was mad as hell. I sat there for a moment, at a student's desk, not a dinner table, and asked Dan what "the Forum" would accomplish? And he said, "We're talking about the impact of technology on society." I said, "I understand that we're *talking* about the impact of technology on society, but what are we accomplishing?" He tersely replied, "We're talking about the impact of technology on society." So, I repeated my question for a third time and Professor Dennett really seemed quite irritated by my lack of understanding and appreciation that "talking about something" was a valid accomplishment!

I then explained to Professor Dennett that there was a big difference between "talking about something and accomplishing something." As an example, I pointed out that I can't simply go to my office landlord and talk to him about paying my rent; I actually have to hand over the money. And if I don't pay my rent, I'll get evicted. Unfortunately, this story is still relevant today. Many people talk too much and accomplish too little; especially our elected officials. And, as those of us who work long, hard hours, meet a weekly payroll, and pay taxes know all too well: Talk isn't cheap.

The Norbert Weiner Forum turned out to be a bust. I never saw a report or anything else from it and was disappointed that the whole thing was an abuse of the grant money from CSK. Professor Dennett's attitude was alien to this achievement-oriented entrepreneur. It reminded me of all those insurance people who I met at Fireman's Fund who just went through the motions everyday.

Springtime always brings with it a rebirth. Flowers bloom and you just feel renewed. It was now June and it turned out that April and May were my two most profitable months in business. It made me reflect on how I told Peggy that I was downsizing and that we'd have to settle for less money and she said that it didn't matter because she just wanted me to be happy. Well, I thought it was interesting that my decision to become happier also created a more profitable small business. It gave me pause to think about other successful people who were passionate about their work and earned a substantial income, regardless of what they did. The lesson here is to focus on doing what you love, and if you do it with dedication and hard work the money will ultimately follow.

My experience with salespeople taught me that they weren't totally motivated by money. Instead, they were limited by where they saw themselves as earners. It was more of a lifestyle issue than anything else. In other words, the issue wasn't how many sales they made, but how much money they made. I recall with Dan Bowman, who was my best salesman in the beginning of Sales Development Associates, that my biggest mistake was trying to coach him to reach his full sales potential rather than having him happy and productive where he felt comfortable economically. It is no different from a waiter who chooses to work at a family-style restaurant versus a leading steakhouse. The job is essentially the same, but the remuneration varies considerably. If you can't see yourself making the big bucks, then you'll never make the big bucks. Offering big commissions can lead to big disappointments.

Dan Bowman was bright and talented and told me once that he made seven sales in one week and hardly left his house. Obviously, he could have made many more sales per week and earned a lot more money if he strictly employed my sales and territory management process, but he wasn't comfortable with that idea because once you reach a certain level of economic success and do it consistently, it is hard to backtrack. He saw himself at a six sales per week average level, not the 10 per week that I believed he was capable of. Most sales organizations had learned that recognition meant more than higher commissions in terms of motivating salespeople. That's why sales contests provided winners with a plaque, trophy, fancy wristwatch, or related items they could show off to their friends.

Dan Bowman's experience was no different from what took place in many other work situations. Again, those waiters and waitresses who work at low-end establishments do essentially the same work as their counterparts at the most prestigious steak houses. The big and critical difference, though, is where they see themselves fitting into the world socio-economically.

In my case, I saw myself at a certain economic level and

regardless of what changes that I had made at Sales Development Associates over the years, I ended up earning more money than I did previously. My self-image had come a long way from the middle innings of our Family Olympic Games. Business remained brisk throughout the rest of the year and I gave Paul LaBelle a nice, well-deserved raise. He wasn't making sales to earn high commissions; it had simply become part of his job and he was enjoying it immensely.

16

LOW PRICING CAN KILL YOUR BUSINESS

Working alongside one assistant, I'd been growing sales and profits by expanding our service offerings to existing clients. Typical additional sales besides international publicity to different global regions, included newsletters, small advertisements, sales lead qualifier brochures, catalogs, and printing. I'd create the concept and copy, sketch out the design and have a graphic designer finish it for presentation to the client and prepare it for printing. I had a sensitive balance, though, because I didn't want those other marketing materials to reduce the number of publicity orders a client placed annually. Those orders had a much higher profit margin. In other words, I didn't want to rob Peter to pay Paul.

Back in the early eighties I had to inform George Berbeco, the owner of Charleswater Products, Inc. that I could no longer handle all his advertising and marketing and hoped that he would understand. It was a sensitive resignation because I still wanted to handle his product publicity. Charleswater Products alone was paying us $180,000 per year, much of which was consulting to me personally at $125 per hour, and that was putting too many eggs into one basket for me. George wasn't concerned about what he was paying me, of course, because he was growing rapidly and I was doing a great job contributing to that growth for him.

At that time, our annual sales were around $560,000. Fortunately, George understood my situation and I continued to do Charleswater's publicity every month, working closely with him. I also continued giving him marketing ideas, naming products for him, and providing sales advice. My belief was that as long as I was working consistently with a client then I would give them all the help and ideas that I could. It simply improved my value proposition. Many years later George would post on LinkedIn, "As valuable as the publicity is (and it is remarkable in volume and quality), Steve's insights and advice on positioning products and companies is even more valuable."

Well, my approach turned out well, but I still needed to develop a strategy to get new clients, and at that point I no longer wanted to make cold calls via telephone. So, I developed a direct mail campaign consisting of letters with reply cards and beautiful, full-color post cards. We sent something out to a list of about 500 prospective companies every six weeks. I also created a pamphlet entitled, "The 10 Most Common Mistakes Companies Make When Preparing Press Releases," and prepared a news release about it. The response in terms of publicity and interest was tremendous, but it didn't generate any business for us.

The post cards did generate business, though. One previous client who hadn't used us for several years, Dave Ring from Applied Plastics Co., Inc. in Norwood, MA telephoned me and said, "Hey Steve, I received your post card and have been meaning to call you for a while, can we set up an appointment?" We met and ended up working together monthly for over 20 years. What was fascinating, however, is that when I met with Dave, the post card that he was referring to was thumb-tacked to his bulletin board and it had been mailed to him three years earlier! If not for the repetitive mailing of post cards he may never have called me.

Another byproduct of the aforementioned Crabapple venture, besides the Norbert Weiner Forum at Tufts University, was an invitation to lecture to a public relations class at Boston College. I accepted and enjoyed sharing the distinctive Sales Development Associates business model and approach with the students. Naturally, I explained that we specialized in product publicity which was a subset of public relations. I went on to describe our publicity programs and explained that they were "packages" that were sold, rather than billed by the hour like conventional public relations firms. I wanted to give them a sense of the real world in terms of small business and how we fit into it.

A week after the lecture, I was pleased to receive a letter from Donald Fishman, Chairman of the Department of Speech Communication and theatre at Boston College. He applauded me for what he thought was insightful information that had never been discussed in his class before. I later went on to replicate this experience at my alma mater, Northeastern University. It offered me a great way to give back to the community.

Meanwhile, I did want to grow my client base. We were starting to lose clients to China and with businesses that were sold. Charleswater Products was one significant example. George Berbeco sold the business to Armstrong World Industries, Inc. and continued to run the company himself, hiring me with no interruption. But, when Armstrong subsequently sold Charleswater to a company called DESCO, who was also in the static control industry that was the end for me.

Even though I personally helped George build the company from one product to several million dollars in annual sales and handled all of their marketing programs for much of their tenure, I was the odd man out. I understood the dynamics. The buyer wanted to bring in his own team. What irked me in the Charleswater case, though, was that the buyer was so arrogant that he didn't even want to have lunch and pick my brain about my role with the company he just bought. For Sales Development Associates and me, Charleswater had become dead in the water.

I had seen several small companies over the years who didn't want to grow. Even though the alternative to growth was death, they were comfortable with where they were and didn't want to generate more business and have to hire more people. As I've previously mentioned, hiring was typically a nuisance for small companies. Most were understaffed and had no human resources expertise or department. Again, the owner was typically an engineer or technician and not a manager. From a sales standpoint, to get through to those biased anti-growth owners, I had to convince them that my publicity program was essentially an insurance policy to maintain their business at a reasonable level for a reasonable fee. That category of client typically hired us four times per year and that level of activity generated a steady flow of sales leads for them and they could select the ones that they felt were best. My main concern was sales predictability and cash flow. We usually had lots of sales in January, July, September, and December because of those quarterly clients. There's safety in numbers and those clients appreciated the fact that we left them alone and weren't always trying to upsell them.

Businesses are organic and like all living organisms, the alternative to growth is death. One of the frustrations that Sales Development Associates had was that people didn't really understand what we did unless we explained it to them. Literally, nobody else did what we did. Even though our program was a publicity order, the results varied, depending upon our approach. In fact, the perception of what we did changed with each client. Some thought we were advertising for them, others thought that we were generating sales leads for them, and still others thought we were doing market research. Naturally, when the internet age arrived, we were creating content on the web and driving traffic to company websites, affecting SEO (search engine optimization) and so forth.

Early on in my career, I would try to educate clients by explaining that we were publicists and not advertisers, but as time went on, I didn't bother. As long as they hired us and their checks cleared, I was happy. We used product publicity as a marketing tool and we were different things to different people. Clients bought our service because of the benefits that we provided for them and those benefits were defined by their marketing requirements or business goals not ours. That's important to remember.

In June of 1985, Paul LaBelle decided to resign. He was young and wanted to see a career path in front of him and I understood. He was a valued employee for three solid years. So, it was my assistant Penny and I and we had automated our mailing process with an envelope sealer and postage meter plus a separate envelope labeling machine. We also had our custom software modified to improve several other administrative functions and print the mailing labels in the appropriate format. E-mail hadn't entered the picture yet.

In addition to our marketing program using direct mail letters with reply cards and postcards, I decided to try to recruit a salesman again, and I hired one who lasted about four months. It was a bad decision on my part to try something that I really didn't enjoy. Part of my thinking was that I had successfully hired good sales people in the past and with a fresh, positive mindset, perhaps I could do it again. But, I couldn't. It just didn't feel the same. It wasn't fun. Then, I concluded that rather than wasting money and time recruiting and training, I'd continue our marketing program and I actually enjoyed meeting new people and selling without the pressure of having to actively prospect. So, if our marketing generated sales leads for us it would be great. After all, sales leads were an invitation to sell because they already expressed interest in what you had to offer them.

I sent out one direct mail letter with the subject line, "Do you know the three most important factors in industrial marketing?" and it got an incredible response. In the real estate business, of course, it has long been said that the three most important factors when selling a property are "location, location, and location." The answer to my question for industrial and technical marketers was "Repetition, Repetition, and Repetition." Think about how many TV ads that you see repeated within minutes and how many Coca Cola signs adorn restaurants and gasoline stations everywhere. *Repetition* works.

Repetition puts a company's products in front of prospective customers when their need arises and repetition reinforces perceptions about your products and company. In other words, repetition gets attention, builds brands, and most importantly, generates inquiries. Repetition matters so much because it is typically an external event that stimulates the prospect's buying behavior and creates a sales opportunity for you. But, you never know what will prompt an inquiry for your product. A company might be in the process of expanding operations and they may send a request for a quotation that requires your product, or perhaps their current vendor just had a price increase or botched a delivery and now they need a product like yours. You never know what will prompt the inquiry.

The key, therefore, to converting sales leads into sales is to be in front of prospects when the event arises which stimulates their buying behavior. Product publicity is so effective as a marketing tool because the exposure is typically widespread and in a variety of credible trade magazines and websites, making it highly repetitive. Simply stated, publicity increases a company's likelihood of being visible to a prospect at the right time, when the prospect recognizes they might need your product or service. It might seem obvious: you can have the greatest product in the world, but if someone doesn't need it, they aren't going to buy it.

Consistent with the above, your brand, value-proposition, and pricing need to be consistent. I had an interesting international publicity sales appointment at a major medical company in Medfield, MA. It was one of those days that you don't ever forget like JFK's assassination, the Space Shuttle Challenger explosion, O.J.'s acquittal, and 9/11. Although it took me a while to understand why, I remember exactly where I was the day I lost a sale because my fee was too low! It was February 12, 1990, also my dad's birthday.

Medfield, MA is a sleepy suburb about an hour and a half drive southwest of Boston where I met with three people in the medical company's international marketing department including the Vice President in charge. The building had a casual feel and we were in a nicely appointed conference room. The prospects seemed interested as I showed them samples of the press releases that we had prepared for Western Europe and the corresponding foreign magazines where the publicity was published. Those publications featured high-gloss paper and full-color photographs and were clearly a higher quality than our domestic publications.

The high-level international marketing participants were asking relevant questions about our approach and the specific services that we provided. Clearly interested and impressed, a key member then asked, "How much does this all cost?" That, of course, was the ideal scenario: the quality of our work persuaded them to ask me and I didn't have to ask them for the order.

When I told them my fee, the room went silent. You could have heard a pin drop. My answer changed the tone of the meeting. Because of their previous experience with international marketing, they couldn't believe that I could achieve the results I showed them for our $2,695 fee. Frankly, I didn't fully realize it at the time, but the issue was my credibility. They couldn't imagine how I could achieve similar results for them for the low fee that I quoted, regardless of the evidence presented with respect to our highly efficient business model. They were suspicious of my Porsche performance at Ford prices. The meeting was over and I left empty-handed.

It took a few months for me to realize that my problem was one of "positioning." In other words, my presentation was high-end and my low fees didn't match. It was the same problem that the automobile company Volvo had when they transitioned from a boxy safe car to a more stylish car that was equally safe. People didn't think that the more stylish

Success and Self-Discovery

Volvos were safe anymore and were confused, at least subconsciously, and sales declined. So, by May of 1990 I had decided to "reposition" Sales Development Associates and increase all of our fees dramatically. The people at the medical company were right: our fee for publicizing products in Western Europe was too low. It was too low despite the fact that most of it was pure profit. But that didn't matter in the positioning equation. Our fee is what mattered and it was too low.

It reminded me of another time when I was quoting a full-page, full-color advertisement for a client and my fee was very reasonable but I lost the sale to a fancy advertising agency in Newton, MA. What was interesting is that the client went with the agency instead of Sales Development Associates and we were using the same graphic designer! In fact, I was at the designer's office one day and saw him working on the ad. The client chose to pay much more money for a prestigious advertising agency and didn't realize they were getting the work done by the exact same creative person who I would have used had if they hired me. Perception and positioning are everything. Sales Development Associates was *perceived* as low cost and I needed to change that *perception* from low-cost to high-value.

The medical company taught me a lesson that would make me a lot of money for many years to come. In June of 1990 I changed our company name from Sales Development Associates to Venmark International, developed a rich new logo based upon the IBM typeface and color, and proceeded to generate more business than we could handle during the next several weeks that summer. Over $10,000 per week! The new "brand" more accurately reflected our "position" as a high-value service provider.

Venmark International

So as not to offend my longstanding clients, I gave them each a substantial discount from the new fees. Another lesson surfaced: everybody wants to be treated as if they are special and get a good deal. And if they perceive their deal to be better than the deal others get; that's even better. I successfully repositioned our company with a 30 percent across the board increase in fees and was able to increase fees to existing clients by at least 10 percent. And none of them balked. That was further confirmation that the repositioning Sales Development Associates to Venmark International was the right thing to do. In retrospect, it was fortuitous that I lost that sale. As Ace Remas my old Newsmaker partner would have told me, "The judgment of failure needs to be put into a larger context."

The bottom line was that the quality of our work and the results we achieved for clients easily justified the additional fees that we implemented. Our sales message and new fees were totally congruous with the repositioning and Venmark International had become recognized by clients as well as many media outlets as one of the best product publicity firms in the country. That was our brand. We weren't the cheapest, we were the best.

So, my advice to anyone involved with selling a product or service is to review your lost sales; especially the ones that didn't feel right to you. Make sure your messaging and pricing are consistent and that your pricing isn't too low compared to the benefits provided by your product or service. Make sure that you're positioned properly, and remember; low pricing can kill your business!

17

BUSINESS SUCCESS AND LIFE-ALTERING REVELATIONS

The early nineties was a good time for Venmark International. I was invited to address the IEEE (Institute of Electrical and Electronics Engineers) and talk to them about the subject of "Advertising and Public Relations." The seminar coordinator subsequently sent me a letter in which he wrote, "I would rate the event an unqualified success. We had over fifty participants and all of the responses were very positive. I hope that you will consider speaking at our next event, probably in early 1993."

Following me on the program was George Berbeco, formerly of Charleswater Products and on the prowl for new business opportunities. He spoke about the "Purpose of Business." The key concept that I remember from George's presentation was his statement, "the purpose of a business is to create assets." The Oxford dictionary defined assets as a "useful or valuable thing, person, or quality." Suffice it to say, something of value was what he meant. And that something of value, either a product or service, was exchanged for currency. George said that he woke up every morning trying to figure out how to make money. He is a real entrepreneur.

People have asked me why I didn't change my company name to Steven M. Stroum, Publicity Consultant and the answer, in my view, was simple. People would rather work with an institution or company than a person. An institution or company provides more substance and credibility. I doubt anyone would write Steven M. Stroum a check for $22,000 yet I've had several checks that large written out to Venmark International. I believe that having a corporate identity is another side of "positioning," especially for firms that provide an intangible business service.

Periodically I would correspond with editors about their editorial statements, which were usually in their magazine next to the table of contents. One time, an editor wrote about losing a parent and I responded by email, "I just read with interest about the loss you experienced and I agree, you can be prepared for that passing and you can expect it, but you're never really ready for it because the experience is so new and intense. I am so sorry for your loss." She then copied me on an internal email, forwarding my email to a colleague. She wrote, "This note is from Steve Stroum, the president of Venmark International, they are a big company." My positioning was working. Many editors preferred working with a big company. Apparently, the perception was that a bigger company was more substantial and stable.

In terms of personal sales, profits, growth in new clients, and vacation time, 1992 was my best year ever. Since my well-documented work style was typically a 12-hour day, five days per week plus most of Saturday, I needed some kind of break with time off every 12 weeks or so. Throughout the year, Peggy and I would take a two-week vacation together, then we'd take a vacation as a family with Marc for two-weeks and each of us would also take a four-day weekend or full week vacation for ourselves. Our vacations would recharge us individually and as a couple; because we always missed each other. Funny, after each two-week vacation I'd come home from work by 6:00 p.m. which I would hope to establish as a new norm. But the work hours would gradually extend after a few days. Before we knew it, I was back to working 12-hour days. The frequent vacations were a healthy integration into my work schedule which helped me prevent burn-out.

On one relaxing mini-vacation to the Cheeca Lodge in Islamorada, FL where I frequently went bonefishing with a guide, I had an unusual experience after returning to the Lodge. I returned from a fantastic day on the water with my guide and was back at Cheeca Lodge on their beautiful long pier where people frequently fished from a large platform at the end. While I was staying there, President George H.W. Bush who was an avid fisherman, was also a guest. Because of his being there, I wasn't surprised when I was on the pier and turned around and saw a video crew about six feet away focused on me. I was wearing a black tee-shirt, had a full beard, and was smoking a cigar while leaning against a pier support. At first, I was annoyed by the invasion of my privacy, but being a veteran and thinking more about Presidential security, I accepted the situation without reservation.

After hanging out on the dock, chatting with other fisherman and enjoying my fine Dominican cigar, I returned to my room to call Peggy to see how she and Marc were doing. It was about 5:30 p.m. and she answered the phone, "Hey movie star!" I said, "What do you mean?" She replied, "I just received a phone call from your cousin Maxine who saw you on CNN smoking a cigar at Cheeca Lodge!" That was funny and sure explained what the video camera crew was doing.

Can you imagine, though, if I was videotaped chatting with a beautiful woman on that dock? That could have created a problem!

At this time in my life I was feeling good, but something still bothered me. I felt as though I was missing something; an inexplicable void. So, I decided to call my old friend Rabbi Kra who I grew up with as our leader at the synagogue we attended in Waltham, MA. He was a terrific man and knew my family well. He was especially close to my father who had been president of the synagogue and was also close to my mother, having counseled both of them about my brother Jerry. The Rabbi officiated at my Bar Mitzvah and at our wedding. I really liked and respected him a great deal.

So, I phoned Rabbi Kra and asked if he would like to join me for lunch. I told him that I felt great about my life emotionally and physically, had a wonderful marriage and son, and was doing well financially, but thought I lacked something spiritually and wanted to get his insight. He was delighted to hear from me and invited me to join him for lunch at the Jewish Rehabilitation Center in Roslindale, MA where he was the Chaplain. I accepted his invitation and we scheduled a luncheon date.

When I met Rabbi Kra for lunch it was great to see him. He was a small, thin man with a distinct limp when he walked. He looked much younger than his 73 years. Long gone was the mustache that he wore to look older when he was the rabbi at our synagogue. After we sat down to eat lunch, I asked him with great interest about his decision to become a Rabbi. I was expecting a "heavy answer," maybe something that would trigger a spiritual response from deep within me and he said, "Steven, to be honest with you, I always wanted to be a businessman like you." I was totally taken aback by Rabbi Kra's response and jokingly said, "Rabbi, you're not helping me." He explained, however, that when he was a young boy in Poland, he suffered from a disease in his hip which ultimately became fused, and being a sickly child, he couldn't play baseball and other sports outside with his friends. Consequently, he became a bookworm and spent all his time indoors reading and studying, which later led to the path of a Rabbinical student and ultimately a Rabbi.

As it turned out, Rabbi Kra was the only person who had the key to unlock my family's past. He especially mentioned my mother's need to fantasize and cover things up. He explained that she used fantasy as a coping mechanism to maintain her sanity. He said, "Your mother had a tremendous capacity to alter reality when it didn't suit her." I could clearly see how I had done the same thing at Sales Development Associates with Charlie Fox and John Kenmore. They weren't the people I wanted others to think they were, so I created the fantasy that they were much more capable than they actually were. Just like my mother had done when she told me to tell them at school that my father was a Display Manager and not just a lowly store window trimmer.

The other fascinating part of my conversation with Rabbi Kra dealt with my grandfather, Nathan Stroum, who died before I was born. The Rabbi revealed that my grandfather had spent time in prison. "He molested a girl," the Rabbi said was the reason why he was jailed. As he put it, "Imagine the shame which the Stroum family lived with in the small community of Waltham." The Rabbi was not holding back one bit and I welcomed his revelations. He brought the subject up and somehow must have thought it would be helpful to me.

Perhaps that's why we never heard too much about my

grandfather Stroum when we were growing up. All we heard was that he was a veteran of the Spanish-American War and owned a furniture store that was lost during the great depression. My father always told us that he was a very kind and generous man and that the reason why he lost his furniture store was that he didn't have the heart to collect monies due the store from needy families. Instead, he lost his store and had to auction off the contents. I'll never know what really happened. Perhaps he was imprisoned around that time?

Rabbi Kra didn't accept my conclusion that everything was okay in my life except my question concerning spirituality. He knew better. Then he began talking about my father. "So, your father isn't that bright or accomplished, so what?" he said, his voice rising somewhat. "But your mother couldn't accept that," he continued. According to the Rabbi, my father was incredibly insecure and my mother had to put him on a pedestal to make him feel important because she made more money than him, was better educated, and was more accomplished. She was an elementary schoolteacher and took the initiative to get her Masters Degree when she was 47 years old. The Rabbi did say that my father was a good man who was loyal to him, and he used the term "contamination" to describe the effect of my brother Jerry on our family when I was growing up. It was an interesting word and I think he was right.

As we were concluding our fascinating and shocking luncheon conversation and bland kosher food, the Rabbi looked me directly in the eyes and sternly said, "Your father was a tyrant when you were younger!" Indeed, he was, I thought, and remembered that his name was carved into the boys' bathroom wall at our synagogue, "Behave or Iron Mike Stroum will get you." Rabbi Kra continued, "You're now over

40 years old; it is time to get over it!" In other words, your issue isn't spiritual, it is emotional and he was right; it was time to let it go. What great advice from a very perceptive and wise man. I considered Rabbi Kra my dear friend and I miss him today.

I left our luncheon feeling as though a weight had been lifted from my shoulders. Rather than learning more about spirituality, I had a clearer idea of why I became driven to succeed and how I had mismanaged my employees by treating them with the same control and rigidity that my father used on me as a child to conform and behave the way he wanted me to. I had been a tyrant too. It was also crystal clear that this was all in the distant past. At the time of our luncheon, my dad was 75 years of age and retired in Delray Beach, FL. He was no longer the tyrant who I feared while I was growing up. He was no longer the father exchanging punches with my brother, Jerry, when I was 11 years old. In fact, he was a man who had two multiple heart bypass surgeries and had become much more kind and much less judgmental. In his later years we had a marvelous truth-based relationship fused by mutual respect.

My Dad passed away on April 8, 1993 at 78 years old and we had no unfinished business. He had apologized for projecting his issues onto me and wrote me a beautiful note that included a key to his safe deposit box. He assigned me as the executor of his will. He wrote, "We know you will handle things properly when the time comes. Love to Peg and Marc. Stay well and happy." Love, Dad.

It was great to have an epiphany without depression. Meanwhile, during the early nineties, Penny Dayes, my assistant and I were contending with the many changes in our business operations that were being precipitated by the internet. I was working with a brilliant young website developer who introduced me to a software engineer who would convert all of our MS-DOS-based software into a more user-friendly Windows-based version. MS-DOS stands for Microsoft Disk Operating System and was the Microsoft-marketed version of the first operating system (OS) to be widely installed on personal computers (PCs) during the eighties. Clearly, the upgrade was necessary.

Without notice, the software engineer abandoned our upgrade project and moved to San Diego. I had to lean on my website developer to get him to release the software code to us so that I could hire someone else to continue the project. That's when I met a fellow named Ryan Williams. He was looking for a second, part-time job and my office was close proximity to his day job. He'd come over after his day job and work on our project for two or three hours while I was there at the office writing for my clients. It was perfect. If a question arose, I was able to provide the answer for him instantly.

He was converting the software from MS-DOS to Windows® and it applied to every system that we had from order entry to media list development to creating labels for distribution to client letters. Originally developed in 1985, our custom program was called, "The Venmark Marketing System," and recorded our client information, including project and sales data. It also enabled us to research and compile media lists as well as create postal mailing labels to distribute them. The software had an accounting function too and our own direct mail procedure for communicating with our clients.

As email became more popular, we had to figure out a way for our custom software to distinguish between publications that accepted email and those that didn't, and in turn send out the appropriate form of communication to them.

The shift from postal mail to email for distributing press releases was evolving rapidly and was challenging because the 8,000 publications weren't changing to email in unison. We had to create a simple questionnaire and poll the editors in order to learn their preference for receiving press releases. It turned out to be a great benefit to Venmark International because the editors appreciated the fact that we were interested in serving them more efficiently. Besides, editors like being asked for help. Think about it, don't you feel good when someone asks you for help? There's a great book that relates to the topic titled, *When I say No I Feel Guilty* by Manual J. Smith, PhD. It was a best-seller that helps you understand why we feel that way and offers techniques for learning how to get your own way.

While the rapidly evolving world of technology was creating all sorts of administrative challenges for us, there were also greater sales and marketing opportunities. I was voraciously reading articles on the topic and listening to clients when they shared what was most important to them. Part of this involved paying attention to what the more progressive clients were doing. Most importantly, I shared this information with clients at our regular publicity meetings. My value proposition included more than product publicity by then and I told them, "Look, as long as we're working together consistently, I'm going to share whatever knowledge I have that I believe will help you, at no additional charge. It is all part of what Venmark International can bring to the table."

18

THE INTERNET CHANGED EVERYTHING... AND NOTHING

Mike Kempkes, Vice President Marketing, of Diversified Technologies used to call me a "honey bee" because I was getting great ideas from smart and successful clients and sharing them with him. Naturally, I wasn't sharing any proprietary information, just the general ideas. As the internet began playing a bigger role in our business lives, I was watching with great interest what my clients were doing differently, especially the more sophisticated ones. And then, I'd share the generic approaches with other clients, where applicable. I love helping people, but more than that, as a businessman and service provider, I wanted to constantly increase and reinforce my value-proposition.

Another reason why it was important for me to bring more information to my clients about internet marketing was because many of them were not marketers. Most were engineers who had built their business based upon their expertise, word of mouth marketing within their industry, and through the use of independent sales representatives. So, marketing was changing faster than many could adapt without someone like me playing an active role and making them aware of new opportunities.

Bill Gates, the co-founder of Microsoft wrote in his 1999 book *Business @ the Speed of Thought*, "A fundamental new rule for business is that the Internet changes everything." There's no doubt about that! And when you relate his statement to marketing, you've got to understand what marketing is. According to the *American Marketing Association's website*, "Marketing is the activity, set of institutions, and processes for creating, communicating, delivering, and exchanging offerings that have value for customers, clients, partners, and society at large." In practical terms, marketing involves a series of activities required to bring a product from manufacture to the marketplace. Historically, those activities included advertising, direct mail, promotion, public relations, branding, packaging, and distribution. They were often referred to as the four P's: product, price, place, and promotion.

Obviously, Mr. Gates was right. The internet changed everything. And it also changed nothing! Everything includes the ease with which we can access information today, the new on-line distribution channels and their respective advertising opportunities, e-commerce, viral marketing, and the general speed and breadth of communications offered on the world wide web. The "nothing" involves the fundamentals of marketing and peoples' decision-making process. Those haven't changed. Generating high-quality sales leads, brand development, and presenting your company as a problem-solver in the marketplace are more important today than ever before because of the convenience of online searches on any topic or product available.

What had changed also with respect to the internet by

the early nineties was the definition of news and publicity. It often became referred to as content. Venmark International created "content" for our clients as it related to the internet. What's more, the content enhanced their product visibility in search results. I remember, early on as the internet was becoming a bigger part of the marketing mix, I lost a great client who had been hiring me twice per month for 26 straight years. What upset him was that the publishers weren't sending him sales leads in the form of stick-on labels that were ready to attach to an envelope to mail and that he wasn't getting the number of leads he used to and, therefore, my services weren't as good as they used to be. As a consequence, I was no longer needed.

Clearly, in his view, it was my fault. I tried to explain to him that he was getting the same number of sales leads or more and that he could see them in the website analytics provided by Google. Those leads would show up as visits. Plus, he could determine how many pages people visited and what they were most interested in. His reply was, "I only bother checking on my website every few weeks." Regardless of what I said, he had made up his mind and decided not to listen to me, announcing that he didn't want to hear another one of my diatribes about the internet. Despite the fact that he was smart and successful, there was nothing more that I could do. Getting some clients to accept the impact of technology on marketing was challenging in the early days of the internet because it happened so fast. Paradoxically, they had no problem integrating technology into other aspects of their manufacturing businesses.

The above client's attitude was not unusual at the beginning of the internet era. It reminded me of a Peter F. Drucker quote from his book *Innovation and Entrepreneurship*, "Entrepreneurship is 'risky' because so few of the so-called entrepreneurs know what they are doing. They lack the methodology. They violate elementary and well-known rules. This is particularly true of high-tech entrepreneurs." Mr. Drucker was recognized as the dean of America's business and management philosophers by *The Wall Street Journal*.

On the other hand, I did have clients who were internet savvy. They realized that the transition from physical to electronic sales leads was occurring and it was beneficial. I received an email from another client, which included a copy from an internal company memo he wrote that dealt with the transition where he pointed out to his employees in detail how many visitors were coming to their website, what products generated the most interest, and how many pages each visitor viewed, how long they were there, and so forth. He was using his Google analytics reports to make better marketing decisions. Thankfully, those decisions included Venmark International.

The fundamentals of marketing have not changed. People don't change that rapidly. Technology changes at a much faster pace than people can assimilate. What has changed, however, are the tools available for marketing. Many engineers, especially, assume that if somebody needs a particular product, they'll "Google" it and, therefore, all you have to do is have a strong internet presence with SEO (search engine optimization). That is partially true. But, as Peter Nielsen of *Sail Magazine* wrote about a product he chose to publicize for one of our clients, "This is one of those handy little gizmos you never knew you needed before you saw it." That says it all. Effective marketing stimulates and preconditions prospective customers to recognize that your company offers solutions to their problems; even problems they never knew they had.

What caught Mr. Nielsen's attention in *Sail Magazine* was that we illustrated how a mounting shaft collar, typically used in an industrial setting, can also solve a problem on a yacht. He recognized the value that we proposed and chose to present it to his readers. So, whether you're communicating with two tin cans and a string or you're on the internet, you still need to illustrate how your products can solve problems and benefit your prospective customers.

As every industrial and technical business owner knows, problem-solving is a key to being successful. Often, however, the prospective customer is unaware that he or she has a problem. Of equal importance is that they might not be aware of a potential solution. As Henry Ford once said, "If I asked people what they wanted, they would have said faster horses." Although there is no evidence that he actually said it, the quote has been attributed to him and the point is clear. In my business people called me to do advertising when they really wanted exposure for their products which I could provide better through publicity.

The attitudes of some clients never ceased to amaze me. I had one small company in central Massachusetts invent a universal chuck for a Bridgeport manual industrial milling machine that made life much easier for the operators. Venmark International got him a tremendous amount of publicity in the most influential trade journals and when I followed up with the client and asked him how sales were going, he said, "I haven't sold too many because most prospects want a handle on it." I replied, "Fantastic, so give them a handle" and he said, "No, it doesn't need one." He demonstrated that he'd rather be "right" than successful. For goodness sakes, when you get very clear market feedback like that, you should pay attention to it. I suggested that he add an optional handle, but he wouldn't listen to me.

The challenge in the internet age is to be recognized through all the noise and clutter; both electronic and postal. And the best way to accomplish this is through product publicity because editors select the information which they believe will interest their readers and present it to them as *news*. As such, there is an implied "third party endorsement." Part of the "nothing has changed" aspect of the marketing paradigm [in this internet age] is that publicity is still "news and information" selected by editors and web hosts and published to inform their readers and visitors. Consequently, it has more value than an advertisement or a sponsored message and it always has. Today, however, the job of a product publicist is more challenging and important than ever before because of "cyber-clutter." He or she must be even more creative in describing a product's features and benefits as well as illustrating visually how the product solves a problem.

Y2K came and went without incident. Y2K meant the "Year Two Thousand" and the big fear at that time was potential computer errors related to the formatting and storage of calendar data for dates in and after the year 2000. Many programs represented four-digit years with only the final two digits, making the year 2000 indistinguishable from 1900. In the first few years of the new millennium, it seemed as though all of our news release distribution would evolve to all email. After minimal software revisions, that was what actually occurred. Our cost for postage and mailing equipment rentals became a thing of the past and our labeling machine became a relic while profit margins increased.

For Venmark International the adoption of the new technology was great. On national publicity orders I simply gave my new assistant, Laura, a list of codes, representing media outlets from a catalog, and she fed them into our computer and subsequently printed the media lists out for me to give to our clients and then she would distribute the releases automatically via email. International list creation was different. We worked with a vendor called Marketwire and on each international news release I would speak to my representative there and we compiled the media lists together. It was a very worthwhile collaboration and I learned a lot about his thought process. In reality, the business had truly become a terrific professional practice. Every advancement in technology helped Venmark International improve our output and profit margins.

As time went on, our vendor that provided media outlet updates for our database decided not to automatically provide them to us anymore. Our custom software could visit their website on a monthly basis and secure name and address changes, etc. It was very easy in the beginning, but the vendor sold out and the new buyer considered us a potential competitor. So, Laura had to manually research certain media outlets and we also received emails that would let us know where changes in our database were required. It became a labor-intensive nuisance, but we had no alternative, or so I was told by Laura. At that point, she was spending about sixty percent of her time working on media list management. After all, if we didn't stay on top of that game, then our successful publication rates would suffer.

I took full advantage of LinkedIn and had a premium membership which allowed me to see who my clients' contacts were and then I would look at my best clients to see who their connections were. I'd then look at each connection's full profile page and see whether they were a good prospective client for me. If they were, then I'd call my client as a courtesy and see if they objected to my phoning their contact and using their name. Clients rarely objected and sometimes they'd even make the introductory call or email to their contact for me. The approach usually ended up with my setting a meeting with their contact which often resulted in them becoming a new client.

I also read a book in 2007 entitled, *The New Rules of Marketing & PR* by David Meerman Scott which was the best book I've ever read describing the benefits of news releases; most of which I implemented back in the late seventies. Mr. Scott wrote, "Don't just send news releases when big news is happening; find good reasons to send them all the time." Beyond that, he listed the benefits of publicity which I was articulating for many years. It was a perfect book for any publicity non-believer and I bought several copies as gifts for the skeptics I knew. Skeptics were often those who said, "I've tried publicity and it didn't work," to which I'd reply by asking to see what they've done. Usually, they had no examples and if they did, they were poorly written advertisements dressed up as news releases.

In addition to sending books to skeptics as gifts, we also implemented a direct mail campaign offering a free book for anyone interested. After I received the email or business reply card back from postal mail, the catch was that I would deliver the book personally to them. It was clever because if they were a lousy prospect, they wouldn't want to take the time to meet and, therefore, wouldn't get the book. But, if they were a worthwhile prospect, I'd persuade them to meet with me and I would usually get an order. Naturally, they also got their free book.

One new client asked me, "How do you have so many clients who have been working with you for over 40 years?" There are three essential reasons, I told him. "First, I clearly and simply explain the services that I provide and what they should expect, second, I then do what I say I am going to do and since I control their expectations, I will usually do a little more. Third, I tell them that I love them by frequently communicating our successes on their behalf, in the form of physical and digital press clippings, and making myself available to them. Number three is especially important because it reinforces to clients that you care about them and it lets them know that you are not taking your relationship with them for granted. Nobody wants to be taken for granted and that is especially important in long-term relationships.

On the topic of human nature and our automatic defenses, I received great advice from a client by the name of Gene Megna. He said, "When asking a prospect or customer for an order, it often puts them on the defensive, so it is much better to insert the words, 'idea of.'" So, rather than asking for an International Publicity Order, I would ask, "How do you feel about the *idea of* doing some international publicity for product XYZ?" As Gene suggested, I'd get a more objective answer from them and then could follow up and make the sale. That was great advice and I still use that sales technique today because it changes the question from a closed-end "yes or no" question that puts pressure on the client, to an open-end question which is intended to gather information and get feedback.

The reality was, as computer technology and software kept advancing throughout the two-thousands, our process became easier to execute and more profitable. By 2007, I was 59 years old and starting to think about selling Venmark International or getting my son Marc involved with the company to ultimately take over and grow the business. It was so damned efficient and profitable that it would be a shame for him not to build it, enjoy the personal freedom of scheduling his own time, while getting rich too, I thought.

Hiring Marc, of course, would be tricky because of my previous painful experience with my brother Rich many years before. Naturally, the last thing I wanted to experience was that sort of falling-out with my son. That was a huge risk and it would have been devastating for both of us. I had to figure out how to guarantee that a falling-out would never happen. We had an extraordinarily wonderful father-son relationship and it meant more to me than anything else in the world besides, of course, my relationship with Peggy.

19

ARE YOU AN S.O.B?

When I told my client and friend, Joe Herbert that I was thinking about having Marc join me at Venmark International in 2007, he was concerned about my management style. "You'll beat him up," he warned. But he didn't belabor the point. In fact, I never fully understood what Joe was saying until Marc worked for me and I had to modify my authoritarian management style.

The first thing that I prepared for Marc and me was an agreement which clearly stated our mutual responsibilities, expectations, and exit options. It was a thorough one-year contract that was based on several meetings and in-depth conversations at a quaint Japanese restaurant across the street from my office. Essentially, after one year, either one of us could decide whether or not to renew the contract. That allowed us to "bow out gracefully" if either was not comfortable moving forward. Hopefully whatever we decided could be executed without screwing up our relationship. That was my major concern and Marc's too. The last thing I wanted was a repeat of the painful experience that I had with my brother Rich back in the early days.

Marc Stroum joined Venmark International in August, 2007 as the Director of Business Development, essentially a field-sales position. To learn the business, he would be starting out as a salesman with the objective of getting new clients. Then I would work him into a writing role. I thought he'd be well-equipped for the position since he majored in communications, with a concentration in journalism and public relations, and a minor in marketing and advertising. What's more, he had already held a sales position traveling the country, visiting prominent universities, and doing a good deal of public speaking for a company called Campus Fundraiser.

Marc began making sales calls in mid-September and was a quick study. I was somewhat concerned at first because he wasn't memorizing the sales presentation. That had always been nonnegotiable for me, but Marc convinced me that by creating his own Power Point Presentation and thinking through the selling points of our sales presentation that he would learn it better that way. I was open-minded because it was the digital age now and everyone does learn differently; especially the younger generation.

The North American Publicity Order fee had increased to $2,495 and photography services at $595 were included most of the time. During the month of November he had produced over $15,000 in new business! That was really exciting for both of us. We would occasionally make sales calls together, usually the second meeting that Marc arranged with a new prospective client. They were always fun for me and I enjoyed having him by my side. In retrospect, quite frankly, I think that I enjoyed showing him how good I was too. We usually had lunch afterwards and discussed what had happened. Those were great times and learning experiences for both of us.

On one particular day Marc had arranged a meeting for us with a company that manufactured food processing systems and equipment. I had a lot of experience publicizing similar systems for another company and felt confident that we could help them get exposure and sales leads. It was Marc who had set up the second meeting after an initial meeting the week before. He had warned me that our prospective client was not the warmest personality. That turned out to be an understatement.

There was nothing unusual about the small industrial building as we drove into the company parking lot. I had seen hundreds of them on both coasts. It was a brisk fall day and the leaves there had already been raked and all of the walkways were well groomed. That was impressive and showed some pride, I thought. Marc had mentioned to me that the president was somewhat of a character who had told him that he had a terrible experience working with his own father and was "glad he was gone." That was a chilling statement, in my view.

Marc and I entered the building and introduced ourselves to the receptionist who ushered us to the conference room where the company president and marketing manager would join us momentarily. After brief introductions, the president of the company looked across the table at Marc and said, "So, you're an S.O.B?" I was seated to Marc's right and we were both puzzled and I asked, "What do you mean?" He said, "S.O.B., you know, son-of-the-boss!" Without hesitation, the president's facial expression changed from stern, at best, to something akin to anger and he said in a loud voice, "I was an S.O.B. and my old man's gone now and that is a good thing!"

The president of the company continued the rant about his father and Marc and I kicked each other under the table. It was bizarre, to say the least. He appeared regressed as though he was talking directly to his father. Then Marc and I tactfully shifted the conversation to his products, the company marketing program, and how we could help them achieve their goals. We left with a Publicity Order and a check to begin a project. When Marc and I got out to the car, I looked at him and said, "if you ever felt that way about me, I would consider it to be the greatest failure of my life."

Then during January and February 2008, the Stroums together generated $191,000 total sales for the first two months of the year, a terrific achievement. But I was beginning to feel that I was providing too much of the wind beneath Marc's wings in terms of positive feedback to keep him feeling good. Being a direct salesman can be very rough because you face much more rejection than positive feedback. I also saw a slowing down of his appointment setting activity and actual meetings. His lack of enthusiasm concerned me and I could see on his face that something wasn't right.

To state it plainly, by May 2008 I noticed that Marc wasn't happy at work. He may have been an S.O.B., but when it became crystal clear that he wasn't happy and fulfilled working at Venmark I felt that something had to be done, but wasn't sure how to proceed. It was my responsibility, though, because I knew Marc was conflicted. He didn't like the work and didn't want to let me down either. It was my move now and how I handled it would be risky. In the old days and with other employees I'd terminate them and move on. For obvious reasons, the tightrope I was walking on was far different.

Not wanting to disappoint me, Marc plugged along for a

couple more months. Despite our achieving $386,000 in total sales through June, by July we began talking about the elephant in the room. Although he performed well when he pushed himself, Marc was no longer pushing himself hard enough to succeed and said that he felt out of his element. You've got to be "hungry" to build a business and Marc wasn't hungry. So, we had a conversation about it and he said, "Dad, I just don't enjoy calling on 60-year-old men by myself all day long. I need to be part of a team."

My initial reaction was to say, "Then build your own damned team!" But I knew that wasn't something that Marc wanted to do. That's not how he wanted to spend his time. He is much more social than I, he didn't have the appetite for it, and I really understood that. I was fully conscious of wanting what was best for him and didn't want to project my own desires onto him. He preferred to be part of a younger team with more varied duties and we chose not to renew our contract that August. Nevertheless, I thought, the original sales model of salespeople selling publicity services was validated and worked well for a year.

It was important to me that Marc knew that I wasn't disappointed in him and I wanted to help him transition into a position and an organization that was right for him; not me. It was really the first time that I had cared more about my employee than I did for Venmark International. One of my clients told me about a career counseling program at a place called The Rockport Institute in Maryland. So, I phoned there and after talking with the founder, I enrolled Marc in their career testing program and it became instrumental in helping him recognize what kind of work he should be doing, with what style team, and in what environment, in order to further define his career path. It achieved everything that I pursued with the book *Where do I Go From*

Here With My Life through a computer assisted series of tests and subsequent analysis and counseling. It was superb.

The Rockport experience worked out great for Marc and his final day at Venmark was Friday, August 29, 2008. We had a nice lunch together at The Sherborn Inn restaurant nearby and reminisced about our experiences and what was hopefully in store for him next. When we returned to the office in Wellesley and Marc gathered his belongings for the last time, reality set in. We hugged and began sobbing like little children. Neither of us expected that parting would be such an emotional and painful experience. We were both disappointed that we didn't make it happen together and hoped that we didn't disappoint each other. Marc asked rhetorically, "I wish I knew why I didn't apply myself?" It seemed like an apology and I sensed that he felt guilty. That didn't sit well with me.

I wrote Marc an email a few hours later with the Subject line: I know Why?????? I wrote, "Don't beat yourself up!! The answer is simple....You didn't enjoy the work. And you latched onto the fun stuff, you and I being together, etc., and sort of hoped that you might like it eventually. Look, I suspect that you knew by January that the job wasn't for you, but you kept your commitment to try it for a year. You kept your commitment. Thank you." I reinforced in that email that I totally enjoyed the time that we got to spend together and was disappointed that things didn't work out, but was clearly not disappointed in him. Quite the opposite, I was proud of him and it was not his fault.

Like Marc, I had doubts about my performance too. I apologized to him for my lack of management skills and wrote that if I hurt his feelings in the process of trying to help him, that I was truly sorry. "I hope that I didn't disrespect you," I wrote, and finally, "I'll treasure forever the memories that we created while working together." Marc and I have a special relationship. When he graduated from college, I asked him what he wanted for a gift and he said, "a two-week road trip to Key West, FL together; just the two of us in your sports car." We had an incredible time and the two of us bonded over great dinners and lots of partying; Key West style.

The Rockport Institute helped Marc identify that he should be involved with academic marketing and business development. As I mentioned previously, before joining Venmark International Marc had worked for a company called Campus Fundraiser as a Fundraising Manager and did very well before the company went out of business. As a postscript, Marc's next job was for Student Health 101 calling on universities with a student wellness tool. He worked there for three years and then took a job at Brandeis University where he started as Assistant Director of Annual Giving and became the Associate Director of Alumni Development.

Marc did very well at Brandeis for a few years until he was recruited to work at his alma mater, The Rivers School, a private prep school in Weston, MA as their Director of Alumni Engagement. As of this writing, Marc has been there for over six years and is exactly where he belongs. He loves the work and being part of the school community. I am a proud and happy father. Proud of Marc and his chosen career and proud of the way that I handled him while he was my employee at Venmark International to be sure that everything I did was in his best interest. I didn't beat Marc up and Joe Herbert would have been proud of me. I was back to working solo with Laura as my assistant and was relieved to have helped Marc find his way professionally.

For me, one of the aspects of driving to and from meetings, besides the fact that I enjoyed driving great sports cars, was that I had time to think and reflect while listening to good music. I remember the day back in the early eighties that Mr. Mitchell, the octogenarian owner of E.C. Mitchell Co., Inc., a supplier of abrasive cords and tapes for cleaning needles and intricate parts of sewing machines, asked me if he could mail his check later instead of giving it to me that day. "I said, sure, Mr. Mitchell, whatever is best for you, I appreciate your business." I was leaving with two orders, but no check. As every salesman knows, an order is not an order until you receive the check. So, I left his building and started my car. But then I was startled by a tap on the window and it was Mr. Mitchell bringing me a check for $4,200. He had tested me and I passed.

Many years later while meeting with Mr. Mitchell, I mentioned that my son Marc's Bar Mitzvah was coming up and that my wife and I were excitedly making plans. Then, at our next meeting, he handed me an envelope with $50 in cash and said, "This is for your boy." I was surprised and pleased that my elderly client thought enough of me to make such a gesture. It felt great.

Mr. Mitchell's situation was interesting because he was heavily involved with the sewing industry and the entire industry was moving offshore to China at that time. That's where I came in and helped him diversify by creating press releases and publicity for him that featured other applications for his abrasive cords and tapes that I conceptualized. I would show them cleaning pipe threads, for example, targeting the piping, process control, utilities, and oil and gas industries. Then I would show them deburring spindles in the woodworking and do-it-yourself industries and so on. It was great fun and I even created a tidy three-fold brochure and reply card mailer for E.C Mitchell featuring all of those nice applications that I dreamt up. It had a great impact on the survival of his business and that felt really good to me.

Those memories and experiences of helping small businessmen compete and survive are what keep me enjoying the game of business. I remember, back in the very beginning, assigning a project to one of my new writers for a client called Custom Fabricators. We previously had them publicized on several leading magazine covers and it gave the impression that the company was huge. Well, my writer was taken in by the publicity too. He was looking for a big building and drove right by their small building. Twice. That's what I loved about publicity, especially in the early days. News was an equalizer and there was no other way that a small company could compete effectively without spending a fortune on paid advertising.

My hope that Marc would become as excited about his work as I have been about mine has become a reality. I spent an afternoon with him at The Rivers School and witnessed for myself how he was viewed and respected by his colleagues, teachers, staff, and students alike. What's more, I was thrilled to see how enthusiastic he was when showing me around the campus. That former S.O.B. is enjoying his important work in academia and the wonderful environment at The Rivers School and nothing could please me more. As it turned out, our father-son relationship was enhanced by working together because we treated each other with respect and both chose to embrace the positive aspects of the experiences that we shared.

20

THE FINAL YEAR THAT NEVER HAPPENED

For so many years, it was the business that defined me. I'll never forget working with a fellow named Don King at a company called Starmet Corporation. Not Don King the boxing aficionado, but Don King the Marketing Manager of this specialty metals company. He was turning 35 and opining that he didn't know who he was and was having a very difficult time with his birthday. He was clearly troubled and I could relate because 35 was my most difficult birthday too. When I shared that fact with Don, in an effort to lift his spirits, he looked at me and said with certainty, "You are product publicity, that's who you are. It's simple. How could you have had trouble with your thirty-fifth birthday?" Here's a poem that I wrote on October 22, 1983 about my thirty-fifth birthday.

Thirty-Five

The tide washes the shoreline away and it changes
It happens before your eyes but you don't see it.

A child grows taller, sees more, becomes wiser
And it happens so fast.

You look in the mirror and different images appear,
There's your own inner child in touch with the fears;
The defenses have eroded over the years.
A new person emerges at age thirty-five.

Somehow you can see way deep down inside
There's much more to see and nothing to hide.
Old folks are dying and you want to be near
But there are changes occurring and always the fear;
Soon you'll be dying and no one will hear.

With the old life half over and the new not yet here
You feel somewhat alone after many a year.
What can be said about living your life;
Just to accept, and endure, the struggle and strife.

Somehow you'll grow, change and be alive.
But that's not enough at age thirty-five.
There's so much you want, but it's hard to explain.
To live and be happy;
A child again...

Don King's view of me reinforced my brand as president of Venmark International. After all, we had a business relationship and to him I was product publicity. That said, the view that I held for myself was multi-dimensional. I saw myself as having much more to offer than product publicity and writing allowed me to express myself in that regard.

On January 4, 2010, I started a new journal and I titled it, "The Final Year." My grand plan was to make a poignant daily entry and then compile it into a book about my final year in business. But I allowed life to get in the way and ended up skipping days, then weeks, and then months. Obviously, I wasn't ready for the project or to retire for that matter. One big thing that you learn from entrepreneurship is that you are responsible for your own behavior. Period. And once you understand that, your life changes forever. You can no longer blame anyone else for your choices. They are yours; you own them.

So, here I am several decades later and far from the conflicts written about on my thirty-fifth birthday. Today's conflicts are far different and weigh less on my mind. Perhaps that's because I've enjoyed the freedom of charting my own path, continue to take risks and learn from my mistakes, and have experienced so much growth emotionally and financially. Also, there's an internal compass that says everything will be okay when you're confronted with difficult choices. For example, when I suffer from occasional bouts of depression now, my experience reassures me that "this too shall pass." As they say, "nothing succeeds like success." That applies to personal development as well as business growth.

What muddles up decision-making and choices sometimes is what I refer to as my "rubber band theory." A rubber band stretches a long way before it finally gets really tight and that's what happens when you're involved in the same situation for a long time. Often you don't notice changes along the way. But, at some point, you realize that you're now at a different place and time; even if you're at the same physical place. As you stretch a rubber band it goes a long way and then tightens up at the end of a stretch and can't go any further. That was me in 2010 when I began spending more time in my study at home writing essays, articles, and blog posts. Close to a hundred of them over the following few years, if not more, while my assistant Laura did a marvelous job taking care of the tasks at our Wellesley office. All the while, I was still earning over a half-million dollars per year net profit while appreciating my new reality. A new rubber band was in place and was tightening up much faster during the next few years as I became more comfortable with where I fit in the world.

Reflecting back on the 1980s, though, it was clear to me that self-deception was an easy trap to fall into when you're in pursuit of a dream. And it didn't help that I was raised by a mother who routinely altered reality to suit herself. Ironically, when my brother Rich lost his job at 55 years old and couldn't find another corporate job, my mother told people that he was retired. I said to her one day, "Mom, you know that isn't the truth, why do you keep saying that?" She answered, "because it makes me feel good; that's why." Sadly, she always cared way too much about what other people thought.

It still puzzled me that prospects weren't knocking my door down or asking for more information through my website. Nobody Googled and searched for a product publicist. Peggy always reminded me that it was the nature of the business because of my unusual approach of using publicity as a marketing tool to achieve so many marketing benefits attributed to costlier forms of advertising and promotion. Again, one of the keys to Venmark's success was being different things to different people by using product publicity to achieve their marketing objectives. I was achieving those objectives by illustrating how their products could solve problems for their prospective customers.

Anyway, it had become very frustrating for me that I had to continue making sales calls in order to build the business.

I did that job for many years and wanted to get off the merry-go-round. I was tired of it; plain and simple. Even though I considered myself semi-retired at age 63, my sales in 2011 were over $655,000 and my accumulated net worth was sufficient to let me retire fully with a substantial six figure annual income and no mortgages or outstanding loans. I was financially independent with a large and diverse investment portfolio. But, since I enjoyed making money and doing the work, I continued selling, but not as aggressively as I had in the past. That's what entrepreneurs do; we make money in exchange for goods or services. It is in our DNA.

I worked the same way for a couple more years and concluded that it was time to find a business broker and sell Venmark International. I had my nicely decorated office suite in prestigious Wellesley where I was for over 30 years, but my sales were not increasing, and I wasn't on the hunt for new clients. What was also interesting was the fact that several of my clients were aging too and selling their companies. Naturally, whenever there was a new owner in the picture, they always wanted to bring in their own people and create their own team. Another thing that happened was that some clients had grown enough after my handling all of their marketing monthly for 25 plus years that they created a new position and hired a marketing person.

When it came time to sell Venmark International, I always believed that my initial insurance company-like sales model was viable, especially after my son Marc proved that a non-publicist could still sell publicity effectively per my original business model after all these years. My friend George Berbeco recommended a business broker to me named, Walt Huskins. Walt had sold the Harvard Coop in Cambridge, MA, a classic business that had been in operation for many years, and was an extremely successful business broker.

Walt phoned me and set up a date to come to my office and despite the fact that he was retired, he was very impressive. He was working with me for pleasure and to stay busy, in addition, of course, to any fee that may have resulted from a sale of Venmark International. I could sense that he cared and it was a good feeling. Walt Huskins was a no bullshit type of guy. I liked that, despite the fact that he told me that I couldn't sell the company as anything other than the professional practice it was at the time because I didn't have a recent successful track record with a sales team. Another thing that I had to answer for was declining annual sales. They were declining because my personal activity was declining.

Walt had a very thorough process for evaluating a business for sale. It began with a conversation, naturally, and then he gave me a homework assignment. Central to the assignment was the development of a three-year average Seller Discretionary Cash Flow (SDCF). In other words, all of the money that went for my salary, bonuses, benefits for insurance, deferred compensation, automobile, 401(k), travel, Red Sox tickets, other forms of entertainment, and the like. The other questions were:

1. Why would someone want to buy Venmark International?
2. What is going to worry the buyer?
3. What is your brand strength?
4. How do I know your clients will stay loyal to Venmark International?
5. What could go wrong for a new buyer?

The questions were all quite thought provoking. Walt also mentioned the fact that I would likely have to work for the buyer for several months to a year. It was 2014 and I recall that I had considered myself semi-retired since 2011 and the idea of working for someone else for a year and having to get up early every day to work 40 hours per week, and take them out on sales calls didn't sit well with me. The one common thing I've observed with clients who have investigated selling their business was the fact that they always valued it more than it was really worth. I was no different.

Walt Huskins told me that the way a business like Venmark was valued was based upon the SDCF times 2.5 to 3.5. So, I figured that maybe the company was worth about $1.2 or $1.5 million and after taxes maybe I'd walk away with $600,000 to $750,000. Then, without too much extrapolation, it occurred to me that by working for at least three more years I'd be ahead of the game on a net basis without the aggravation of working for someone else and being bound by a contract, risking conflict with the buyers, and potentially alienating clients.

About a week and a half later, Walt visited with me again and I asked him point blank, "So what do you think?" And Walt Huskins, the highly experienced business broker, looked at me and said, "I think you have the best one-man business that I have ever seen and you would be a fool to sell it." I was speechless! We had arrived at the same conclusion about selling the business from our very different vantage points. Then Walt suggested that we have lunch.

A couple of months later I was approached by an extremely bright and pleasant woman by the name of Celia Brown who was a career development coach. She said that she had noticed something that I posted on LinkedIn and found it quite interesting and wanted to spend a few minutes with me. So, I invited her to come to my office. Celia was a low-key professional and made me feel very comfortable. We talked about many topics and all the while, she was "selling" me on how she could help me transition from full-time work to retirement when I sold the business or closed my office.

Celia Brown followed up a week or so later and invited me to lunch. We had a pleasant conversation over a couple of healthy salads and glasses of white wine at The Cottage, an upscale restaurant, nearby my office. The essence of what I learned from her was that achievement-oriented business owners like me don't stop being that way when we retire. The need for achievement doesn't go away; the definition of what it is that we want to achieve is what changes. She pointed out that "achievement" needs to be looked at in today's terms, as a 65-year-old man, not as Steve Stroum the young entrepreneur. As Socrates said, "know thyself." I never hired Celia, but I sure valued the advice she gave me. It was invaluable and ultimately led to me writing this book.

All the while during 2014, my assistant Laura was telling me how her husband was tired of working full-time and was considering retirement. He was well past retirement age. Laura and Rich commuted to work together every day. He drove her to our office in Wellesley and then trekked off to his job in Sudbury and back to Wellesley at five o'clock. Add on the fact that they came from Reading, MA which was over an hour away during commuting times and it was clear the routine was getting old for them. They left home at 5:00 a.m. and didn't get home until 6:30 p.m., typically. Laura frequently opined about her commute and long hours and I understood her situation and how she felt.

It was November 2014 and I met with a previous client

by the name of Harry Black. Harry was the sales manager for a metal stamping company. We had met several times before he actually became a client and at each meeting, he didn't really listen to me and I couldn't get through to him. At every meeting he asked the same questions, created the same objections, and never followed through on books or articles that he agreed to read which would have validated my value proposition for his company. Instead, he judged me not on the basis of my work and recommendations, but by evaluating "how hard I tried to sell him." Ultimately, he did become a client and hired me for several projects over a few years.

One could argue that I should have known my prospect, Harry, better and "sold" him, closed harder, and played his game; especially after I understood what was taking place. That "sell-me-or-else" behavior is fascinating. As a young entrepreneur in my twenties, I remember feeling the same way about people who made sales calls on me. If they weren't hard-selling, I thought, they didn't believe in what they were doing. It was an attitude that challenged them to "prove to me" that they really wanted my business.

The fact is; the "sell-me-or-else expectation" reveals a lack of confidence in that person's ability to evaluate the product or services being presented to them. Effectively, the person is saying, "since I don't have the confidence in my ability to evaluate what you are selling, I will evaluate you on *'how you are selling,'* and I want you to tell me what to do."

Harry was a few years older than me and was retired. During our luncheon conversation he told me that he was writing a book about his son who unfortunately had died from a drug overdose. I mentioned to Harry that I was also thinking about writing a book and he asked me what was keeping me from writing it. Before I could answer, he continued, "for me it was because I didn't think that I was good enough." Well, as my old friend Sam Paris once said, "that made the hair on the back of my neck stand up!" That was consistent with Harry's lack of confidence in our early sales calls and also was consistent with how I felt about writing a book during the final year that never came.

By this time the rubber band was tightened fully and I had really grown to appreciate that I had created a true lifestyle business as a product publicist and an independent writer and was ready to cut back some overhead at the office and spend more time writing articles, and perhaps, even my book. This book. I've wanted to do it since the early 1980s and saved all of my appointment calendars and personal journals since 1976. So, when the day came to write the book I'd be ready.

21

MY BUSINESS IS MY ART AND MY ART IS MY BUSINESS

According to the Oxford Dictionary, the definition of Art is: the expression or application of human creative skill and imagination, typically in a visual form such as painting or sculpture, and producing works to be appreciated primarily for their beauty or emotional power.

During the process of writing this book, I've reread all of the journals that I've saved since 1977 and all of my appointment books too. That's a collection of calendars from 1976 through 2023, as of this writing. Like the artist-businessman that I am, though, I just wasn't ready before. Perhaps, as Harry Black said, I didn't think that I was good enough. That was part of it for sure. The other part involved revisiting unhappy times and reading, in my own handwriting, how depressed and conflicted I was.

What makes me an artist is that my palette has been my business. From the very beginning when I created those business cards with the big right facing blue arrow in raised thermographic printing and the words Sales Development Associates in white letters out of the blue, I thought about the image we wanted to convey. Those cards were very expensive and I used to watch prospective clients feel the raised arrow between their thumb and forefinger. I swear that it reinforced the legitimacy that we were trying to convey as a brand and a lot of sales were subconsciously influenced through their thumbs.

Our sales presentation and sales materials were not only designed to help our salespeople sell, but it also made them feel secure knowing that they were involved with a professional organization and a leader who knew what he was doing. Back then, our employees were buying me on faith and I had to constantly reassure them that they made the right decision. We were visiting industrial parks making sales calls and convincing the owners and presidents of companies to hire us and write checks on the spot for an intangible business service. Not an easy task.

The first step in the selling cycle was constructing a list of prospects to telephone for an appointment. We always asked for the president by name. When I receive calls from salespeople asking for the owner or the person in charge of a department, I always blow them off. If they aren't smart enough to take the initiative to find out who I am then I don't want to talk with them. Today, all it takes is a Google search.

There's an art to telephone appointment setting and I created a script that showed consideration by asking the prospect if I was interrupting anything important. If he said yes then I would ask him or her what would be the best time to call them back. Most of the time they would ask me to continue. Usually, the prospect would try to get us to make a sales presentation over the phone and tell him more about what we want to discuss with him so that he could blow us off. But my response was always related to the reason I called; which was to schedule an appointment. I would say, "John, that's exactly why I'd like to chat briefly with you, I can assure you that at the very least you will find our meeting informative and that your time will have been well spent. Would Tuesday morning at 10:00 a.m work for you or would Wednesday at 1:00 p.m. be better? Sometimes we'd go around a bit, but I always stuck to my goal which was not to sell, but to secure an appointment.

Then there was the CRM (customer relations management) program that I developed. Our new clients were contacted by phone, in writing, and in-person no less seven different times from several Sales Development Associates employees within their first 30 days of being exposed to us. It was all designed to build a total relationship with them and reinforce our company's brand. What's more, it would also help prevent our employees from stealing clients and becoming competitors. That was the art of business preservation and it worked well as evidenced by the phone call that I received from the president of National Duraform Co., Inc. about Charlie Fox after I returned from Korea.

In addition to providing art direction to my photographer in order to create images that communicated visually what I was writing about, another aspect of "art" was my writing formula itself. I literally kept a copy of the formula in front of me while writing the first 50 or so product news releases. The structure fit the media outlets' available space and that made their lives easier. The copywriting was also concise and to the point. It was also essential to control the copy approval process because every client wanted to become William Shakespeare and put in their two cents if you left copy behind or mailed it to them. It was all about control. Our process was to include everyone in the initial interview who would be involved with the approval of the copy and our approvals took place while we visited the client in person. We would even drive for an hour for a 10-minute copy approval meeting.

It was sacrosanct that we never left the copy behind for them to manipulate, twist around, and show their neighbors before approving it. We had a script for the writing interview and approval too. During the interview we specifically told our client that the approval was for "technical accuracy" only and not for style or grammar. Our argument to clients was simple and straightforward. I trained our writers to say, "you hired us because we know how to get product publicity and we know that you will be pleased with our results, so please let us do our job and if you're not happy, then don't hire us again."

So, that was the art of getting copy approved. We took no chances. The copy approval paper, which we called "Copydraft" was a nice quality heavy paper with their product news release written on one page. It had a two-line headline and four concise paragraphs of a certain size and structure. The final copy the client received when the publicity release was distributed said, "News" in large letters with "For immediate release" underneath and was also a piece of art; printed on a distinctive canary or buff colored paper.

Even today, in the digital age when all of our news releases are distributed over the internet, we still send our clients a nice glossy photograph and letter when it is distributed. We do this because it makes a positive impression and our clients typically save them in a file. Consistency was and still is essential to our brand and we received numerous letters and emails from editors applauding our work. They liked the fact that our copy was concise, to the point, and free of advertising-like puffery. Every performance claim we made in the copy was substantiated with fact. For example, if we wrote that a product was fast, we'd provide a speed. If we claimed it was precise then we'd provide a tolerance or specification to substantiate the claim. Editors appreciated that.

When I began designing brochures for clients, it was another form of art which my business took. I had never written a product news release until I sold one and the same was true about brochures. I said to myself, "what's the worst thing that can happen? I'd give the client their money back if they were dissatisfied." I used good graphic designers and photographers who could execute my vision and rudimentary sketches. The same thinking applied to Newsletters and Press Paks. The business of art and the art of business demanded a certain presentation and execution.

The packaged services that I created were all "firsts" for me as an entrepreneur and I was confident that I could pull them off. I had the essential motivation of an entrepreneur, and that was, and still is, a desire to make money. My friend George Berbeco said that he used to get up every morning and ask himself, "how am I going to make money today?" He even did that after he became very wealthy. That's the nature of the entrepreneurial beast. We live our lives by taking risks and love the process of making money. It's nice to have an extensive stock portfolio and to be financially independent and not beholden to anyone. After all, isn't that the American Dream?

Finally, in August of 2018 I actually moved my office from Wellesley to my home. Looking back, I still can't believe that I didn't move home three years earlier. My rent was $2,000 per month, half of one of my North American publicity orders, so it wasn't that bad. It took a fraction of my time each month to earn that money and pay the rent. That was the artist speaking, not the businessman. It didn't make economic sense, but I was comfortable there and just couldn't let it go. When I did take that final step, however, it was a huge relief and I've never looked back. I felt liberated, in a sense.

We tried to give away all the office furniture and nobody wanted it, not even charitable organizations. What's more, we had to have a security company come in and destroy 41 years of client files and thousands of CDs containing clients' photographs. On that final day, Peggy and I popped open a bottle of champagne and toasted each other, recalling that back in 1977 it was eight and a half months before we even left the office together at the same time to grab an ice cream next door. But frankly, I was relieved to be making the change and excited to start operating from my office at home. I had a 450 sq. ft. study over our garage which was attached to the house, with a nice work setup. There was a big window in front of my desk where I could watch the deer, wild turkeys, and an occasional fox or coyote cross the lawn while I was standing up and writing on the computer or talking on the phone.

I'm now in my seventies and the greatest lesson that I've learned in life is who I am and how I want to live my life. I still violate boundaries because I'm only working with a dozen clients now and I've been working with most of them for over 40 years. It became clear long ago that my client relationships were based upon my performance and getting results for them. So, having become friends with them is an added bonus. I don't know how you can see someone monthly or bi-monthly for so many years and not become friends with them. Venmark International is truly a lifestyle business.

Three of my clients have asked me to assure them that I'll keep working and not retire. For now, I won't quit because I enjoy the work, making the money, and the fringe benefits. Besides, it only takes about a week of my time each month and I'm doing over $300,000 in business annually. If Celia Brown, the career development coach, asked me how I'm enjoying retirement I would tell her that my goal as an achievement-oriented person was to take the best from Venmark International and weave it into my more dominant personal life and I've done that with great success.

Beyond the financial independence of having transformed Sales Development Associates into Venmark International and subsequently to having fun working at home as a senior citizen, I enjoyed the feedback and many testimonials from clients over the years. For example, I received an email a few years ago from a client, Brook Reece, President of Adcole Corporation, a manufacturer of sophisticated measuring equipment for the automotive and aerospace industries that read, "Hi Steve, this may not come as much of a surprise that I retired last Wednesday. It was the end of my 32-year run. Much of it was working with you which was a high spot. Warm regards, Brook."

The most touching feedback that I received was from Dave Ring, President of Applied Plastics Company, Inc. Recall that Dave was the guy who had a marketing post card that we mailed to him on his bulletin board next to his desk and he had, "meant to call me for three years." Well, Dave sold his company for a small fortune and called me a year later and said, "Steve, I've been meaning to call you for a while to thank you for all of your work with us since 1978." I was largely responsible for all of their marketing. I created their brochures, their website, their trade publication advertisements, and all of their product publicity. I was a real partner and loved it. Dave continued, "if not for you, Applied Plastics would have never entered the medical marketplace which has become the biggest part of our business. It was your insight, creativity, and product publicity that introduced us to the medical market back in the 1990s and I truly appreciate it. What I would like to do is make two charitable contributions for you: one on your behalf and one on behalf of your wife. So, please tell me what your two favorite charities are?" I felt honored, proud, and grateful. Dave was a real mensch. For those of you who don't know, "mensch" is a Yiddish word that means a person of high integrity, decency, and morality.

I've seen several posts on social media recently from millennial entrepreneurs and high achievers agonizing over their life-work balance, or lack thereof. So, having been there myself, and being a reformed workaholic, perhaps I can provide some insight for them. If not for my wife understanding me, my type 'A' personality and need to achieve, I don't know what road I might have traveled. She kept me grounded and committed to our relationship and family. We got married in my third year of college and she knew that I was intense back then, given my academic record and making history as a co-op student at The Paul Revere Insurance Company plus starting Sales Development Associates together.

Consistent with knowing who I am, which is the biggest life lesson that I have learned, the corollary is 'don't fight who you are.' I remember, when we lived in San Francisco, everybody preached living a balanced life. So, I thought I would just hang out on Saturdays at a local bar, shoot pool and have a few beers. But, it wasn't comfortable for me. That wasn't me and it felt like a waste of time. The truth is that I felt guilty for being so unproductive. At that time I was 25 years of age and even went to University of California Berkeley for vocational counseling to find out why I was so "driven to succeed." I was counseled and tested and the bottom line was that it was my true nature to be driven. That's who I was. It took a while to stop fighting the balanced life concept and I ended up working Saturdays for over thirty years and loved it. My nature was to work my ass off and do my very best. I left nothing on the table and never quit, even though I thought about quitting at times.

Believe me, as I've shared with you throughout this book, I made plenty of mistakes. And as you know, some big ones; very big ones! I never "tried" my best though; I always "did" my best. Hopefully you understand the distinction which is an important takeaway from this book. Trying is irrelevant. *Only doing your best is acceptable.* That's all that truly matters: doing your best. Full accountability to "self" is essential for an entrepreneur. I've seen several businesses fail and the entrepreneurs attribute their failure to a lack of funds. That's an easy excuse. Blame it on an inanimate object rather than yourself.

When I packed up my office in Wellesley to move Venmark International home, I had a stack of projects tucked away in my bookcase that were never completed. One was never even started and all were paid for in advance. They amounted to over $200,000. That's mismanagement personified. In most cases all I needed was for the client to send me parts for photography. In fact, I always contacted them at least five times before setting their files aside. I said to myself, "if they don't have the sense or interest to take care of their businesses, then that's their problem, not mine."

Learning time management is critical for entrepreneurial success. For everyday tips on the subject, there's a great book by Allen Lakein, *How to Get Control of Your Time and Your Life.* On a broader level, realizing that my nature and workaholism would lead to burn-out or illness, I scheduled time to vacate. I'll interject right here that if you think going on vacation and bringing an iPad or smart device along and calling the office every day or so is really vacating; you're an idiot. Let me repeat: an idiot! Period. The root word of vacation is "vacate." It takes five or six days without business to totally decompress and come down from the rush of high-achievement. Then you can relax, renew, recharge, and think more clearly when you return to work. And then the wonderful cycle of madness resumes!

Embrace the lifestyle if that is your nature. Ultimately it is your subconscious choice. I used to work 12 to 14 hours plus per day Monday through Friday and about six hours on Saturday. However, I took four to six weeks of vacations throughout the year. And for one of them I was totally alone in order to recharge my mind, body, and spirit to prevent myself from burning out. I knew my nature and my workstyle and never ever called my office while I was on vacation. My assistants were competent and knew to call me if they thought it was necessary. None of them ever called me when I was on vacation.

Peggy and I used to rent a villa in St. Maarten, right on the water, every winter for a couple of weeks and I remember the first year that a personal computer was included, I logged on and checked my Venmark International email and felt totally violated. That was the first and last time that I did that.

Frequently when I returned from vacation I'd "reason" with myself and leave the office by 6:00 p.m. But, no matter what I did after returning from vacation, I always went back to working like an animal. I was passionate about my work. I loved helping clients. I loved the "action" of making money and couldn't control it, but learned to live with it. It helped that I had a very clear purpose in my work which was to help small businesses survive and prosper. I established that in 1976 as part of my life's mission. It also helped immeasurably that Peggy was totally supportive.

To monitor and hold myself accountable, I kept a daily journal which helped me sort out the self-deceptive behaviors that can accompany stress in high pressure situations and cause depression. When I made journal entries, I included the date and time of day in order to help see any interesting patterns of behavior and when I was most or least productive. The journal also improved my decision-making because I could see issues more clearly and avoid emotional traps.

Eventually I gave up working on Saturdays and began coming home from work earlier. Then I gave up working on Fridays. Ultimately, I gave up working three weeks a month and all of those changes in scheduling happened naturally for me. It became "my" clear choice instead of pure "drive." I was finally ready to slow down and it was my decision. As Socrates said, "Know thyself."

22

ENTREPRENEURS ARE THE REAL AMERICAN HEROES

During the summer of 1976 when I was going through the *Where do I go From Here With my Life?* book exercises to decide once and for all what I wanted to do with my life, I ended up with a large sheet of paper with satellite circles around a center circle of "Top Skill Clusters." They included such topics as, "Ultimate Life Goals, "Philosophy of Life," "Ideal Job Specifications," and "Preferred People Environments." "Each circle listed from five to 10 comments that were extracted from the numerous essay assignments.

One topic was entitled, "What needs doing [in America]" and here are the five things I listed:

1. More considerate interpersonal behavior
2. Equitable taxes and law enforcement
3. Growth of the small businessman and enhancement of free enterprise and competition
4. People need to be more responsible for their own actions
5. More vocational training.

Success and Self-Discovery

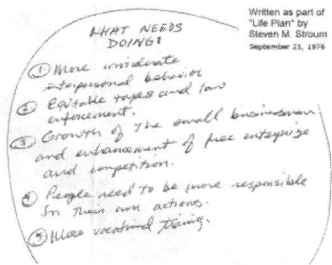

Unfortunately, it is nearly a half century later and there has been very little progress, if any, regarding the above very important things that I believed "needed doing" in America. In fact, I think we're worse off today. Nevertheless, I've dedicated my life to number three and in a small way, one client at a time, I have contributed to the growth of the small businessman and enhancement of free enterprise and competition. Obviously, I haven't made a dent in the bigger problem, but for those clients who I've served; especially the ones for over 45 years, I've played a significant role in their lives and it has felt really good. What's more, I still find it very rewarding. After all, you walk a mile one step at a time.

Consistent with my interest and the loads of research that I did on the topic of small business, I discovered a congressional report that was published in 1978, entitled, *Future of Small Business in America, a Report of the Subcommittee on Antitrust, Consumers and Employment of the committee on Small Business House of Representitives Ninety-Fifth Congress.* For those interested, the report was number 95-1810. In that report, it became crystal clear how important small business was to American culture. The report concluded, "The essence of the American economic system of private enterprise is free competition. Only through full and free competition can free markets, free entry into business, and opportunities for the expression and growth of personal initiation and individual judgment be assured."

The report continued, "the preservation and expansion of such competition is basic, not only to the economic well-being but to the security of this Nation. Such security and well-being cannot be realized unless the actual and potential of small business is encouraged and developed. It should be declared policy of the Congress that the Government should aid, counsel, assist, and protect insofar as possible the interests of small business concerns in order to preserve free competitive enterprise, to ensure that a portion of the total purchases and contracts for supplies and services for the Government be placed with small business enterprises, and to maintain and strengthen the overall economy of the Nation." Finally, the report warned, "Unless direct and concerted action is taken now, small business, the mainstay of a truly competitive system, will continue to decline. The decline will have disastrous consequences for the American Economy considering the proven contributions of small business to areas such as job creation and innovation."

Among the specific recommendations from the *Future of Small Business in America* report was that tax legislation should be passed which further graduates the corporate tax rates and specifically targets small business as receiving "preferential capital gains treatment." The report also noted that "small business is one sector of our economy capable of resolving the unemployment problem and providing benefits rather than additional tax burdens to the consumer." Highlighted throughout the report was the relationship between free enterprise and personal responsibility. We as small businessmen and women take responsibility for our own behavior: our success depends upon it. This has traditionally been the "American way, the American Spirit."

The report also noted that small business was the Nation's largest job creator and at that time, more than 98 percent of the commercial establishments in the country were small businesses. It also discussed small business as a source of leadership. One quote from testimony before the subcommittee on antitrust, consumers, and employment was of particular interest, "Without the small businessmen and women of America, we will become a Nation of computers, profit-and-loss decision-makers, automated robots who cannot give proper attention to the essence of living – the human spirit of our society and nation." A particular concern to me dealt with "Manufacturing Assets and the Decline of Small Business." The data revealed a pattern of increasing market control being exercised by the largest manufacturing firms. Testimony presented to the subcommittee was virtually unanimous in agreeing that this trend would continue unabated unless immediate and forceful steps were taken.

Another conclusion from Chapter Three of the *Future of Small Business in America* report really hit home with me because of my own experience working and socializing with small business owners. It was, "This country's small business people are believers in the rights and responsibilities of citizens, and strong participants in the spirit of independence on which this Nation was founded and with which it must continue to prosper. Our small business leaders are those who can and do create new methods of solving problems. Their high regard in local and national communities is not so much a result of their business role as much as their willingness to break new ground, maintain the virtues of freedom and independence and do their own thing."

Innovation and profit have always motivated entrepreneurs. Consider the Apple story. Steve Jobs and Steve Wozniak started Apple Computer, Inc. out of a garage and incorporated in January 1977. Today, Apple, Inc. employs over 164,000 people. Bill Gates and Paul Allen had a similar start with Microsoft and today the firm employs 221,000. Jeff Bezos' story is also the same. He started Amazon from his garage and today they have 1.5 million employees. The Home Depot's idea was born in a coffee shop by Bernie Marcus and Ken Langone and today the firm has 500,000 employees. Fortunately for all Americans, I could go on and on with this list of innovative businessmen and women. Their feats and contributions would not have been possible without the freedom we cherish as Americans.

Louis Brandeis, former Associate Justice of the Supreme Court believed that profit is an essential condition of success. He wrote, "In business the earning of profit is something more than an incident of success. It is an essential condition of success; because the continued absence of profit itself spells failure. But while loss spells failure, large profits do not connote success. Success must be sought in business also in excellence of performance; and in business, excellence of performance manifests itself, among other things, in the advancing of methods and processes; in the improvement of products; in more perfect organization, eliminating friction as well as waste; in bettering the condition of the workingmen, developing their faculties and promoting their happiness; and in the establishment of right relations with customers and with the community."

What makes entrepreneurs the great American heroes isn't just their success as job creators, but also their impact as philanthropists. Ken Langone, for example, a co-founder of The Home Depot gave $100 million to help make NYU's medical school (New York University) tuition-free for all students. The Bill and Melinda Gates Foundation fights poverty, disease, and inequity around the world and has attracted other wealthy donors including Warren Buffett to pledge huge amounts of money to the foundation. Marc Benioff, the founder of Salesforce.com and his wife were listed by *Forbes Magazine* in their list of top philanthropists and have donated hundreds of millions of dollars to worthy causes. Fortunately, the Forbes list is quite large and the overall contributions by philanthropists yield tremendous benefits to all American citizens and many others around the globe. Small businesspeople also play a large role in philanthropy by sponsoring all sorts of events ranging from local hockey tournaments to charity walks and road races to bake sales and other fund-raising schemes.

Abraham Lincoln really brought the idea of entrepreneurship down to the individual level. Lincoln wrote, "The prudent, penniless beginner in the world labors for wages for a while, saves a surplus with which to buy tools or land for himself another while, and at length hires another new beginner to help him. This is the just, and generous prosperous system which opens the way to all, gives hope to all, and consequently energy, and progress, and improvement of conditions to all."

Lincoln's idea of entrepreneurship is more akin to the vast majority of entrepreneurs in our society today. Many small business owners value their independence more than anything else. Others had to find a way to support themselves and their families and had no other choice but to start a business. Survival is a much stronger motivator than innovation or making a profit.

All small business owners contribute to their communities by providing goods and services and most that I've met and worked with are extremely generous with their employees. Statistically, very few become millionaires and billionaires. Nevertheless, they are the real American heroes who employ the vast majority of people in America. The high-profile entrepreneurs like Steve Jobs, Bill Gates, and Jeff Bezos all started small, but they are the exceptions; not the rule.

My hope is that this book ends up inspiring people to strike out on their own. People who were brought up in a working-class family like me who, even though I had a college degree in Business Management, I had no idea how to get started in business for myself. Desperate, I recall buying an oversize orange covered book for $15 entitled, *100 Small Businesses You Can Start from Your Home*. It was a sham and simply listed a hundred examples of small businesses but didn't include any information about the "how-to" of starting a business or who to contact. There was nothing resembling a process included or other advice about what to do and what not to do in order to run a business.

Even if my story doesn't inspire you to become an entrepreneur, hopefully it will help you avoid some of the pitfalls and painful mistakes that I made during my business career and give you some ideas that might improve your own situation. If this book helps you face your demons, that's all the better. We all have demons, but few of us make the concerted effort to address them. All too often we let them have a negative impact on our lives and relationships; personal and business. And the sad part is that many people keep repeating dysfunctional behavioral patterns and have no idea that they have the power to change them if only they made that choice and put in the effort.

My advice to any would-be entrepreneurs or job seekers, for that matter, is to make a list of the favorite ways that you like to spend your free time. Maybe you have a specific hobby or you like to read. Whatever it is, make a list of them and then start at the top and research all of the companies and organizations that are involved in that interest area. For example, if you like hiking, then look at all of the companies associated with hiking. In 2022, there were 4,749 Hiking & Outdoor Equipment Stores and businesses in the US. There are makers of footwear, clothing, backpacks, binoculars, and all kinds of accessories. In addition to manufacturers, there are distributors, wholesalers, and retailers too.

The specific jobs that you pursue within those companies will really depend upon your training and specific interests. What will make you happy, however, is spending time with people who share your interests. If you're an avid hiker, what could be better than working with and associating with fellow hikers all day long? So, while learning more about the opportunities available within your own area of interest, you'll be socializing with like-minded people. That's not only good for enjoying your work life, but is can also set the stage for entrepreneurship through collaboration with others.

One of my favorite Muhammad Ali quotes is, "No one starts out on top, you have to work your way up. Some mountains are higher than others, some roads steeper than the next. There are hardships and setbacks but you must not let them stop you. Even the steepest road, you must not turn back. You must keep going up. In order to climb the mountain, you must climb every rock."

So, if you do have the courage and good fortune to become self-employed, remember the quote that my client, Manny Affler, sent me that I displayed on my office wall for over three decades. It said, *"The man who follows the crowd, will usually get no further than the crowd. The man who walks alone is likely to find himself in places no one has ever been before. Creativity in living is not without its attendant difficulties, for peculiarity breeds contempt. And the unfortunate thing about being ahead of your time is that when people finally realize you were right, they'll say it was obvious all along. You have two choices in life: you can dissolve into the mainstream, or you can be distinct. To be distinct, you must be different. To be different, you must strive to be what no one else but you can be..."*

Manny Affler was in his fifties when he hired us several times per year. He owned a company called Pleasure Knit Corporation and I publicized their active wear clothing for skiing and other outdoor activities. He was one of those clients who I could relate to and enjoyed kibitzing with. He recognized that Venmark International was a different kind of company. It was early in our business life when Manny began hiring us and in addition to validating our good work with repeated publicity orders for several years, he encouraged me to be different.

On the topic of creativity, there's a great book by Dr. Rollo May entitled, *The Courage to Create* which explains that there's a process to creative thinking. I've spoken with too many people over the years who claim not to be creative. Nonsense! As May points out, the power to create exists within each of us. We need to believe it and create the environment which fosters creative thinking. For example, he points out that we often get creative thoughts in those times between intense work and relaxation or for men, thoughts while shaving, is a "between activities time." For me, I get some of my best ideas at night when my subconscious mind is busy and I'm falling off to sleep.

During my half-century of working with entrepreneurs and being one myself, I've read a great deal about the topic and I thought I'd offer two specific observations that apply to all types of entrepreneurs; blue-collar and white-collar alike. In fact, these observations apply to anyone. First, as has been attributed to the psychologist Abraham Maslow, "Your greatest strength is always your greatest weakness." In the context of a salesperson, if he or she is articulate and can think well on their feet, they might have a tendency to rely on those skills rather than taking the time to properly prepare for a sales call. Maslow wrote about it in reference to a fear of success and the avoidance of one's own potential.

Making a sales call is like getting ready for a football game. The team spends an entire week preparing and practicing for a one-hour game on Sunday. My second observation is that regardless of your college degree or title, your approach to problem-solving is either as a technician or as a manager. In response to a problem, the technician thinks, "How can I solve this problem?" On the other hand, a manager's first thought is, "Who can I get to solve this problem?" Obviously, there's a huge and significant difference in the two approaches. I learned that I am a technician and my son Marc is a manager.

I have created a list of the 7 Must Have Character Traits for Entrepreneurs:

1. Empathy and a genuine desire to help others
2. Personal accountability and discipline
3. Know thyself and trust your instincts
4. Curiosity and a thirst for knowledge
5. Drive to succeed and persuasive ability
6. Belief in your product, service, or mission
7. Positive attitude, tenacity and integrity

Lastly, in writing this book I had the help of my weekly planner appointment books that I saved since 1976 and personal journals (diaries) that I kept since 1979. Without them, I doubt that I could have written the book. There were so many entries to review. In fact, many of my notes prompted me to recall my childhood and what sort of activities made me happy. It was interesting that some of my fondest memories took place while I was alone. I especially remember lying on the flat roof of the garage behind the house next door from us during the summer and enjoying the solitude. The garage was located far behind the house.

After buying a Popsicle from the ice cream truck driver who visited our neighborhood regularly, I'd climb up on the garage roof and with my head propped up by a small rise in the roof itself, just relax and enjoy the flavor and refreshment of my Popsicle while looking up at the blue summer sky through the shady trees and daydreaming. Entrepreneurship can be extremely isolating and lonely, and daydreaming is essential for success. Again, your most creative ideas will come to you at times between intense work and relaxation. Know thyself and set yourself up to win by controlling all of the variables you can, and when you get knocked down, get up again, fight the next round, and never quit. Being your own boss, being true to yourself and creating freedom for your family are wonderful... Good luck!

If you enjoyed my story, please take a moment to post a review on Amazon.

For more information please visit my website at https://www.smstroum.com/

ACKNOWLEDGMENTS

This book never would have been written had it not been for my dear friend Ellen Gibson-Adler who told me when I began thinking seriously about it not to be intimidated by the thought of writing an entire book and to just write one chapter at a time. An author of three excellent books herself, the feedback and encouragement she gave me was immeasurable. Peggy also read each chapter and offered feedback. Her support bolstered my efforts, as always.

A special thanks to Matthew McKee Photography for creating exceptional photographs for Venmark International these past twenty plus years. Matt's ability to interpret my vision is extraordinary. He has also given me the honor of mentoring him at our creatively engaging weekly meetings. What's more, he's a great fishing partner. Matt was one of the first to read this book before it was edited and gave me very candid and helpful feedback.

Thanks also to George Berbeco and Bruce Forman who were kind enough to read my manuscript and provide feedback before I engaged a professional editor. Their help was invaluable and I may not have expressed that adequately to them. My dear friends Bob and Phyllis Totaro, Wendy Plottel, and Reed Hillman also deserve a special "shout out" because of their immense proofreading help. Thanks so much for taking it so seriously, guys. Thanks also to Marc at Long Dell Inn for gifting me the back cover photo. His Inn at Cape Cod is an excellent place to relax.

Finally, thanks to Kate Anslinger, my editor, for making so many insightful edits and for teaching me how to write this book properly. Our collaboration was one of the best creative experiences I have ever enjoyed and I applaud her expertise and patience. I could go on-and-on about how great it has been working with her, but she wouldn't allow it. Thank you again, Kate.

BOOKS TO CONSIDER READING
[NO PARTICULAR ORDER]

How to Get Control of Your Time and Your Life by Alan Lakein

22 Immutable Laws of Marketing by Al Ries and Jack Trout

Positioning: The Battle for Your Mind by Al Ries and Jack Trout

The Fall of Advertising and the Rise of PR by Al Ries and Laura Ries

Limbo: Blue Collar Roots White Collar Dreams by Alfred Lubrano

Inbound Marketing by Brian Halligan and Dharmesh Shah

On Becoming a Person by Carl Rogers

The New Rules of Marketing & PR by David Meerman Scott

Winning Through Intimidation by Robert Ringer

Power: How to Get it How to Use it by Michael Korda

To Sell is Human by Daniel H. Pink

Exceptional Selling by Jeff Thull

When I say No I Feel Guilty by Manual J. Smith, PhD

Overcoming the Fear of Success by Martha Friedman

The Courage to Create by Rollo May
Innovation & Entrepreneurship by Peter F. Drucker
The Angry Book by Theodore Rubin, MD
Your Erroneous Zones by Wayne Dyer
When all You've Ever Wanted Isn't Enough by Harold Kushner
The E-Myth Revisited by Michael E. Gerber
Winners & Losers by Sidney J. Harris
Where Do I Go From Here With My Life by John C, Crystal and Richard N. Bolles
Hidden Persuaders by Vance Packard

ABOUT THE AUTHOR

Steven M. Stroum grew up in a working-class family in Auburndale, a village of Newton, MA. After briefly attending Northeastern University in 1966, he enlisted in the US Air Force and served in Thailand during the Vietnam War. In March 1968 he received a medical discharge, became a Disabled Veteran, and in September returned to Northeastern University. The youngest of three boys, he was married to Peggy Lawrence in 1970 and received a BS in Business Administration in 1973.

Stroum started his business from a spare room at his parents' home in Newton, MA with only $300 and within a few short months moved to nearby Wellesley. By the end of his first year in business his firm had ten full-time employees and hundreds of clients. In recognition of his company's contribution to the success and growth of numerous small companies, Stroum was selected to serve on the Commonwealth of Massachusetts Small Business Task Force and was later appointed one of 18 Small Business Advisors to the Governor of Massachusetts. He was also selected by the International Rotary Foundation to tour South Korea for six weeks as an ambassador, was later appointed to The Norbert Weiner Forum at Tufts University to study the impact of technology on society, and served as publicity advisor on the Board of Directors of the Smaller Business Association of New England.

Steven M. Stroum, a seasoned product publicist,

marketer, and entrepreneur has been featured in INC Magazine, Sales and Marketing Management Magazine, Marketing Magazine, OMNI Magazine, USA Today, Business Week Exchange, The Christian Science Monitor, Boston Globe, Boston Herald, Middlesex News, San Francisco Chronicle WHDH-TV, WJAR-TV, WKOX radio and others. He has also been a guest lecturer at The American Marketing Association, Babson College, Boston College, Northeastern University, and numerous business and civic groups.

For more information contact:

Steven M. Stroum
success@smstroum.com
www.smstroum.com